Becoming a
Network Consultant

Becoming a
Network Consultant

Matthew Strebe

with

Marc S. Bragg, Esquire

and

Steven T. Klovanish, C.P.A

SYBEX®

San Francisco • Paris • Düsseldorf • Soest • London

Associate Publisher: Guy Hart-Davis
Contracts and Licensing Manager: Kristine O'Callaghan
Acquisitions & Developmental Editor: Maureen Adams
Editor: Rebecca Rider
Book Designers: Franz Baumhackl, Kate Kaminski
Cartoonist: Daniel Ziegler Design
Graphic Illustrator: Tony Jonick
Electronic Publishing Specialist: Franz Baumhackl
Production Editor: Leslie Higbee
Associate Production Editor: Jennifer Campbell
Proofreader: Laurie O'Connell
Indexer: Ted Laux
Cover Designer: Daniel Ziegler Design
Cover Illustrator: Daniel Ziegler Design

Library of Congress Card Number: 00-100626

ISBN: 0-7821-2661-8

Manufactured in the United States of America

10 9 8 7 6 5 4 3 2 1

To Nathan,
I hope you like this wacky place as much as I do.

ACKNOWLEDGMENTS

My wife makes my life so easy to live that I have time for such frivolity as writing. Without her, my life would be a complete waste of time.

My clients have provided so much rich material to write about that they certainly deserve mention, although hopefully they'll never read this book. I won't tell them about it, and I'd appreciate it if you didn't either.

Marc S. Bragg and Steven T. Klovanish unselfishly provided their expertise to make this book more accurate and useful. Besides being experts in their respective fields, they're both all-around good guys. Adrienne Crew took the time to explain Marc's commentary on the critical work-for-hire issue in more detail, for which I am eternally (or until this book goes out of print, whichever comes first) grateful.

This book would not exist without the hard work and dedication of many people at Sybex, especially Maureen Adams, acquisitions and developmental editor, and Guy Hart-Davis, associate publisher, who both liked the idea in the first place and championed the cause. And thanks to Rebecca Rider, editor, who made my incoherent rants both more readable and gentler on the stomach. There are numerous unsung heroes at Sybex who deserve to be sung. They are Franz Baumhackl, electronic publishing specialist; Leslie Higbee, production editor; Jennifer Campbell, associate production editor; Laurie O'Connell, proofreader, and Ted Laux, indexer. Many thanks to one and all.

TABLE OF CONTENTS

INTRODUCTION

Many people don't bother to read the introduction, which causes us sensitive authors to feel slightly slighted. To foil those non-introduction-reading people (a group that obviously does not include you), I've incorporated the former introduction as the first part of Chapter 1, and included this paragraph because I felt like there should actually be some text below the Introduction title. Clever, I know.

Matthew Strebe
16 February 2000

Consulting:
Quit and Grow Rich

1

"Owner of NetServ? I thought you worked for the phone company..."

"Whoa—wrong card! Hold on..."

In the middle ages, feudal society revolved around the concept of villagers, called serfs, who were bound by law to work for their lord. They didn't necessarily lead bad lives (that depended mostly on how well the lord ran the demesne), but they weren't free to choose their daily activities, either. Free folks, who were usually skilled workers like carpenters, millers, or smiths, had far wider latitude—they could move if they wanted to, and they made a much better living than the serfs. Arguably, they had more freedom than the lords, who also were not free to move around.

Fast forward to the 20th century. Modern corporations act much like feudal society, with employees who have no choice but to do as they're told or quit. Employees can't choose which projects they want to work on, how much they want to work, or how much they want to try to get for their services once they've accepted a job. Consultants are the free people of the corporate world. They move from job to job and company to company, taking on as much work as they want, charging what they can convince clients to pay, and taking time off whenever they want for activities like surfing the waves or the Web. In this book, I will detail what you can do to escape from feudal corporate work, and how to establish yourself as a free agent. In essence, you will begin the progression from serf to surfer.

Anyone can become a consultant. There is no professional association you must join, no jury or council from whom to obtain a license, and, in most cases, there is no government regulation on most types of consulting. All you have to do is convince clients to pay you for your expertise. Unfortunately, that's more difficult than passing a licensing exam.

There's a popular notion that consultants do nothing and make a ton of money. Both points are true, but not at the same time. Consultants either do nothing or make a ton of money.

Successful consultants, those who know how to find new customers, retain old ones, and deliver solutions consistently, are always busy. They make a ton of money, and they have no time to spend it, so it just accumulates until they retire. Unsuccessful consultants complain about how they can't find work, how crappy their customers are, and how they'd be more successful if their car didn't keep breaking down.

This book is designed to help make you successful as a consultant, because driving a crappy car sucks. I know this from experience. When I started consulting, I drove a used Hyundai Scoupe. Within a year, I bought a used Infiniti J30 (paid cash), and a year later, I traded that in for a new Mercedes Benz E-Class (financed, because the interest rate is lower than the return on my investments). I'm not mentioning this to brag about my success (yeah, right) but to show by example that no matter what your financial situation is now, you can use consulting to get to wherever you want to be.

This chapter will help you understand consulting and demystify the roles of people you may know who call themselves consultants. It will also explain what you need to know to become a network consultant, and help you decide whether you have both the talent and the personality to become successful at consulting.

How I Lost My Job and Found My Calling

The company I worked for was sinking faster than *Titanic* analogies. Since the company was a small defense contractor in San Diego, the military drawdown struck them swiftly and hard. Both of the military contracts the company had depended on were completed, and the management staff had no idea how to market for more business in the face of stiff competition from the large defense contractors who were now scrambling for a piece of a much smaller pie. Suddenly, the small contracts on which we subsisted (which we were overlooking because we were working larger contracts) were being snatched from us. It was like being the smallest orphan in the poorhouse.

The owner had refused a buyout offer from one of the largest defense contractors in the country over a difference in valuation, thus virtually assuring that we'd all lose our jobs. When the company had to hold my paycheck until the next payday rolled around, I decided to negotiate my own layoff since I could just as well do nothing if I wasn't going to get paid. The company was closed down for good less than four months later. I quit on the third anniversary of my hire date, and I had no idea what I was going to do next.

Just after I'd quit, a sales manager for a local network-cabling distributor called and said he'd heard that I was no longer encumbered with a job. He had a customer who needed help with a networking problem and asked if I could help. It seems that their network was extremely sluggish. I had no idea what the problem might be, so when they asked for a firm, fixed-price contract to solve it, I figured it would probably take me a week to figure out. I multiplied 40 hours per week by $62.50 to determine the contract price. (This number seemed unreasonably large at the time; it was what my former employer charged for my time when they billed my time to their customers. My employer paid me $25 an hour.) I then told them that if I didn't solve the problem, I wouldn't bill them. They were happy with that, so I started to work.

Less than four hours later, I'd identified a malfunctioning bridge that was transmitting broadcast storms. It connected an obsolete section of Thicknet cabling to the network, and was hidden in a ceiling—none of the current IT staff even knew it was there. I had identified its Ethernet address using an Ethernet packet-sniffer diagnostic tool and wound up tracing cables until I stumbled across it in the ceiling. After shutting it off, the network became completely stable and fast again.

I went home, fired up my copy of Excel, and used the default Excel invoice template to write up a bill. After that, I realized I could make three weeks' pay in a day, and I would never have to sit in a cubicle again. I've never looked back.

When I first became unemployed—er, I mean, a consultant—I looked far and wide for a good book on consulting or the process one would go through to become one. I didn't find any good books on becoming a consultant. I did, however, find a few books with lots of meaningless facts (like what FoxPro programmers in New York charge per hour) and bad advice (like cold calling was apt to be my best strategy to find customers if I didn't happen to already know everyone in town). I threw those books out and decided to figure things out on my own since nearly none of the advice offered seemed to apply to me. (I now wish I'd kept the Tax chapter, but that's a story for a later chapter.)

I have vague memories of my former cubicle—staring fixedly at my monitor, filling out vacation request forms, and listening to irate customers complain about problems I was powerless to solve. I remember my boss telling me I didn't have enough vacation time on the books to get married and take a honeymoon. I remember taking a urinalysis for insurance purposes. I remember sitting through endless meetings trying desperately to keep my eyes open while people debated ceaselessly about matters that had nothing to do with my work or me. It's been three years for me though, so the memories are fading fast.

I love my lack of a job. I'm excited to get up in the morning, happy to execute my daily routine, and satisfied at the end of the day. I have a solid body of work to look back on proudly. The money I make is limited mostly by the amount of work I want to take on, and my customers feel like they're getting a great deal. Being a network consultant allows me to schedule my life the way I want to, and it allows me to work as much as I feel like working. Best yet, I make about four times what I made when I did the same thing for a company.

My work is different now. Although the phone is even more insistent now than it was then, the conversations are far more positive. The attitude of my customers is my responsibility—and because I can control the work I do, everything stays positive. I rush around quite a bit, but I like driving, and I don't mind the hurry. I don't waste much time at all—I spend time in traffic either on the phone updating customers or my schedule (on a hands-free cellular phone), or dictating books on consulting. While waiting at a customer's site, I respond to e-mail on a hand-held computer that I synchronize with my desktop computer at the end of the day. It's a hectic life, but I like hectic.

People ask me how I tolerate the uncertainty of working for myself (which they apparently equate to being unemployed). I have a hard time figuring out how they tolerate the uncertainty of a single paycheck. I've never liked putting all my eggs in one basket; when my former employer went out of business a few months after I was laid off, I realized that nothing is certain. At least as a consultant, I'm in charge of my destiny, as far as it can be made certain. Without sounding glib, having six customers pay me on a regular basis makes it nearly impossible to lose all my work at once. Even if I suddenly lost three of them for some inexplicable reason, I'd have plenty of income to get by and plenty of time to find more customers. To me, consulting is far less risky than working for a single company whose finances I don't control.

Concerning Consulting

Consulting is the business of providing specific expertise on a job-by-job basis. Unlike employees, consultants are hired to solve a very specific problem. That problem either has well-defined specifications, time periods, and budget constraints, or the consultant is hired to define the problem, time period, or budget needed.

Hiring a consultant makes sense for businesses when one or more of the following is true:

- ➤ The business needs to solve a problem in an area that none of the employees understands sufficiently.

- ➤ The business can't afford to hire an employee to solve the problem, or the problem isn't important enough to warrant a new hire.

- ➤ There are recurring short periods of time when the business requires outside expertise.

- ➤ The business needs help on a single specific project with a defined time period and budget.

Businesses hire consultants because they are less expensive than hiring an employee to perform the same function—this is the case because the function is most likely short term, perhaps for a period of days, weeks, months, or even a year, but it's not permanent. For these short-term projects, hiring a permanent employee doesn't make sense because there won't be a long-term need for the specific expertise once the project is finished.

In other cases, there may be a continuous but infrequent need. For example, I consult for numerous small businesses that need me to stop in only once every two or three weeks to set up a new workstation, add new server software, or modify a firewall policy. Having someone sit around full time for these infrequent tasks doesn't make sense, so hiring a consultant part-time is less expensive.

Of course, as a network consultant, you'll work for yourself, so in addition to all of the technological knowledge you will need, you'll also need the following business skills, which I call "The Seven Business Skills I've Enumerated for No Very Good Reason":

Negotiation   To make certain you provide what your clients need at a price that's fair for everyone.

Financial acumen   To stay ahead of the myriad of expenses, receipts, tax issues, and accounting.

Ethics   To keep your dealings above board and your attention to customer service in the right place.

Discernment   To find the clients with whom you can work best.

Public speaking   To address large audiences during training sessions and sales presentations.

Good humor   To relieve stress and make people feel good about you.

Technical writing   To document your results and provide information to your clients.

Chances are, you're more worried about the business skills than the technical skills. If you're already a network administrator, you're pretty familiar with what your job as a consultant will be. But negotiating a contract? Finding clients? Picking up on subtle clues that indicate a potential client has financial problems? Getting a client to pay? Doing taxes?

Don't worry. Everything in the above list is a learnable skill (yes, even the good humor part) and it's all easier than building a Linux-based file server with a RAID adapter and a wireless interface.

Types of Consultants

The majority of consultants are freelance technical experts, and this book is geared toward them. Technical experts design, implement, and maintain hardware and software network systems for businesses; they are network consultants, systems integrators, and application developers.

In the course of my consulting, I've identified a few other types of people who call themselves consultants. If I were a conservative writer, I would, of course, euphemistically describe them according to their merits. But I prefer to throw gasoline on the raging debate about what actually constitutes consulting because it bothers me that the word consultant has recently (and unfortunately deservedly) become something of a joke in the business community.

In order to demystify the sort of consulting that this book covers, take a look at the list and descriptions that follow. See if you can classify yourself into one of the following five types of consultants. I've included recommended reading for those types of consultants who will not find this book useful:

➤ The Unemployee (Purchase *Job Interviews for Dummies* or *The Complete Idiot's Guide to Getting the Job You Want.*)

➤ The Glorified Temp (Purchase *Consulting for Dummies.*)

➤ Celebrity Experts and Soothsayers (Purchase *7 Habits of Highly Effective People* or *The Goal: A Process of Ongoing Improvement.*)

➤ The Application Developer (You'll find this book useful.)

➤ Network Consultants (This book is for you.)

Unemployees

Unemployees are unemployed middle managers or technical experts who don't actively consult, but they do hand out business cards with their own logo on them while they seek gainful employment. They might accept a contract job or two, but their primary goal is to get plugged back into permanent employment as soon as possible. Essentially, they describe themselves as consultants to avoid the embarrassment of being unemployed.

I personally don't find being unemployed embarrassing—some of my fondest memories are of being unemployed. If I could live without working, I'd do it in a heartbeat. If you're actually unemployed and don't really intend to become a consultant, don't muddy the waters by calling yourself a consultant. You'd be surprised how pleasant employers find forthright people looking for work without pretense.

Glory Temps

A new trend among temporary employment firms (also called "brokerages," as if humans were a commodity trade item; don't even get me started on "human resources") is to call their pool of temporary employees consultants and farm them out for a higher price than your usual Kelly temp.

People who work through brokerages or temporary agencies are not consultants, they are "glory temps." Temp doesn't sound as cool as consultant, but temporary employees who call themselves consultants muddy the term for real consultants. If you're paid via an IRS form W2, you aren't a consultant, you're a temp.

According to the IRS, if you work for a single employer for the period of a fiscal year, you are an employee, and if you work for just one client, you aren't a consultant; you're a contract employee. This may mean you pay your own taxes, but paying your own taxes doesn't make you a consultant, it just makes you self-employed. I know that thousands of contract programmers and application developers disagree with me, and because the word consultant is somewhat fuzzy, they have their case.

For the scope of this book, though, a consultant is a technical professional who intends to work for multiple clients. If you're just looking for a job, there are better books for you.

Celebrity Experts and Soothsayers

Management consultants who use the early success of their technical books or high-profile jobs to make themselves a permanent niche in the speaking and writing fields are called "celebrity" experts. You can't decide to become a celebrity expert—you must have already achieved success as a consultant or writer before you can begin your nationwide speaking tour.

These celebrity experts become soothsayers when they find themselves sucked into the vacuous realm of the mahogany-paneled, high-rise Fortune 500 boardroom explaining technology to those who believe they are the masters of the world because their expertise is money. In this way, management consultants are the soothsayers to the modern emperors of capitalism. As with any feudal society, this role actually trickles down to small business fiefs, so you may actually find cut-rate management consultants hovering around little presidents as well.

You can identify the management consultants by their characteristic use of the word "paradigm." If you ever hear this word come out of the same person's mouth twice, they're either a management consultant or they want to be one. You'll find these consultants making ill-defined or blatantly obvious statements like "we need to rethink our process for maximum efficiency."

Application Developers

Application developers create custom business solutions for their clients. They do everything from designing databases, to writing custom workflow software, to creating e-commerce solutions and Web sites. Custom application development is often necessary for businesses that want to encode their unique business model in software.

The line between an application developer and a systems integrator/network consultant is very blurred. Technically, one group deals mostly with software and the other deals mostly with hardware. Most practicing consultants do both, however, depending upon their specific expertise.

Avoid becoming the dreaded Addiction Developer, however. Addiction Developers build themselves jobs by delivering systems nobody else can work on. The binding thread among this group is that they tend to build themselves permanent clients—once their system is implemented, it's nearly impossible to extricate the consultant without abandoning the system. Because the system is proprietary, and because the consultant is the only one who knows it inside and out, it's prohibitively expensive to have anyone else provide further development.

Developing a group of clients who are addicted to your work is a great way to keep getting paid forever. But a better, and more ethical way to ensure a paycheck is to create systems that are lucid enough for any competent consultant to understand, to document those systems completely, and then to rely on good business relationships to keep you working.

Network Consulting

Network consulting, also called systems integration, is the practice of designing, installing, maintaining, upgrading, and repairing computer networks and their associated software, and peripherals like servers, printers, and client computers.

Network consulting is different than most other forms of consulting. Unlike contract programmers who are little more than temps forced to pay their own taxes, network consultants rarely work full time for a single employer for more than a few weeks at a time. Unlike celebrity experts (like me, for example), who act as soothsayers to upper management, network consultants solve concrete problems. And unlike application developers who invariably wind up addicting customers with software that nobody else can maintain, network consultants are generally easily replaced. These differences make the practice of network consulting somewhat unusual among the computer consulting trades.

A typical network consultant has from two to ten regular customers, averaging around five. Usually, these consultants are called in to either establish a new network or reengineer an existing deficient network. After the initial work is complete, the consultant usually remains on either a retainer or with an established hourly fee for administration and maintenance. The point of hiring a freelance expert is to avoid paying a full-time network administrator or chief technology officer (depending upon the size of the business and the scope of the work involved). By hiring $^1/_5$ of an expert, the company saves money and avoids having geeks wander around the office all the time.

Freelance technical experts like network consultants don't get oodles of billable hours from a single employer the way contract employees do, so their rates are necessarily higher. If you're looking for cushy chair consulting, learn Visual Basic—network consultants are always on the go.

To do this work, you need to completely understand the following:

Network cabling   Especially Ethernet and Fast Ethernet.

Data link equipment   Including repeaters, hubs, bridges, and switches.

Network equipment   Like routers, firewalls, and network printers.

Computer components   Like processors, RAM, motherboards, hard disk drives, and network adapters.

High-end computer hardware   For servers like RAID adapters and tape backup controllers.

Network operating systems   Including Windows NT, Unix, and Novell NetWare.

Network server application and Internet software   Like e-mail services, Web servers, and groupware applications like Exchange and Lotus Notes.

Client operating systems   Like Windows, Unix, and the MacOS.

Client application software   Like Microsoft Office, Internet client software, and financial software.

Wide area networking technology   Like leased lines, xDSL, and various alternative carrier options.

Don't worry about knowing everything on the above list at first. As long as you have a fast brain and you know at least half of the above, you're ready to start. Pick your clients well to make sure you're inside your range of experience, and learn as you go.

Can You Consult?

So you don't waste your time reading further if in fact you should not be a consultant, take the following personality quiz. This quiz is not technology specific—rather, it weeds out those psychological profiles that might have an especially difficult time marketing themselves. Remember: if you fail this quiz, it's not your fault—it's society.

The quiz is even easier than the ones you'd find in *Cosmo*: Read the question, formulate your response, and then quit if your answer isn't (a). If you don't make it to the end of the quiz, just read this book for the funny parts and don't think about quitting your job.

1. If you went a month without making any money, would you:

A. Learn to love mac & cheese

B. Get divorced

C. Starve to death

2. Have you ever brought a weapon to work?

A. No.

B. Yes.

C. Does it count if I bought it at work?

3. Do you believe that you've been contacted by non-human intelligent beings of any sort?

A. No.

B. Yes.

C. I have strange scars I can't account for.

4. How many pets do you own?

   A. 0-4

   B. 4-8

   C. 9+

5. How many times have you been convicted of a felony?

   A. 0-1

   B. 2-3

   C. 4+

6. With whom do you live?

   A. Self, domestic partner, roommate, kids

   B. Parents

   C. Other members of my commune/church

7. Complete this sentence: I believe the world is...

   A. Round/spherical

   B. Flat

   C. Hollow, with an interior sun and a sub-technological society living in peace on the inside

8. How often do you shower?

   A. Daily

   B. Weekly

   C. Monthly

9. Why do you want to be a consultant?

   A. For the independence

   B. Sounds cool to say you're a consultant

   C. Because I keep getting fired

10. Have you ever changed your name to match that of a beloved celebrity?

   A. No.

   B. No, but I've thought about it.

   C. Yes, because Cassidy is easier to spell.

11. Have you ever had a sex change?

A. No.

B. Yes.

C. I'm back to my original sex.

Now remember: this quiz isn't designed to make you feel badly about your lifestyle choices, it's to prepare you for the fact that your lifestyle may be a marketing problem in today's business environment. Of course, your lifestyle choices may be normal in your neighborhood, so your marketing mileage may vary depending upon where you live. Feel free to try anyway, and if you find your niche, you have my greatest respect.

In an ideal world, factors like religious preference, sexual preference, and body-piercing preference wouldn't matter. But we don't live in an ideal world, and no law exists to protect consultants from discrimination. If a client doesn't like something about you, they don't have to hire you, and there's absolutely nothing you or anyone else can do about it. If very few people in a contracting position agree with your lifestyle choices and your eccentricity can't be hidden, you won't maintain enough work to keep consulting.

FROM THE TRENCHES

The following story is true.

As the network administrator for the College of Law at the University of Utah, my fellow consultant and friend (who shall remain nameless) was on the steering committee for the development of a work automation application for the college of administration. One of the developers, a consultant whom I will refer to as "Bob," was a competent and hardworking member of the team. The team met every Friday to discuss progress, feature changes, and so forth.

One Friday, Bob showed up to the meeting wearing a dress, makeup, and heels. At the beginning of the meeting, he announced that from that point on, he was to be referred to as "Roberta." He then calmly went about explaining the features of the new version of the software while the other members of the team sat in stunned silence, gripping their coffee mugs and trying to maintain their composure. After finishing the presentation, "Roberta" left the meeting. The group was unable to provide useful comment on the software at the end of the meeting, because they'd been totally distracted during it.

Conclusion

When you become a consultant, you're in charge of the trade-off between time and money—you can sell or keep as much time as you want. Want four-day weekends? Take them. Want to accumulate money faster than a car's grille collects gnats? Work seven days a week.

Because the demand for good network integrators is so strong, you won't have to worry about competition; in all of my consulting career, I've never had to compete against another consultant. The only competition I have had was the customers' preconceived notion of how much service should cost. By avoiding the metric they used to compute that cost (the hourly rate) by using firm, fixed-price agreements and retainers, I've managed to provide better, faster service, lower overall costs for my clients, and higher profits for me.

The techniques I use are all explained in the rest of this book.

A Day in the Life of a Consultant

2

"Oh, so you're a consultant.... Well, don't worry, you'll find a job soon."

I'm now going to present a day in the life of Me, as a final warning to the faint of heart. If you read this and find it energizing, exciting, and action packed, then keep reading this book; consulting is for you. If you read it and find it scary, exhausting, exasperating, or annoying, then put this book down and go buy a book on Visual Basic.

The remainder of this chapter constitutes the true-to-life details of "The Wednesday Before I Wrote This Chapter."

6:30 A.M. Wednesday

A combination of sunlight and anxiety woke me up. I rolled over and glanced at the clock: 6:30. I rubbed my face and braced myself for the morning cold. As I tramped into the bathroom, my mind seemed to automatically pick up where it left off the previous night: a client's sales staff would be leaving for a trade show at 11:30 A.M. Of the 18 new laptops they ordered for the show, only four had arrived. And the proxy server they were using on my recommendation still wasn't reliably connecting to an Internet service provider.

This client was moving into their trade-show season: three teams of salespeople would simultaneously hit 12 trade shows in a 10-day period. The regular logistics of plane flights and hotel accommodations were a nightmare, but not my problem. My problem was that the budget to purchase equipment for this circus didn't come through until Monday. With two days' notice and the help of just one of their employees, I had to get three complete trade-show demonstration systems running and shipped.

I thought about the dial-up problem as I showered. Most of the hotels hosting the trade shows did not have Internet service capability. My client sells their e-commerce directory at these trade shows, so they needed high-speed Internet access at the shows. No problem, I had said: we'll bond multiple dial-up phone lines into a single aggregate connection for speed, and then use a proxy server to cache most of the site locally, once it has been browsed. Simple.

Or so I had thought. I'd wanted to use USB modems to establish the multi-link channel because I'd read reports of Windows 98 users successfully getting 16 modems online in Windows 98. That would certainly do. But browsing on Microsoft's site revealed an annoying limitation: multilink in Windows 98 supported only four simultaneous connections. Still, that seemed good enough.

We had used my road-warrior laptop and four identical USB modems to prove the concept on the previous Friday—except that it didn't work. We'd get all four modems dialed into the Internet service provider, establishing an aggregate speed of 160Kbps. Then Windows 98 would crash with a Windows protection fault in the NDIS.SYS driver—the basic interface through which all network communications had to stream.

Not a problem, I thought—I'd dedicate a new hard disk to a fresh install of Windows 98 Second Edition—the latest and most stable edition of the Windows operating system. That should certainly take care of the problem. It didn't. Exact same failure. As I washed my hair, I remembered thinking "Okay, it's probably something wrong with running four modems over USB." So I pulled those and put two highly stable PCMCIA modems in. I dialed in, and voila! it crashed again, same problem. The issue had nothing to do with USB. It had to be a bug in the operating system. Since I was on a fresh, uncorrupted version of the latest operating system, I had two choices: call Microsoft and spend two days on the phone while I got escalated up the technical support chain, or cut to Windows NT. Friday was over, so I had decided to go to NT Monday morning.

With those thoughts, I finished my morning routine and hit the road. My wife, being pregnant with our first, didn't stir when I got out of bed.

7:30 A.M.

In the usual morning traffic congestion, I pondered the problem further.

The budget for the shows came through Monday morning, so an employee and I went on a shopping spree to purchase three identical servers locally, 18 large flat-screen monitors, and 18 identical laptops. The laptops we'd specified (Toshiba Librettos for their extremely small footprint, which was crucial in the trade-show environment) were out of stock everywhere—we got just two in town that day. When we got back, we searched the Web and found a supplier who had five—enough for the first show that would be leaving today. The next show left Thursday, and the final show left Saturday morning.

We did find a good deal on WebGear Aviator wireless network adapters—$200 per pair, or about what a regular PCMCIA network adapter would cost. Since I had the OEM cousins of these adapters, the Raytheon Raylink adapters, operating at my house, I knew they'd be perfect for the trade shows: an Internet speed network without cables all over the place. We stopped by Fry's Electronics and bought out their entire stock of 22 adapters (18 for the laptops and three for the servers, plus a spare).

This made a nice little network for the trade shows: the proxy server would dial the Internet and caches pages for the Librettos, which connected over the wireless adapters to the proxy server and showed the sites off to customers with the large flat-screen monitors. The combination of Librettos and flat-screen monitors allowed the salespeople to stand behind the podium and drive while the client looked directly at the monitor—a much more comfortable position for customers than peering over the shoulder of a salesperson as they browsed the Web on a large laptop. And considering the low cost of the Librettos and the reasonable price for the flat-screen monitors, each station cost about the same amount as a good large-screen laptop anyway.

As I barreled down the freeway at 80 mph, chili cheese burrito in one hand and steering wheel in the other, I thought about the four modems I needed for the proxy servers. Given time, I would have purchased a single quad-modem built for Remote Access Service (RAS). But there's no way to acquire server-specific hardware like that in just one day—it's difficult to even find references to it on the Net. So I decided to just put four modems each in the NT machines. Because the machines would be ported all over the country, it was important to make the setup and teardown simple—external modems were not an option. And since finding a motherboard with more than two ISA slots these days is an exercise in futility, I knew I'd have to go with PCI modems.

I then got back to work on the server problem. Because I had spent all of Monday shopping, I'd just barely gotten NT installed on the first new server by quitting time.

Descending from the freeway into town, I thought about Tuesday. Tuesday was totally exasperating. Having purchased four identical PCI modems that supported NT, I learned quickly that my knowledge of modem technology was rusty—I hadn't used a dial-up modem since I got a cable modem in my house. All my customers had direct Internet connections, and so they didn't require modems. I assumed that modems hadn't changed much. I was wrong.

PCI modems aren't really modems in the old sense of the word; they're just PCI to phone-line interfaces. All the modem functionality is handled in software by the microprocessor. There's no similarity to the old-style serial port and modem controller.

None of this really matters much except that the drivers that are included with these modems can't bind to more than one card in the same machine: I could put four U.S. Robotics fax/modems in one machine, but the driver would talk to only one of them.

I killed Tuesday learning a new lesson in keeping up with what I'd considered to be obsolete technology. Tuesday night, I ran back to Fry's with a new solution: four different modem chipsets would require four different drivers, each of which would bind to its own card. I identified four completely different PCI modems and stored them in the car for a new attempt this morning.

8:30 A.M.

I arrived at my client's building at 8:30. Alex (not his real name [I've always wanted to say that]), the lanky young network technician who worked for my client, greeted me.

"Hi, Matt (my real name). Have you figured out what to do about the modems?" Alex is always very direct—he doesn't mince words.

I turned to the coffee machine and poured a cup. "I think so. I picked up three different modems last night. They'll all have different drivers, so they should be able to bind to their own adapters correctly."

Alex shook his head when I offered to pour him a cup. "Sounds good. You know the trade-show group is leaving in three hours, right?"

"Yes, I know. Let's get to work. By the way, did you guys find the other Librettos?"

"The ones that were supposed to arrive in yesterday were cancelled because the company doesn't take our credit card. We had to order some yesterday, but Bill found a place on the East Coast that had 18. We shipped them FedEx Priority. They should be here any minute."

I drained my cup and then replied, "Okay. As soon as they come in, get somebody to help you copy the wireless adapter drivers to the hard drives and get them installed. You'll also need to set up Internet Explorer to connect to the Internet through the proxy server's private IP address."

"We'll get right on it." On that note, Alex turned and headed for our test bench.

"I'll be mucking with the server," I called out after him.

I went to the test bench and opened up the first proxy server. Pulling out the extra three modems, I put in one of each type of modem I'd just purchased into the machine for a total of four installed modems. I then repackaged the old modems so that they could go back. While I was doing this, I couldn't help but remember that if I'd have known about the software modem driver problem, I could have saved myself an entire day.

By the time I had put in the three new modems and gotten their drivers installed, the laptops arrived.

NOTE   In an effort to keep my friends and clients after they've read what I said about them in this book, I've changed most of the names of people and companies I work with. So in case you don't recognize anyone, that's why.

9:30 A.M.

Alex and Eric (not his real name) walked into the IT room (a euphemism for whichever room has an extra table) carrying stacks of laptop boxes—14 in all, which, with our previously acquired four, made the entire complement of 18.

"So, how do we set these up?" asked Eric, who was not a network technician, but a helpful and cheerful fellow nonetheless.

"First of all, plug in six of them and boot them up. Plug in the external floppy drives, and then start opening up the boxes of wireless adapters." I then told them that the reason we were hooking up only six was because only six machines would ship today; we'd deal with the remaining 12 after we got these out the door.

"Cool," said Eric, as he always replied. Alex and Eric busied themselves with that while I reinstalled RAS for NT.

"Okay, they're up. What's next?" asked Eric.

"Copy the contents of the floppy that comes with the network adapters to a folder on the laptop's hard drive. Create a folder in the C: drive called software, then create another folder called wireless. Put the contents of the floppy in the wireless folder on all six machines. When you're done with that, unplug the floppy drives and plug in the wireless adapters."

"Cool."

They kept going. I plugged a phone line into each of the four modems and tried to dial. The dialing went well, PPP established a connection, and the machine received its IP address. But I couldn't ping anything. This annoyed me.

"Okay, a dialog has popped up asking about the driver," Eric said.

"Enter the path to the driver you just copied," I replied.

"Um, what's the path?" asked Eric. Not being a computer technician made working with him somewhat difficult. I had to resort to "cargo cult" methods of simply telling him exactly what to do because I don't have time to explain myself. Alex was chugging away on his own, with two laptops already configured.

"C:\software\wireless," I told him.

"Cool."

"Hey, Matt, do you have the wireless adapter in the proxy running?" Alex asked.

"Not yet. Hold on." I inserted the wireless adapter floppy disk and copied its contents to the proxy server's hard disk. I then installed the driver, set the TCP/IP configuration for the adapter, shut down the machine, installed the wireless adapter, and booted it back up.

"How will we know if it's working?" asked Alex.

"If the laptop gets an IP address from the proxy server's DHCP server, then the wireless network is working. You can ping the server if you want more proof."

"Okay good, then the wireless network is working," Alex said.

"Good," I responded. I then turned my attention back to the dial-up problem.

10:30 A.M.

After attempting to dial a few more times, I still had the same problem. Dialing with a single modem also didn't work. It was getting late—the trade-show shuttle to the airport would be arriving in one hour.

I remembered seeing this exact same problem a long time ago—PPP connections that seemed to establish correctly but then wouldn't pass TCP/IP. I checked the TCP/IP configuration panel and mulled over the problem, trying to remember that old solution. It was getting even later and I still hadn't installed or configured the proxy server software.

"Alex, I need to get an Internet connection over Ethernet into this machine so we can test the proxy configuration. Is there a live outlet around here somewhere?" I asked.

"Sure." Alex stepped away from the Libretto he was configuring and went over to the computer of another employee who was away at the water cooler. He reached under the desk and extracted the network cable attached to the employee's computer.

"Here," he said, as he walked over and handed me the cable.

"Don't you think that guy will miss his network connection?" I asked.

"His work is not as important as ours right now." I couldn't argue with his logic.

I configured the proxy server's Ethernet adapter and rebooted the machine. After it came up, I had a connection to the Internet.

I downloaded the proxy software we decided to use. Our criterion was that the software had to be easy enough for a salesperson with no computer expertise to switch back and forth from various dial-up connections or Ethernet connections to the Internet. We settled on WinProxy, which is also fairly cheap.

After configuring the software to use the Ethernet adapter to reach the Internet, we were ready to test the Librettos. Alex set the first one to connect to the Internet using a proxy server and began browsing. It worked flawlessly, proving out the wireless network and proxy service. The only remaining piece was the dial-up multilink connection.

I listened to Alex tell Eric to repack the Librettos in their shipping boxes with the network adapter and tape them up for the trip to the trade shows. Alex continued to configure and test Librettos.

I turned my attention back to that problem. What was different now? We'd had multilink working earlier in NT on my laptop with two PCMCIA modems. We now had four modems that all worked when we tested them by dialing another machine in the office, but when we established a PPP connection to the Net, they'd get their IP address but not pass traffic.

It was a bizarre problem—data must be moving for the PPP session to get an IP address and establish the link without errors. The dial-up monitor showed each modem happily connected, and the remote server accepted the logon information I provided.

This meant it had to be a problem with TCP/IP. I checked and rechecked that configuration, and removed and readded the protocol, rebooting the server each time.

Nothing worked.

11:30 A.M.

William (not his real name), the company president, approached.

"Matt, buddy, how's it going? The shuttle's here, so we need to get going."

"We may have to ship the proxy later tonight. I haven't got the multilink dial-up working yet."

William stared at me. "What's wrong?"

"I'm not sure." I considered resorting to a string of jargon to explain exactly what was going on and confuse William into acceptance, but I decided against it.

"You're not sure? Wow, we don't pay you to not be sure. We've got to get rolling, man. The trade show starts tomorrow morning. I want to have the server set up and tested tonight."

"There's no point in sending it if we can't dial-out. I'm seeing something very strange here, as if there's a bug…" as soon as the word "bug" formed in my mind, so did the answer. I immediately turned around and located my big case of CDs.

"What's up?" asked William.

"I think I know what's wrong."

"What?"

"Hold on." I didn't want to say it and then be wrong. I searched through my CD case for the disc, and upon finding it, pulled it out and slapped it in the proxy server's CD-ROM reader. I searched the disk until I found the correct file, and launched it. A few clicks later, the program ran on its own.

"What is it doing?" asked William.

"I'm reapplying the latest service pack." I couldn't believe it took me this long to remember the mantra of Windows NT administrators. I'd wasted probably 45 minutes that I didn't have wallowing about because I didn't remember to reapply the service pack.

After a few minutes, the installer finished its work, and I rebooted the machine. When it came back up, I opened the dial-up networking control panel and dialed into the client's ISP.

All four modems fired up with their weird chorus of bonging, screeching, and whistling to negotiate the highest practical baud rate. After a moment, they all settled. The dial-up monitor indicated an aggregate connection speed of 160Kbps—significantly better than an ISDN line.

I fired up Internet Explorer, and lo, everything worked.

"We're up." I shut down the Web browser and launched WinProxy so I could reconfigure it to use the dial-up connection.

"Great! You're the man, Matt! So, how are these wireless things going to work in the convention halls?" William asked as I finished the WinProxy configuration and shut the server down.

"They'll be fine," I replied. "I've been using this model for quite some time on my own network. They have great range and rock-solid reliability. I've never had a problem with them."

"Man, this is going to be awesome if it works out."

"It'll work." At least I hoped it would. "Eric, you can pack the server now. Tell them to hold the shuttle until we get it in."

The Remains of the Day

Rather than bore you with a play-by-play of the rest of the day, I'll summarize what happened. Alex and I loaded the modems that wouldn't work into the trunk of my car so we could exchange them for the types that did work for the server that would be shipping out the next day. I then headed over to the office of another of my clients. I had to delay my work for them because of this time-critical proxy problem. The purpose of my trip was to buy the Chief Finance Officer lunch—that usually worked when I needed to delay. This client was in the process of implementing a new, more secure firewall system and security methodology that was going to take some time (that I did not have at the moment) to configure correctly.

After lunch, I went back to my office to check my e-mail. I could have checked it from the road, but I needed a sanity break. I had an e-mail from my editor asking about my overdue chapter (this one), a few pieces of junk e-mail, and an inquiry from a potential client about my qualifications. Nothing too important, so I hit the road again and went back to the client site to configure the next server.

When I arrived, Alex was already mostly finished, except that he didn't know the settings for the proxy server. I showed him how to set that up, and we got most everything running for the trade-show contingent leaving the next day. I told him I'd run back to Fry's after I left to return the older modems and get different ones that would work.

Of course, during the commute on the way to Fry's, an inattentive driver rear-ended me while I was parked at a stoplight. Assessing the damage, I tried to open the trunk, but could not. All the modems I was supposed to exchange that night were now trapped in my trunk.

I went to Fry's and picked up the modems they'd need, putting the cost on my own credit card. They'd have to go out tomorrow, regardless of the condition of my car. I then headed to a business dinner I was already late for with a friend who ran a network-cabling firm. We'd been talking for some time about joint marketing, and he wanted to put the details together over dinner. Everything went well, and after a few hours we put together a reasonable agreement.

I arrived home at 10:30 P.M. and said hello to my wife for the first time that day.

Conclusion

I spend between two and three days a week consulting, another two days writing, and another two days working on another business I'm starting. If I only consulted, I would have made about twice what the average salaried network administrator makes in a week in those two to three days.

But on the days when I consult, I work long and hard. You'll have to, too. I find my natural limit is about six simultaneous retainers for the amount of consulting I want to do—yours will vary. I made the conscious choice not to hire employees because I don't want to turn into a network integration firm.

A Project from
Cradle to Grave

3

"Badda-bing. No problem."

When I tell people I'm a consultant, they usually ask what that really means (unless they're feigning interest to be polite, in which case they humor me with something like "Oh, that's nice."). Consulting really means that you work on a project-by-project basis. Chapter 2 gave an example of a day in the life of a consultant, but it didn't say much about the process of consulting. This chapter will illustrate this by going through the life cycle of a single project, from finding the customer to delivering the final solution and beyond to follow-up marketing.

A project's life consists of the following stages:

➤ Finding the customer

➤ Establishing contact

➤ Establishing credibility

➤ Learning requirements

➤ Designing a solution

➤ Estimating the cost

➤ Determining the price

➤ Proposing the solution

➤ Establishing the contract

➤ Managing expectations

➤ Performing the work

➤ Documenting the solution

➤ Delivering the final product

➤ Continuing the relationship

Notice that about half of the above items actually require technical talent. The other half require generic business skills like business speaking, sales, marketing, writing, estimating, and so forth.

This chapter will present a generalized job that network integrators might be interested in. The example is based on a job I worked early in my consulting career that came to typify the work I did from then on.

Finding the Customer

Archie Duncan called me one morning about four months after I'd started my consulting practice. Archie is a drywall contractor and a friend of a friend. I fixed his computer once, so now I am doomed to receive a lifetime of help calls from him anytime something goes wrong with his computer. I assumed that was what the call was about.

After telling me that he was now back with his wife, that their dog had just had flea treatments, and that they'd just found this really great steak restaurant where you could get a steak with no excess vegetation, he got to the point. He told me he'd overheard a conversation at a construction job site. A couple of people were talking about how they needed a network installed, and they were wondering how to go about getting it done. Archie managed to insert himself into the conversation and explain that he knew a really good network consultant (me). He told them that he'd be happy to have me call them. At the end of the conversation, he took one of their business cards, and relayed the information on it to me.

At the end of the conversation, Archie asked if I intended to pay a finder's fee. I told him my usual finder's fee was 5 percent of the total amount I made on a job minus expenses, and that I would put him down as the finder for this job.

 TIP Make sure your acquaintances know what you do for a living and that you're always looking for work. I pay a 5 percent (of profit) finder's fee to help ensure that everyone I know is actively seeking work for me.

HOW TO FAIL AT FINDING CUSTOMERS

Consultants fail for one of two reasons: 1) They can't find enough customers to stay busy. 2) They suck at networking. The first of these can be solved by developing useful self-marketing and sales skills. You will quickly discover that finding customers is the most important non-technical work you will do and that all other business skills become secondary to those you will need to sell yourself.

Continued on next page

Why do consultants fail to find enough customers to stay busy? The main answer to this question is that they don't get people working for them to look for customers. Keep in mind that being shy, stingy, moody, mouthy, opinionated, mean, foul-mouthed, obstinate, biased, loud, angry, smelly, disheveled, or otherwise annoying will make it difficult for you to find work. If you are any of these things, the people who do know you will think twice before inflicting you on their associates.

To get started, ask your trusted friends what they seriously think your character flaws are. (If you don't have any trusted friends, you've got a lot of work to do.) Make sure to work out your personality issues before you try to consult because you're going to have to become everybody's friend while you are consulting.

On the other hand, don't worry about things you can't easily change. I'm living proof that you can be too tall, overweight, under-handsome, and left-handed and still do very well as a consultant. Skill and personality are everything in consulting.

Establishing Contact

I was happy that all the time I'd spent helping Archie and listening to his chatter turned out to be worth something. After getting off the phone with Archie, I called the number he gave me and left a voicemail message with my contact information:

> "Hi, My name is Matthew Strebe. I'm a network consultant with Netropolis. Archie Duncan mentioned that you're looking for help with a network and asked me to give you a call. I can be reached at 619.555.1212. Thank you."

About an hour later, I received a call back from the prospective customer, Joseph Steck, a managing engineer for Digital Metrics, a start-up test and measurement device manufacturer. He explained that Digital Metrics was renovating a new facility in which they planned to start their business. The company was funded by venture capital, and though there were currently only nine employees, they expected to have 25 by the end of the year and another 100 the year after that. They were looking for qualified network administrators to help them build their business.

I explained that as a consultant, I could certainly design and install a network that would handle both their current requirements and grow to meet their future demands, but that I wasn't interested in full-time employment. Joseph thought that would be fine, and asked if we could get together for a lunch meeting. We decided to meet at a Chinese restaurant known to both of us because he didn't yet have an office and I worked out of my home.

TIP Although other good methods to find work exist, "networking," or using people you know to find work for you, is the most reliable and most often used method among consultants. Chapter 8 goes into detail about how to establish your network, and it then analyzes various other methods of marketing.

HOW TO FAIL AT ESTABLISHING CONTACT

Remember that when you establish contact, you must make a good first impression. If you make a bad first impression, you may never get the chance to make a second one. Other less obvious ways consultants blow the first contact are by failing to leave a call-back number on the customer's voicemail, or by leaving a message that is incoherent or that sounds distracted. If you need to, practice your opening line a few times to make sure you have it down before you call. Nobody will see you talking to yourself, I promise.

Establishing Credibility

I wore one of my Netropolis logo shirts and a pair of khakis to the meeting with Joseph (The logo T-shirts establish a "real business" image, and the khakis don't presume to be overly casual.) After shaking hands and introducing myself, I handed him two of my business cards and took his.

During our lunch conversation, Joseph asked a few questions about my philosophy of networking. He asked whether I could put together a network that had both Unix machines and Windows NT computers. He then asked what I thought of Novell Netware and the Macintosh platform. When clients ask these questions, they usually already have an opinion of the products in question, and they're really trying to find out what your biases are and how closely your opinion matches theirs.

Although you can't expect to agree on everything (especially if your customer has some sort of platform religion), you can keep from making a bad impression by keeping an open mind. Despite what you may dislike about Windows, Unix, Macintosh, or NetWare, these products all have their fans and their place in the network. Never open up a conversation with "I despise Windows and Microsoft" (or Macintosh and Apple, or whatever) or indicate any other unconsidered bias. When customers press me for an opinion because they want validation of their platform religion, my usual response is something along the lines of "Computers all have their problems and benefits. Operating systems all have their problems and benefits. My job is to find the optimal platform for your situation."

After discerning that I had no general platform preference, Joseph asked if I was certified, so I responded that I was a Microsoft Certified Systems Engineer, and that I had worked on but never completed NetWare certification because I hadn't been doing much NetWare work lately. He was satisfied with that answer. Had I not had at least one strong industrial certification, I doubt the company would have hired me.

Certifications, like any form of accreditation, don't really mean a whole lot among specialists in a field because they know that they're just tests, that they're highly biased toward the technologies and techniques that the vendor wants to market, and that unqualified people frequently pass them while qualified but unprepared people fail them.

Other consultants and network administrators probably don't care whether or not you're certified, but employers and customers do. Why? Because employers and customers realize that they don't have the expertise to tell if you're all talk and no action—the certification proves it to their satisfaction.

RESOURCES: CERTIFICATION

Don't let lack of a certification be a marketing problem for you. Whether or not you agree with the test methods used, and irrespective of whether you actually like the products or not, you will need to be certified in at least one "strong" certification in order to pass many of your customers' smell tests.

Keep your certifications up-to-date and appropriate. Being Novell certified isn't going to help much when a customer asks about Microsoft Windows NT.

Getting certified is easy if you already know the products and if you don't have to spend thousands on classroom training. Any active network administrator can get certified simply by studying certification guides and taking the exams directly.

For a complete list of certifications and how to get them, check out *Computer and Network Professional's Certification Guide* by J. Scott Christianson and Ava Fajen (Sybex Inc., 1999).

After learning that I was indeed certified, that I had an open mind and broad competence, Joseph asked about prior customers. This was a sticky issue: I had just started my consulting business, and I only had one regular customer and one other job that I'd worked. My regular customer was fine, but I was worried about using the other customer as a reference because they thought I had charged too much money. Although I'd solved their problem quickly and completely, I hadn't been invited back, so I didn't feel that they'd be a good marketing prospect.

I told Joseph that I had just begun consulting and that I had one client on retainer. I then talked about the projects I'd worked on for my former employer to establish myself as an able project manager.

TIP Use the experience you have in your current job as a work history. Your clients don't care about your expertise as a consultant (in fact, they hope you're naïve about business); they care about your expertise as a network integrator.

Don't be modest. Half the reason that I come off like an egotistical ass in this book is that I've been selling myself as an expert for so long that it has gone to my head. It should go to your head, too. Your customers aren't looking for character traits like humility; they're looking for good network integrators. You have to market yourself, so shed the shyness and tell people how you really feel about your talent.

Then Joseph hit me with a zinger: "Tell me about a job you've had that went wrong." I was a little floored by this, but I immediately understood the importance of it. He wanted to know how I would behave in an adverse situation, and what sort of attitude they could expect from me if things went south. I knew right off the bat that answers like "I had this really bad client" would immediately cast me in a bad light.

Again, honesty is the best policy. Given this question, I shored up my ego and told the story of the job I felt the worst about: a commercial research ship I'd worked on when I worked for my former employer. I had brought the job in myself as the result of a tip I received from a cable salesperson. My job was to design a closed-circuit video network, a Coast Guard–compliant fire alarm system, an onboard telephone system, and a fiber-optic computer network from scratch. The job took two years to complete, and cost about a half million dollars.

As with all large jobs (and especially jobs involving ships), there had been the occasional snafu along the way: my foreman pissed off the shipyard by making personal calls during the workday, the client was worried about progress at certain times, and so forth. All very normal.

At the end of the job, however, after the ship had been delivered, the alarm system had been proven out, the video system had been proven out, the fiber network had been tested, and the telephone system had been programmed and proven out, we ran into what I considered to be a minor problem: the two-channel voicemail system had persistent static on the B channel. Whenever anyone left voicemail using the second channel, the recorded message had an annoying level of static.

After testing the lines, and swapping the voicemail system out, we couldn't solve the problem. I finally had a representative of the phone system provider, Nortel (their real name), admit that the problem was a design problem of the voicemail system. Nortel knew about the problem but didn't consider it to be a big enough deal to bother fixing. They also wouldn't accept the system back or refund our money due to the length of time we'd had the system while it waited to be installed.

The voicemail system was a $5000 piece of equipment that my company should have replaced with another model to make the customer happy. Since the job was so large, $5000 was nothing. Unfortunately, my company was experiencing severe financial strain, and I could not convince them to spend the money to fix the problem. This put me between a rock and a hard place: I had a customer with a legitimate complaint that I couldn't fix. The voicemail machine issue wound up straining the entire job in the mind of the customer (who was pissed at the shipyard, as well, for other reasons). My company was not able to use the job in their marketing literature because the customer could not be relied upon to give a good reference. A job I should have been able to feel proud of left me feeling very conflicted. Joseph considered all this, and thanked me for my candor.

At this point, I turned the discussion to his company. I asked questions about the general level of computer expertise among users at his company, their method of revenue generation, and how large their sales were. He told me that their staff consisted of engineers and scientists, and that they currently had no revenue but were well funded by a venture capital firm.

NOTE It's important to ask questions about the company in your initial meetings before you become financially involved. You need to be able to estimate the company's ability to pay you before you expend a significant amount of effort. You also need to be able to estimate how much support their users will require. Sophisticated computer users take considerably less support time than novice computer users, so your pricing should reflect that difference.

We then ate lunch and chatted about things like the community, traffic, and so forth. At the end of lunch, Joseph told me he'd talk to his people and give me a call the next day.

HOW TO FAIL TO ESTABLISH CREDIBILITY

Your clients don't know you. If you can't provide them with a shred of evidence to show that you are a skilled network consultant, you'll find yourself doing more talking than working. If you can't bring yourself to get certified, or if there is no accepted certification for your specific expertise, you should get a long list of positive references that you can provide for your clients. A note from your mom isn't going to do it. If you don't have a lot of clients under your belt, you'll probably have to work a bunch of cut-rate jobs for cheapskate companies until you do.

You'll also fail to establish credibility if you don't act like a business. Things like company letterhead, uniforms, a company vehicle with your logo painted on it, business cards, and so forth can help you establish yourself immediately as a serious and professional consultant. I don't recommend spending a ton of money up front, but you will be competing with serious professionals, so as your business grows, so should your image.

Learning Requirements

Joseph called me the next day as promised. This time, instead of the conversation being about his company and my qualifications, we talked about their network problem. This was a good sign.

He explained that their immediate need was for 25 users, but that the company expected continuous sustained growth of about 100 users per year indefinitely.

I first asked about the way they use computers. What did the typical user need to be able to do? The answer was pretty generic: share files, printers, and scanners; pass messages amongst themselves; and share scheduling information.

Then I asked about specific applications: did they have a database, a material requirements planning system, financial applications, or any other applications that would need to be supported by or compatible with the network that would be produced? He told me that they currently used only desktop applications like CAD, office document software, and PC-based accounting. In the future, they would implement some sort of database system, but that was too far away to design for specifically. Their immediate need was simply for file and print services.

I then asked about Internet access: would they need Web access and outside e-mail? Joseph said that they would, but that at the moment, they didn't want to spend a lot of money on the problem. E-mail access was far more important to them than Web access. I asked if remote access to the network was a requirement; Joseph said that it was not and that they'd like to make sure that they had some reasonable level of protection against exploitation from the Internet.

At this point, I suggested splitting the solution into two phases: a design phase that would produce a specification that they could use to request bids from a number of different vendors, and an installation phase that I would perform if I won the bid. Joseph thanked me for the offer, but said they preferred to simply receive my design with a bid to implement it.

I often offer to perform requirements analysis and design work as a separate contract. Occasionally, customers will receive your proposed solution and bid, elect not to hire you, and then use your design to solicit lower-cost integrators. And many integrators tend to jump right into the solution without producing "build-to" documents that the customer signs off on. By splitting contracts into a low-cost initial design contract and an implementation contract, both problems are solved. In cases like this one where the client declines to hire design services, I put an obvious copyright on the document and a clause that makes it clear that the document is not to be used to solicit outside bids.

I then directed the conversation toward the existing infrastructure. Joseph told me that the company had already purchased a number of Dell desktop computers, which ran a mixture of Windows 98 and Windows NT. I asked if the company had a platform preference for the servers, and he indicated that while they did not, that the platform should be easy enough for a skilled computer user to administer, at least at first. The company was also partial to Microsoft Solutions, and preferred to use Dell for all their computer hardware. Finally, I asked if they had any workgroup printers, such as HP LaserJets or other large printers that had network interfaces. He said that they did have two HP LaserJet 4 printers, but that they did not have network interfaces.

I asked if he wanted me to resell the network equipment to them or if they preferred to purchase the equipment directly. He said that they would purchase the equipment, so my bid should be for labor only, but they did want a complete bill of material including vendor, estimated price, and source for each item required.

At this point, I had just about everything I needed to know. I asked Joseph if he wanted me to arrange for network cabling, or if he wanted to handle it based on my specification. He responded that I should include the subcontract in my bid. I then told him that my subcontractor would contact him directly to perform a phone interview, or a job walk if necessary, in order to return a bid for me.

HOW TO FAIL AT DEFINING REQUIREMENTS

The easiest way to fail at defining the customer's requirements is not to do it—simply assuming that you know what they need without verifying everything will have you presenting a solution that makes no sense to them, and which they'll decline.

The next most common way to fail at defining requirements is to be incomplete. If you don't have enough experience to figure out what your clients will want to do, go to the end users who will use the system and collect a wish list from all of them. Compile this wish list into requirements by merging them all together, throwing out pie-in-the-sky items, and then passing it on to the person who will be signing the contract before you design your solution. They'll appreciate your thoroughness.

Finally, you can fail at requirements by forgetting something your client told you they needed. Always take copious notes when you talk to a client. I use a Palm organizer to write down everything a client tells me they want done. You can use a small spiral notebook and a pencil if you want, but when you're at customer site, keep it with you at all times and get in the habit of writing while you listen.

Designing a Solution

The only thing unusual about the network solution the company needed was the sustained growth—the solution I identified would have to be able to scale indefinitely.

The immediate network was easy: a Windows NT–based file server was the obvious solution since their staff already had some experience with Windows and Windows NT. A single server was more than sufficient for 25 users. Access to the Internet was a little more problematic. In the days before DSL, access to the Internet for them would mean a Frame Relay line, which, for many companies, was prohibitively expensive. A firewall would also be required, and in those days firewalls were also very expensive.

HOW TO FAIL AT SYSTEM DESIGN

Systems that are inefficient will either cause you to lose the bid to a more efficient consultant, or they will ultimately disappoint your customer. Desktop computers and software should run about $3000 per user for normal business users (figure $5000 to $7000 for engineers, scientists, and programmers). Network infrastructure (everything else) should cost about $1000 per user. If your solution is way outside this realm (unless there are mitigating factors) on the high side, you'll lose the bid or convince the customer that networking is too expensive. On the low side, you'll create a fragile network built on cheap components, frustrating software, and unsustainable management practices.

Estimating the Cost

To estimate the cost of the project's hardware and software, I logged onto my favorite Internet-based, online network equipment vendor (then uvision .com, now shopper.com) and priced all the equipment. I fired up Excel and listed every piece of equipment I could think of, going by my initial network diagram. Table 3.1 shows this list.

TABLE 3.1 **Network Equipment Costs**

Item	Model	Vendor	Cost	Qty	Total
Server	PowerEdge	Dell	$7500	1	$7500
100MB hub	PowerStack II	3Com	$1200	2	$2400
100MB NIC	Etherfast	3Com	$120	27	$3240
Tape backup	20GB DAT	Sony	$1500	1	$1500
Network cables	Cat 5, 3'	Fry's	$3	27	$81
Network cables	Cat 5, 15'	Fry's	$5	27	$135
Windows NT	Server 4	Microsoft	$700	1	$700
Client Licenses	Server 4	Microsoft	$40	25	$1000
Backup Exec	NT	Arcada	$500	1	$500
E-mail service	NTMail	NTMail	$800	1	$800
				Sum:	$17,856
				Tax:	$1786
				Total:	$19,642

The network portion was easy. After computing the costs directly, I rounded the number up to $20,000 for my proposal.

The hard part would be cost-effective Internet access. I checked the Web sites of a number of different business-oriented ISPs and eventually found a service offered by PSINet that included the circuit costs. I also found a service the client could use to filter their Internet connections, which would provide a simple firewalling service and obviate the cost of what, at that time, would have been a $5000 firewall. The circuit was 56K Frame Relay, and the monthly cost with the filtering service was about $500, including circuit charges. The setup charges totaled $800, which included registration of their domain name.

The last piece of the contract was the network cabling. I called a friend of mine who owned a network cabling company; we had worked together at my former employer's, and I knew I could rely on his quality. He told me to figure $150 per network location unless the construction was unusual, meaning not drywall and drop ceilings. Since we'd worked together, he knew that I knew how to estimate network cabling costs myself and that he could rely on my report about the customer's premises.

Given that, I assumed a cable plant price of $4000, which allowed for two extra drops in case the server was located away from the hubs.

So the total cost of the initial network was $20,000 + $4000 + $800, or $24,800. I rounded this price up again to $25,000 for my documentation.

HOW TO FAIL AT COSTING

You can fail to cost something correctly by leaving components out, or forgetting about things like the physical cable plant. Failing to think the problem all the way through will definitely offend your customer: Cost overruns are probably the most serious problem you can cause. If you're just providing budgetary numbers, pad them by 10 percent. If you're competing, be as precise as possible.

Determining the Price

After I knew the hard costs, it was time to determine my fee. Working on a firm, fixed-price basis meant that I would estimate my time and multiply that by my hourly rate to determine how much to charge. My spreadsheet is shown in Table 3.2.

TABLE 3.2 Consulting Fees

Service	Hours	Qty	Rate	Cost
Install and configure server	8	1	$100	$800
Configure hubs and closet wiring	1	1	$100	$100
Install and configure clients	2	25	$100	$5000
Integrate Internet access	1	1	$100	$100
Sum		60		$6000

As you can see, I don't show charges for things like my bid, time on the phone, travel, and other miscellaneous items. In my experience, customers hate to feel like they're being nickel and dimed by a cut-rate consultant, so I simply raise my hourly rate so I can build in incidental expenses. I actually never charge for anything that costs less than $100 in a month.

As you can see, I estimated 60 hours, or 1.5 work weeks, for $6000. This amount would cover my entire month, so if I got the job, I would only need to work 1.5 weeks that month. You can see how consulting will help you free up as much time as you'd like as long as you can keep steady work coming in.

By this point, I had the network design, bill of materials, and estimated cost, so I was ready to write my proposal.

NOTE In most cases, whether or not you actually provide the equipment and software, you will be responsible for specifying it, finding a source, and providing budgetary amounts to your customer so they know what to expect.

HOW TO FAIL AT PRICING

There are two ways to fail at pricing: charge too much, and charge too little. Customers expect a certain price range for professional services. I estimate my prices in a range from $62.50 per hour for preferred customers and work I'm very interested in, to $150 per hour for work I don't want to do. But I never reveal my true hourly rate to customers; rather, I "hide" my hourly rate by using firm, fixed-price contracts and fixed monthly retainers. The amounts I come up with using this method have never caused any problems, and they have actually provided a higher net income for my time spent because I rarely spend as many hours as I estimate. Chapter 10 details how I set my prices and how you should, too.

Proposing the Solution

I use a standard Word template for proposals, which is included as an appendix to this book (Appendix A). Basically, the document is a cover page, pages defining the scope of work, pages defining the cost and payment terms, and pages that specify contractual stipulations to protect both parties. Network diagrams and other technical details are added to the document as attachments, enclosures, or exhibits (pick the term you like best). Refer to Appendix A to see the document as applied to a similar job.

The scope of work that I mentioned above was simply a list of bulleted items taken from my service estimate workup:

➤ Install and configure server.

➤ Configure hubs and closet wiring.

➤ Install and configure clients.

➤ Integrate Internet access.

For the final portion of the scope of work, I wrote in a list of tests that will prove everything is working, such as:

➤ Perform a user logon.

➤ Attach to a network drive.

➤ Copy a file to the file server.

➤ Secure a folder against all but one user, and show that only that user can access the data in the folder.

➤ Browse a public Web site.

➤ Send and receive e-mail from an Internet e-mail account.

➤ Backup the server and restore a file from backup.

These lists define my total responsibility and prove that I've accomplished the work. Ultimately, the document created forms both the proposal and the contract.

HOW TO FAIL AT PROPOSALS

Proposals that are unclear or incomplete are problems. If your customer mentioned something you forgot in your proposal, you're on thin ice. They expect you to be complete and precise, and since your proposal is the first product they see from you, and because there's no contract in place, you can lose the deal before it starts.

Avoid proposals so full of jargon that your customer has to ask for an interpretation. Your proposals should be written in plain English that can be understood by any businessperson. The worst possible thing you can do is make your customer feel stupid.

Establishing the Contract

Upon completing my proposal/contract (Chapter 9 discusses writing contracts in detail), I called Joseph and asked him how he wanted it delivered. He asked me to fax it to him, so I printed it to my fax/modem at the number he specified. After that, I merely had to wait for him to call. He called after receiving it and said that the company would be receiving proposals until their meeting next Tuesday, at which time they would select a bidder. He said he'd call me then to tell me if I got the job.

I was a little worried at that point: Had I known they were accepting bids from other integrators, I probably would have reduced my labor rate. Alas, the proposal was out, so the deed was done. I decided not to worry about it since I couldn't change it now.

When Tuesday rolled around, I worked in the office all morning, anxiously awaiting Joseph's call. It came around 2:30 that afternoon. When his first question was to ask how soon it could be up, I knew I had the job. We agreed to meet the next morning to sign the contract; after it was signed, I would start immediately.

I asked him how the other bids looked in comparison. He told me they'd received three other bids: one that was incoherent, one that specified a network architecture that was far outside their budget (the consultant specified a central ATM switch to allow for future growth), and one very similar bid from a company that charged only $50 per hour. I found it surprising that they'd offer me the job when the other company's labor rate was half of mine, and he responded that the cut-rate consulting firm would work only on an open-ended basis; their bid estimated two weeks' installation time, but it did not put a firm fixed price on the total job—if it took them four weeks to finish, the company would have to keep paying while they worked. Essentially, this meant that the company would rather pay twice as much up front for a guaranteed maximum price.

We met the next morning to sign the contracts. I asked Joseph if I could meet with the executive committee (the people who run the company directly) to explain the network architecture and its installation progress, and to answer any questions they might have about its operation. Joseph appreciated the idea, and said I could take 15 minutes at their regular Tuesday meeting.

After that, I went to their purchasing department to help write the requisitions for the network equipment and software.

HOW TO FAIL AT CONTRACTING

Some consultants work without contracts. I find this to be about as sane as driving without insurance. I've never had a legal problem with a customer—a fact I attribute to well-defined contracts. Contracts project professionalism, they define the expectations the customer should have of you, and you of them, and they spell out costs clearly. Contracts, while useful in legal disputes, are far more valuable in avoiding legal disputes.

Managing Expectations

About a week of wait time occurred while ordering the network equipment. On Tuesday, I met with the executive committee at the beginning of their regular meeting.

After introducing myself to the room of about seven people, I explained the network that I would be installing. Starting with the purpose of the network, I moved on to features and the functionality provided. Last, I explained the products we selected to build the network, and drew a basic network diagram on the whiteboard.

When I was finished, the various executives asked questions about the basic network functions, upgradability, security, and so forth. I explained that certain things like a tape backup policy and the e-mail software the company used would change when the network grew beyond one or two servers, but that purchasing enterprise solutions for those functions now didn't make much sense. I wanted to make sure that they were aware of the fact that some small portions of the design would be obviated as the network grew, so they didn't feel like I hadn't considered the problem or had wasted their money initially.

After the Q&A session, I explained the timeline for the installation, the need for user training (which I would not be providing beyond the basics of logging in and using the file server), and the type of documentation I would provide. I agreed to put together a user's manual pamphlet that described basic network functions like logging on, using shared documents, and sending e-mail.

HOW TO FAIL AT MANAGING EXPECTATIONS

Managing a customer's expectations is an important part of keeping customers satisfied. The only way you'll fulfill their expectations is if you know what they expect and if their expectations are reasonable. The best way to accomplish this is to let the customer know exactly what's going to happen the whole way through the contract.

Give yourself plenty of breathing room on the timeline—make sure your customers don't expect you to have miracles performed in two days. Of course, this is a bit of "Do as I say, not as I do," since my example in Chapter 2 was exactly that—but give yourself as much room as you can with timelines. Also, make sure you know what the customers think is important.

Performing the Work

Once all the equipment had arrived, I started work. The first thing I wanted to get done was the server. It didn't make sense to start with the data-link layer because I wouldn't be able to test connectivity easily without the server running.

The first thing I did was get a notepad to write down every element of configuration I performed; these notes would later form my as-built documentation.

Although purchasing a server from Dell was more expensive than building one myself, it saved me a considerable amount of time. NT Server was pre-installed; all I had to do was complete the installation and configure the server. I then installed the tape backup software and the e-mail service software.

Once the configuration was finished, I set up DHCP, name services, and the default user policies. Although the specification called for neither, both would save me time. After that, I set up the disk shares and permissions. Finally, I added user accounts with home directories and configured user accounts for the e-mail software.

Upon completing the server installation, I started a tape backup to keep a copy of the initial system configuration. I then set up the stackable hubs in the central closet and attached them to the hub. Because there were over

100 network drops in the building, I couldn't install jumpers until I knew where all the client computers were, so I attached only the file server. By the time I finished this, the first day was over.

The next morning, I went around the facility and identified the locations of each client and left a cable and network adapter in each room. I also recorded the port number from each room so that when I returned to the closet, I could jumper the network ports to the hubs. This way, I could simply go from room to room configuring clients without running back and forth to the closet to attach jumper cables.

Then, I grabbed my cordless screwdriver and went to work on client computers. At each location, I opened the machine, installed the network adapter, closed it, booted it, installed the driver, configured the network stack, rebooted, and logged in as the intended user, leaving the computer on the "You must change your password" screen so the ultimate user could type in the password they wanted.

I ran into a snag about halfway through four 486 class machines that didn't have PCI slots. When I asked about clients, Joseph told me they had only Pentium machines. This was important, because at this time, 10/100 autosensing hubs didn't exist; equipment was either 10MB or 100MB. I had purchased exclusively 100MB equipment, and although I'd heard of a company that made a 100MB ISA adapter, I had no idea where to procure them or how long it would take. This was a serious problem.

At the end of the day, I brought the issue up to Joseph. He actually went over to check the machines, and was surprised to find out that they weren't Pentium-class computers. When I explained that I would not be able to get them up on the 100MB network, he asked what the options were. I told him that we could either install a second 10MB NIC in the server and attach a 10MB hub ($500), or we could put in a 10/100 switch, which at that time ran about $5000, or we could replace the computers with more current computers, which would cost about $10,000. Joseph took notes and asked me what I recommended. I said I thought the best thing to do would be to replace the computers, since it kept the network architecture pure and would have to be done eventually anyway. He said he'd get back to me.

I skipped those machines and finished the rest of the clients over the course of the next two days. When I'd completed most of the client work, I went back to talk to Joseph about the 10MB machines. He said they hadn't decided what to do about the computers yet, so I should start on documentation rather than continue.

The next day, Joseph said that although they'd prefer to replace the computers, the company's IT budget for the near future was already gone. I should go ahead and attach a 10MB hub to the server to complete the work. He authorized my expense for five 10MB NICs and a 10MB hub so we could complete the work as quickly as possible. I ran down to a local computer store and purchased the equipment, and upon returning, installed the 10MB NIC in the server and installed the 10MB hub in the closet. I then configured the four 10MB machines, thus completing the fourth day of the installation.

HOW TO FAIL AT PERFORMANCE

The obvious way to fail at performing the work of a contract is to get in over your head and be unable to complete the job. There's no way to fix that problem—you can pretty much forget being paid if you can't complete the work.

Other minor ways to fail are to create negative impressions of your work through sloppiness or by not paying attention to detail. Failing to document what you have done, clean up after yourself, or present a professional attitude will all create negative impressions.

Don't cut corners or take shortcuts. Don't get into the habit of thinking you'll remember everything when you're finished—take copious notes while you work. It'll save you a lot of hassle when you're finished.

Documenting the Solution

I spent the first half of the next day writing the network documentation. This consisted of a formalization of my installation notes into what amounts to a set of instructions to a mythical network integrator on how to re-create the network. I find that writing in this style provides a good framework for providing every piece of configuration information the customer will need to know. I also included an as-built network diagram showing fixed IP addresses and routing information. The documentation for this job is included as Appendix B.

HOW TO FAIL AT DOCUMENTATION

Failing to document is unprofessional, although I see it all the time. I wind up cleaning up after lazy integrators all the time—in fact, I've performed a number of contracts where my job is simply to go in and survey an existing network to produce the documentation that should have accompanied it in the first place.

Of course accuracy is key, but accuracy of documentation is easy. Completeness is also easy if you simply document every change you make to the system as you go.

I learned to document with my first customer, a pharmaceutical company. Their documentation practices were so heinous that I actually had to tape a play-by-play of my activities as I worked. I then had to transcribe myself because they wanted a record of literally everything that happened to their equipment. I also had to perform hour-long validation tests of computers each time I opened one up for any reason. It sucked, but it taught me how to create useful documentation easily for my other customers.

Delivering the Final Product

Once the documentation was complete, I was ready to finish the job. I went back to Joseph's office that afternoon and delivered my documentation, which he browsed through for a moment. I then told him that I was ready to perform the testing according to the original contract, so I used his client computer to walk through the test steps, and he signed off on each test line item. After the testing was complete, I showed him the network closet and we walked around to a few client stations.

HOW TO FAIL AT DELIVERY

It amazes me how many consultants don't go through a formal delivery procedure. "Okay, I'm done now! I'll mail you a bill," seems to be the method a lot of people use.

Customers need closure. By clearly defining the point when you're finished, you can avoid calls asking when you're coming in today, or needy customers who just want you around for a few days after you've completed your work. Having a test procedure you can use to prove you've completed the contract is also invaluable: it shows the customer in no uncertain terms that you've done what you've said you were going to do, and that if they want some additional work performed, it will have to be under the auspices of a new arrangement. It clearly separates work that is part of the contract from work that isn't.

Continuing the Relationship

While we walked around the client stations, Joseph mentioned that the company was very impressed with my performance as a consultant; they'd never seen a consultant work as quickly or with as much dedication. I told him that I thought that was more a function of firm fixed pricing than of motivation—the sooner I finished, the more money I made. He laughed about that, and then asked if I wanted to work there full time. They were looking for a network administrator who could handle a rapidly growing network. The position could eventually grow into the company's Chief Technology Officer. He offered me $75,000 on the spot.

I was floored. The salary was $20,000 more than I'd made at the job I left two months earlier. Although I wanted to consult, I didn't have any illusions about my marketing ability—making more money than that would be damned difficult. I told him I'd think about it and get back to him on Monday.

That night, when I got home, I fired up QuickBooks and faxed Digital Metrics the invoice for the work I'd done.

I thought about the job offer all weekend. I had just been asked to help a friend of mine out with a technical book he was writing, which I would have to give up. I really like the idea of being published, but I really didn't think I'd make any money at writing—perhaps $10,000 at most over the life of the book. Still, my ultimate goal in life was to write fiction, and starting with a technical book seemed like a good way to get my feet wet.

Then there was the issue of my other customer, the branch office of a major pharmaceutical manufacturer. They paid me a $1200-per-month retainer for what amounted to about two hours of work a month. I had a contract with them that I didn't want to drop.

Then there was the freedom issue. By completing this contract, I'd already made a month's worth of money in a week. If I could sustain this average, I'd have time to write full time—essentially, I'd be able to pursue my ultimate goal.

On Monday, I went back to the job site to make sure there weren't any problems I didn't know about and to help users begin to use the system. I stopped by Joseph's office and we talked.

I explained to him that while their offer was more than generous, I wanted to try my hand at consulting. I then offered him a retainer: I would administer their network on call for $50 per user per month plus $200 per server or wide-area trunk line (for example, their 56K Frame-Relay circuit). My retainer would automatically grow as the company grew, and I'd use that money to add people when necessary as their needs grew. The retainer would cover adding client computers, but adding servers or network infrastructure work would be handled as separate fixed-price contracts.

Joseph called the company's CFO into the meeting directly, something that seemed somewhat out of character for him. I repeated my offer to the CFO, whom I could tell was running the numbers in his head. He asked questions about my availability; I promised a next-day response to any call and a two-hour response to work stoppage issues during the workday. I'd arrange for constant coverage if I was out of town, and I'd put in full-time staff whenever their needs required it.

The CFO told me to write up a proposal and fax it to him. As long as they could get a month-to-month deal, they'd do it. I also had to promise to train any IT staff they wanted to add on their own if they decided to discontinue their relationship with me, which I naturally agreed to.

I was happy with this. I had another retainer, making my recurring monthly income about $3000 after just two months as a consultant, along with the $8000 I'd made in fixed-price contracts. It looked like things were going to work out pretty well.

HOW TO FAIL AT CONSULTING

You need to keep your customers. The vast majority of the work I do (and this is true of most consultants) is for existing customers. I probably add only one or two customers per year. By keeping your old customers coming back, you can obviate the hardest part of consulting: marketing.

I use retainers to create a fixed income for me and a fixed-support budget for my customers. It works well for everyone involved. Make sure your customers know you're interested in finding new customers—they all know other businesspeople. A lot of your new contacts will come through existing customers.

Conclusion

As a consultant, you will become a full-time project manager—every bit of work you do from now on will be a project, and you'll have to handle all the details of each one. The remainder of this book details how to handle various aspects of project management, and Chapter 11 discusses project management specifically.

If you don't have any project management experience, don't worry. It comes pretty naturally once you start working as a consultant. At first, you'll have to compensate for your lack of experience by being very detail oriented, but with time you'll learn what you need to explicitly keep track of and what you don't.

Habit Forming

4

"Casual Friday, right?"

This chapter is about your personal habits: your speaking habits, your work habits—yes, even your grooming habits. I'm even going to touch on your illegal habits. It's about the habits you need to acquire and the ones you need to break. I placed it early in the book because you can begin to practice these things now while you are still employed. Then, by the time you start consulting, you'll have acquired the habits you need and you'll have broken the bad ones (except the ones you really like).

There's a big difference between the way employees communicate and the way consultants communicate. The interface between clients and customers is far different than the interface between coworkers. Now that you'll be going from a coworker relationship to a consulting relationship, you'll need to relearn a lot of business communications skills.

Everybody thinks that they are funny, amicable, and well groomed. I thought I was all of these things, but I was mistaken; most of this chapter is based on things I've learned the hard way, so read carefully and avoid making my mistakes.

Forming Work Habits

Perhaps the most difficult part of being a consultant is the lack of rigorous structure to your life. It's great to be able to go sailing in the middle of the week (trust me, it's great), but the price you pay for that freedom is a lack of imposed structure. If you let it happen, your work habits will decay to the point that you don't really work at all; if this happens, you won't make any money and will ultimately fail at consulting. Diligence and self motivation are required to keep you going because nobody is around to check the clock or force you to maintain a routine.

Fortunately, you also probably have a few bad work habits now that will go away on their own once you're your own boss. Procrastination pretty much goes away by itself because you're doing the work you created for yourself and because there's such a close relationship between working and getting money; the longer you take to finish, the longer your clients will take to pay you. Given this natural dynamic, procrastination takes care of itself, along with its cousin—complete lack of motivation.

Help, I'm Lazy and I Can't Get Up!

The first day after I left my last job, I slept in till noon—just because I could. I've been struggling to break that habit ever since. We've all heard that smoking is as addictive as heroin. Well, I quit smoking, but I can't shake this sleeping-late thing, so, assuming a transitive property of addiction, sleeping late is more addictive than heroin. The Latin root of the word narcotic means sleep, so it's a safe bet that the ancient Romans also knew all about the seductive quality of sleep.

The only advice I can give on sleeping late is don't start. From the day you begin consulting, treat your consulting practice as a job. If you get in the habit of working late and then sleeping late to make up for it, you'll find your customers making fun of you in the best case, and being annoyed with your lack of sensitivity about their schedule in the worst. Schedule your workday the same way the rest of your time zone does: from 8:00 A.M. to 5:00 P.M.

About half of my trouble calls come first thing in the morning because something has gone down during the night. You will get calls starting at 8:00 A.M. routinely, so you need to be prepared to accept them at that time. I get really tired of the "Hi, Matt. Did I wake you up?" joke that my customers seem to think is funny. It's difficult to convince them otherwise in my raspy morning voice.

The morning can be your most productive time of day—especially if you have children. You may find it's easiest to go to bed with them at 9:00 P.M. and to get up at 4:00 A.M. You'll get at least two solid hours of work done before others start to stir, perhaps more if your children are younger. Then you can get them off to school as your customers start calling. Then you'll have until they get out of school to work without interruption.

Schedule customer visits in the afternoon (if you've made arrangements for the care of your children after school) so that you don't lose valuable work time in your home office while the kids are away. If you have toddlers or infants, you may find that you'll need daycare, or perhaps even an office away from the home in order to conduct your business professionally.

The evil twin of sleeping late is working late—another bad habit I'm caught up in. I usually have something I just have to have done tomorrow, so I stay up as long as it takes to finish. When I turn in at 2:00 or 3:00 A.M., I'm guaranteeing that I won't be up with the rest of the world. It's also very stressful to be on a different sleep schedule than your spouse. Avoid working evenings except in emergency situations (like your book is overdue), and especially avoid getting in the habit of working late.

Organization and Scheduling

A very good friend of mine knows virtually everything I know about computing systems. He's an excellent communicator, has a strong customer support ethic, and he's a hard worker. As a technical writer, he has plenty of spare time during the day to consult. Yet he does not attempt to consult on his own, and to my knowledge has never contracted except as a sub to another consultant.

Why? According to his own reckoning, he's not organized enough to consult and has no desire to become so. Does this really matter so much? Of course it does. Unless you work contracts that can be completed in a single day, you need to get organized.

You will need to keep track of the following:

➤ Contacts

➤ Projects

➤ Official communications and documents

➤ Appointments

➤ Tasks

Being organized used to require a day planner and an obsessive-compulsive disorder. Fortunately, the advent of the information age has provided us with handheld computers. Geeks, even those who are proud of their slovenliness, have been tricked into buying these organizational devices because they're also nifty gadgets. Give in. You need one.

When I started using an Apple Newton in 1993, it was large, bulky, and so uncommon that it distracted everyone. But then the Palm Pilot came out; it was both inexpensive enough and inconspicuous enough to gain widespread acceptance, even among normal people. 3Com Palms are so prevalent now that they don't even cause eyebrows to rise. Besides, adults never really make fun of people directly, so you'll never know if people think you're silly for using one.

The trick to using an electronic organizer is actually using it. To do this, you have to take it with you everywhere and fire it up every time you talk to someone. Record appointments as soon as you make them. Add tasks as soon as you create them. Add contacts as soon as you get in the car after receiving the business card.

The other side of inserting information is checking it. I actually have no problem putting data in my organizer, but I still have to remind myself to check it on a regular basis. Here again, forming a habit will help. Check your organizer when you start the workday to refresh yourself on the day's events. Check it every time you have spare time in your workday to remind yourself what needs to be done. Pesonally, I check my Palm device when I get up in the morning, and then every time I get into my car. I find that attaching the "checking" function to a specific activity makes it easier to remember and therefore easier to form the habit.

Good Grooming for Geeks

I know, we're all adults and we don't need anyone telling us how to groom ourselves. I'd believe that, except I still run into adults (myself included) who haven't made a habit of absolutely everything they should.

As an employee, you don't have to sell yourself—you did that once, and all you have to do to keep your job is keep from causing a liability problem for your employer. As a consultant, you have to be half technician, half salesman. I'm not talking about being cheesy with gold watches and silk suits, but you do need to look the way people expect you to look as a consultant. Any negative thought a potential customer may form about you should be avoided.

Smell Good and Prosper

There is no good smell in business. Unless you sell fried chicken or muffins, your business day should be entirely odorless. Obviously, you should shower every day—most people have no problem with that. But while working in close proximity to people (as a consultant, you'll lean over people sitting at their computers nearly every time you go to work), I've noticed that some people decay more rapidly than others during the workday. Their aromatic half-life is less than eight hours long, and their choice of deodorant isn't up to the job of keeping them odorless.

I've also noticed that too much deodorant can be just as bad (if not worse) than the natural odor it masks. Similarly, I find that I also have a hard time with the perfume/cologne thing. Both are distracting, and neither are as good as simply having no smell at all. If you consult, avoid both. Perfume and cologne are designed to attract the opposite sex, which should be avoided at work anyway.

Consider choosing odor-neutral or odor-free soaps, shampoos, and deodorants. Make sure that your laundry soap doesn't smell funny either. Avoid handling your pets before you leave in the morning—many people are allergic to pet dander, so showing up looking like a mohair sweater because your cats are shedding may someday cause problems (or at least a sneezing fit) with a customer.

Smoking also creates odor problems, especially if you smoke products other than tobacco. I know, smokers are already the new persecuted people in America, but that status just exacerbates your problem if you smoke: since most indoor smoking has been eliminated in the U.S., the smell of smoke is much easier to detect, and non-smokers are even more vehement about pointing it out. If you have to smoke, get in the habit of smoking before you shower in the morning, outside if possible. Your wardrobe should not smell like smoke. Avoid smoking during the day; if you must smoke, do so outside and never in front of customers who don't smoke. Once you're home for the evening, you can feel free to smoke to your heart's content (or would that be discontent?), but you should get in the habit of smoking outside so your wardrobe won't be suffused with the odor all the time. Don't smoke in your car if you intend to have customers in it.

Proper dental hygiene is also crucial to maintaining an odor-free personal zone. Brushing in the morning is obviously crucial, but you should also keep a pack of sugar-free gum in your car so you can "freshen" whenever you need too.

Ask your spouse to be honest and tell you if you need to brush up on any areas of hygiene. Nobody smells you more than your spouse. If you don't have a smelling relationship with anyone, ask a close friend to sniff you over once and point out any problem areas.

Dressing Up or Down

Clothes for computer consultants can be tricky. When I first started consulting, I remember going to a job in khakis, a collared shirt, and a tie. The customer was very impressed with my presentation, and told me that they couldn't wait to meet with our technical people. There was an awkward moment when I convinced them that despite the tie and my dashing good looks (this was during that two-week period of my life when I was between being underweight and being overweight, the time when I was fortunate enough to meet my wife), I was indeed the technician. We laughed about it afterward, but it drove home a point to me: look the way people expect you to look. Besides, geeks who try to dress up usually come off looking like used car salesmen anyway.

Computer geeks are expected to dress less formally than the standard businessperson. We have geeks to thank for casual Friday and the breakdown of dress codes throughout the business world. But this puts the consultant in a tricky spot: how does a person dress geek-chic? I (originally) couldn't bring myself to show up to a customer site in a T-shirt and jeans, and I've never really liked oxfords. My first attempt was to wear sweaters, but that only works in the wintertime. By the time the first summer rolled around, I'd settled on the right way to dress: uniform shirts, either oxfords or T-shirts, depending upon the phase of the job. Getting a dozen logo T-shirts was probably one of the best image decisions I've ever made. It solved the "what do I wear" problem, since I can now wear the same thing every day without people saying "Gee, didn't he wear that same thing yesterday?" I can also project a more professional image, as if I am part of a large firm. I usually wear them with new jeans, but you can choose whatever type of pants you like. I even wear shorts on a regular basis in the summertime now.

Check your yellow pages under "graphics," "logos," and "uniforms" for companies that specialize in creating custom business uniform graphics. I don't know of any national companies I can recommend, and there are so many local shops that a Web search would be exhausting.

Speaking of Speaking

Life is not fair, and consulting is even less so. As a consultant, you will need to become politically correct in your speech and mannerisms, in the most milquetoast sense of the term. Why? Because by becoming a consultant, you've lost your freedom of speech. You can no longer afford to offend people.

Unlike employees, consultants don't have to be fired—they simply needn't be called back. This makes your position as a consultant for a company far more tenuous than that of a regular employee. Regular employees have to bring weapons to work before they get fired. All you have to do is make a joke that doesn't get laughs. It starts out simply enough—a client shares an anecdote, you reciprocate; client laughs; you're on a roll so you tell another, client's mom is French; you're out of a job.

It's not a two-way street, though. You may find you are consulting for the biggest ingrate on the planet. It's okay for them to be an ingrate. It's not okay for you to be one, too. This portion of the chapter is all about navigating the tricky waters of what to say, when to say it, and most importantly, what never to say.

Clients Are Not Your Friends

Clients are not your friends. Obviously, you should have a friendly relationship with them, but to your clients, you exist to solve a specific problem. Just because people are friendly to you, it doesn't mean that they are your friends. If you slapped a patrol officer and were thrown in jail, you'd call a friend to bail you out. You wouldn't call a client. That defines the essential difference between friends and friendly acquaintances.

The reason you can't simply assume that clients are your friends is that they may have a totally different perception of you than you have of them. Remember that they're involved in a business relationship with you out of necessity, not out of some desire to be close to you personally. And that's the way they usually want to keep it. Cordiality can be easily mistaken for friendship.

Again, in the unfair world of consulting, the reciprocal case is not taboo: if a client asks you out sailing and you want to go sailing with that person, that's fine. As long as the client initiates the change from a business relationship to an actual friendship, you don't have to worry about misreading their perceptions. Of course, that's assuming you want to go sailing with them. If you don't, make up an excuse. Consultants are always busy, so you can always claim to have too much on your plate. Don't tell them you aren't interested in a sailing relationship with them—they'll eventually get the idea if you're always too busy.

In addition to Not Calling Clients for Bail Money, you should avoid the following:

➤ Inviting clients to social functions.

➤ Asking to be invited to social functions.

➤ Asking a client out on a date.

➤ Drinking alcoholic beverages during a lunch meeting.

➤ Dressing like you're in high school when you come to the office.

➤ Clicking your tongue post loudly against your teeth when you talk.

➤ Crying.

➤ Asking personal questions like "If your husband turned up missing, how long would it be before you started dating again?"

➤ Talking about your own personal life, as in "My mom's in the hospital. Really bad corn on her right foot. It's going to require surgery."

➤ Assuming your client will pick up the tab for lunch.

➤ Coming in when you're actually sick.

➤ Making up excuses to come in more than your contract requires because you like the environment or the client.

➤ Showing up at the office unexpectedly without calling first.

➤ Chewing your nails, washing your hands too frequently, or grooming other people.

➤ Showing up at your client's home dressed in an eerily similar fashion.

Opinions Are Best Left in a Salad

Okay, I know that doesn't make much sense, but I've always thought those little red things inside green olives should be called opinions. Then I could order a martini with two opinions.

As a consultant, you should learn to charge for your opinion. Don't express it unless you're being paid to. The absolute worst thing consultants can do (that isn't illegal) is bash their prospective clients over the head with an unsolicited opinion. You'll be branded a blowhard and you'll show them that you aren't truly objective. Opinion in the absence of a specific case isn't really opinion, it's dogma.

Are you a blowhard? Here's a quiz:

1. Which is better, Windows NT or Linux?

   A. Windows NT

   B. Linux

   C. Depends on the problem, available talent, and budget

2. Which is better, Macs or PCs?

   A. Macs

   B. PCs

   C. Depends on the problem, available talent, and budget

3. Which is better, an off-the-shelf package or a custom solution?

   A. Off-the-shelf package

   B. Custom solution

   C. Depends on the problem, available talent, and budget

Okay, granted this quiz is easier than the "Is He Sleeping Around?" quiz from the February '98 *Cosmo*, but it makes my point: unqualified opinions offend people because they indicate that a consultant doesn't have an open mind to evaluate their problem effectively. Even worse is the foot-in-mouth problem of bashing somebody's pet idea just before you find out it's their pet idea, as in this actual conversation from my consulting experience:

Client: So, what do you think about Microsoft Exchange?

Me: I think it's bloated, expensive, and way too complex for what it actually does. Most people only use its Internet e-mail functionality anyway. I wouldn't touch it with a 10-foot pole.

Client: Oh. Well, we just bought it. I guess we'll hire somebody else to maintain it.

Take a hatchet to your skull and open your mind. Try repeating "Bill Gates isn't actually evil" or "Linux isn't actually that hard to use" over and over until you can recommend the right software for the job.

Conversation Taboos

Now that we've established the difference between friendly business relationships and actual friends, I'm going to clarify the topics that are off limits to anyone in your life except your friends, family, and people you dislike.

Bodily Fluids

Conversations about bodily fluids, and the activities that accompany them, are completely off limits in the business world unless you happen to be a doctor, in which case I hope you aren't reading this book.

People who talk about how many repetitions they can do or how much they can bench are incredibly annoying to everyone else, and they're only talking about sweat, the most benign of all possible bodily fluids. Listening to people talk about sex, digestion, or sucking chest wounds is even more disconcerting over lunch. Leave the locker room in the locker room, the bedroom in the bedroom, and the emergency room in the emergency room.

Swearing

Don't swear in front of your customers. This is a particularly difficult one for me (as is avoiding discussions of bodily fluids), but it's an absolute necessity. There's no telling whom you'll offend when you swear, and if your client has the manners I didn't get at birth, you won't know because they won't tell you. You just won't get called back.

If, like me, you find your language taking a walk down the seedier side of town more often than not, I suggest the age-old standby: the substitute swear. Here's a translation table:

- ➤ A------   Person
- ➤ B----   Person
- ➤ D---   Darn, Dang
- ➤ F---   Flip, Flipping, Flipper
- ➤ G------   Gosh Darn
- ➤ H---   Heck
- ➤ S---   Shoot
- ➤ Z----   Person

I actually perform non-swearing exercises by standing in front of the mirror and repeating the words "dang," "darn," and "That Person is a Shoothead!"

over and over until I find myself using the terms naturally. You'll sound like Barney Fife in no time.

Crude Stories

Stories that start out "That reminds me of this time when I was in the Navy" should probably be left out of business discussions (I have a hard time with this one as well). If you were popular in high school, you probably shouldn't talk about that either. Fortunately, I was huge geek in high school, so I mine that rich vein of boredom all the time when I need people to leave me alone at a customer's site.

It always amazes me what people will talk about over lunch, though. It's as if by walking into a Red Lobster, you're suddenly free of the shackles of the business relationship. Don't buy in. And don't believe for a minute that although an employee of your customer might think it's okay to tell fraternity hazing stories, it's okay for you to reciprocate. If you think the story is funny, respond as you will, but when you relate your sordid tale of youthful bed-wetting, remember that blabbermouth is going to tell your story to all the other slackers who spend more time by the coffee pot than in their cubicles. Next thing you know, the accounts payable guy won't ask you to join his Zen meditation discussion group anymore, and your checks will mysteriously arrive a month later than before. You'll have no idea why.

The employees of your client are protected by a bond much stronger than you are. You can't afford to lose a customer over something as stupid as a joke you told to the wrong person.

Politics and Religion

I have a friend who doesn't wear shoes. He doesn't wear them at his house, he doesn't wear them at the store, and—yes—he doesn't wear them at work. He makes the very reasonable argument that by walking around without shoes, he's able to pick up weakened bacteria and viruses from the ground that his immune system can deal with quickly, thus constantly immunizing him against disease. Of course, then he goes off on a tangent about how shoes are causing the downfall of western civilization. To his credit, he never seems to be sick, but he's got really nasty looking feet.

This friend is a database consultant. Oddly, he always seems to be looking for work. If you are interested in a wider marketplace than companies that will let you walk around their office shoeless and with nasty feet, consider leaving your beliefs and opinions at home and opening your mind to the fact that other people don't see things the same way you do.

Besides being careful to hide your freakish eccentricity, keep a lid on opinions that aren't related to your technical specialty. If you don't, you'll find yourself firmly planting your foot in your mouth before long, and you'll be spending more time looking for work than performing it.

Political Affiliation   Take a moment to count the number of people whom you've actually convinced to switch political parties thanks to your polished rhetoric. Enough said. Don't waste time and risk offending customers with your views on political issues.

Gender and Sexual Preference   In the business world, there is only one gender: none. Business is about business; it's not about finding Mr. or Ms. Right or getting into discussions about the good old days before "Ms." when you could tell whether or not you could make a pass at a coworker.

You are not at a customer's office to expound on your theories about how sexual dimorphism predisposes a natural labor division in humans, or to flirt, or to denigrate your ex, or to talk about what the President does in his spare time, or to say how sad it is that you can't tell a joke at the water cooler without offending someone these days.

The same goes for sexual preference. In the business world, if there's no such thing as sex, then there's no such thing as sexual preference. Don't discuss other people's, and don't force your personal choices on the people you work with. If you can't sublimate your sexual preference, you can probably forget consulting as a career unless you deal only with others who share your beliefs.

Early in my networking career (before becoming a consultant), I went to lunch with an attractive female sales representative for a cable company. The conversation went something like this:

> (Waiter seats us at a table)
>
> Me: "Oh, you're wearing Birkenstocks. I thought only lesbians wore Birkenstocks."
>
> Salesperson: "Well, you could be right."
>
> Me: "So, what are you doing after work?"

Needless to say, I didn't actually comprehend that she was a lesbian until the next sentence, which needn't be published.

Two things are wrong with my behavior in this case: 1) I expressed an inappropriate generalization about a shoe company, and 2) I was trying to lead into a discussion about bodily fluids. Now, I've never had a problem with different sexual orientations, but like most people, I'm not all that sensitive to issues that don't affect me on a daily basis. I didn't realize how badly my shoe comment sounded until after I'd put my foot in my mouth, or how inappropriate it was to make a pass at a business colleague during a business meeting. Fortunately, I learned my lesson on my former employer's time and not my own.

Generalizations about any group of people are always wrong in the unique case of an individual. If you forget what you think you know about specific groups of people, you'll stop being surprised by how they are just like everyone else once you actually get to know them.

If you are single (or married and a complete jackass), don't look to your clients for dates. I know it's hard not to be attracted to beautiful people, but you will cause yourself a world of trouble if you mix dating with consulting. In the worst case, you'll lose a job and potentially have to fend off a harassment suit. In the best case, you'll get married and then wind up with a conflict of interest causing you to leave the job. Notice what happens here: good or bad, it doesn't work out for the job.

If it turns out that you find your soulmate working in the accounting department of your latest customer and you just have to try to gain their interest, consider using the tactic of telling them where you usually are in the evenings without asking them out on a date. If the person shows up there and expresses an interest in you, you can develop the relationship outside the working environment. You should make absolutely certain that your amour's personal interest in you has nothing to do with work, and that you'll be able to disengage the relationship without affecting your contract if you should need to.

Race   I'm still surprised by the number of racial jokes and slurs I run across at work. No matter how you try to couch it ("My mom is French, so I'm allowed to tell French jokes"), it's inappropriate. You have nothing to gain if a joke goes over well, and work to lose if it doesn't. If you actually believe that your specific race is superior to others, networking is probably over your head.

Religion   Religion is not a part of business unless you happen to be directly employed by a church. My religion is fine. Other people's religions scare me. To me, few things are scarier than being asked to go to church with someone, unless I'm very close to them.

Finding faith is a life-consuming passion, but trying to share your zeal with those unprepared for your enthusiasm will only freak them out. Until your feet come back down from heaven, you'll probably find that people are avoiding you quite a bit, and that the conversation gets a little hushed when you come around.

Most people aren't looking for a life-changing experience, especially not one that appears out of the blue at work. Accosting people with your testimony of Zoroaster the first time they have lunch with you will guarantee that they will never have lunch with you again. Leave the proselytizing to the missionaries. They have far more effective methods anyway.

Evolution and the Origin of the Universe   Most people think that their own beliefs are purely scientific, so it's not surprising that topics that you consider benign can trigger a sudden and unexpected religious or metaphysical debate. If you subscribe to the theories of evolution and current astrophysical thinking on the origin of the universe, bringing these topics up can move you suddenly into the twilight zone. Consider the following conversation:

> Me: "My mom was pregnant with me during the moon landing."

> Client: "Oh, right. That was totally faked. I can't believe you don't know that."

> Me: "Um, what?"

> Client: "The moon landing. They did that in Hollywood. I mean, look at the pictures. There are no stars in the background."

> Me: "Well, it was daytime on the moon when they took those pictures. Just like daytime on earth, the brightness of the sun obscures the stars."

> Client: "Are you saying I'm wrong?"

> Me: "Well, I'm saying there are other possible explanations."

First mistake: pregnancy involves bodily fluids. This whole conversation could have been avoided. In this example (which actually happened to me), through sheer tenacity and force of will I not only managed to save the business relationship, but gained a much greater personal understanding of the Trilateral Commission, the banking cartels, and the government's role in covering up alien abductions.

Avoid religion, metaphysics, or any topic that appears regularly in the *Weekly World News* with your clients unless you're certain of their feelings on the subject. You may want to get a subscription to the *Weekly World News* so you'll know specific topics to avoid.

Charities   I have real problems with people who think it's perfectly fine to ask me for money for a good cause. I'm capable of determining on my own which causes deserve my time and money. So are your clients. Don't ask them to spend their time or money on your charitable causes.

The reciprocal case is a little stickier. So far I've avoided a refrigerator full of Girl Scout cookies, but when a client asks you to donate time or money to a charitable event, you're on the spot. Best bet: answer honestly. If you admire the charity and honestly don't mind helping out, do so. If you have any problems with it, just make some excuse like your spouse selects the charities or you gave at another office.

Personal Subjects

Living in Southern California as I do, I talk to many people who have seriously strange lives. Take, for example, this conversation:

Me: "Hey, let's go to Chang's Chinese for lunch."

Client: "Oh, we can't do that. This freaky guy from my Narcotics Anonymous meetings works there."

Me: "Yes, let's avoid freaks."

Now, I applaud anyone with the conviction to overcome a drug addiction, but as with bodily fluids, drugs have no place in a business conversation. Avoid the following:

➤ Topics that reveal that you make or have made bad choices: drugs, polyester, drinking, or the number of children you have that you've never met.

➤ Topics that reveal a lack of success: debt, car problems, trailer problems, or your pre-paid cellular phone service.

➤ Topics that reveal character flaws: numerous ex-wives, numerous ex-cats, or restraining orders that are pending against you.

➤ Topics that reveal potential risk for your client: your gun collection, or how often you have your lawyer over for dinner.

Remember that your clients aren't your friends. They don't need to know the sordid details of your life; they only need to know about your skill in solving the problem for which you were hired.

Talk Less, Listen More

My brother told me the story of one of his wife's best friends—a woman whom everyone liked, and whom everyone considered to be their best friend. She had the remarkable talent of listening. After sitting with her for a few minutes, you'd find yourself talking about the personal details of your life, going on about your various successes and failures as if you were talking to your shrink.

My brother didn't notice this talent until he tried to ask her a personal question once. Probably without even meaning to, she turned the question around rather than replying herself. So he was off again, talking about himself and his life rather than about her. He never did find out the answer to his question.

Learning to listen has these remarkable benefits:

> ➤ People love to talk, and no subject is more interesting to them than themselves (this is especially true of me). People automatically like you when you listen to them.

> ➤ People assume the attribute of trust and integrity in listeners. Once people are used to talking to you, they'll tell you just about anything that you want to know. Of course, violating this trust will end your relationship with them.

> ➤ The less you talk, the less likely you are to say something stupid. As my former boss was fond of saying, "It's better to be silent and thought a fool than to open your mouth and prove it." She said that quite often to me, for some reason.

> ➤ Your client hired you to solve a specific problem. Listening closely to everyone involved will help you define all the requirements, including those the client forgot to mention.

> ➤ People like to vent. Listening to small things, like people griping about their boss or their work situation, will help you understand the political and financial situation at your client companies. You'll need to know as much as possible about these things, so listen carefully when people complain.

Once you get in the habit of listening more and talking less, you'll find that many aspects of your life improve without assistance. Your spouse will love the new you.

On the downside, you will find that the emotionally needy start clinging to you like wet toilet paper to shoes. If you find yourself stuck in a meaningless conversation, use the following technique to extricate yourself without offending: interrupt the self-absorbed speaker, claim a serious time constraint, say something very supportive, and wish them luck. Start moving before they can start talking again.

Never, Ever, Get Upset

Clients are frustrating. Employees of your clients never seem to know what they're doing; they break things all the time, and some of them keep causing the same problems over and over. They ask annoying questions, they hang out when you'd rather they went away, and they frequently blame things on you because you aren't around to defend yourself. You may even catch an employee in a blatant lie, but you can't chastise them (you can, however, report the incident to whomever you consider your primary contact to be if you think it's important).

As frustrated as you get, you cannot ever lose your temper in front of an employee of your client (or the client, for that matter). No matter how many different ways you've explained the same thing, no matter how many times you've shown a passive-resistive employee how to log on or change their password, no matter how many voicemails you wake up to about some silly minor configuration problem, you can't lose your cool.

Now, I'm a pretty easygoing person by nature, so I almost forgot to include this whole section. But I've seen other consultants lose their cool and snap at a client's employee. There's no faster way to get the boot. Don't ever let it happen. If you have a temper problem, get a good book on anger management, or call your mom and resolve all your outstanding childhood issues, or count to ten, or call your shrink, or do whatever it takes. You can't be angry, temperamental, or even short with the employees of customers. You must be patient, long suffering, and good-natured no matter what's going on.

Conclusion

Changing your personal habits from those of an employee to those of a professional consultant is mandatory if you want to succeed. Your future client's expectations are vastly different than your current employers. You need to start thinking about the image you project when you present yourself to people. Do they think of you as friendly, competent, and free of smell? If not, start working on your personal habits before you quit your job.

Before You Quit...

5

"Your request for two cases of Post-it notes was denied because you've given your two week's notice."

Now that you're all fired up to tell your boss to kiss your butt and that you quit…Stop! Wait. Don't jump the gun. Your current employment can be extremely useful in helping you establish your consulting career. This chapter covers those things you need to do before you quit your current job. If you love your job, consider it the nurturing mother of your consulting career. If you hate your job, steal every intangible bit of help you can.

Before you leave, you should try to do the following:

➤ Establish a large number of contacts in your local area.

➤ Get your finances in order.

➤ Increase your technical skill.

➤ Get certified.

➤ Sign up for transferable benefits.

Many people won't be in a position to take advantage of the recommendations in this chapter immediately. Even if you find yourself suddenly out of a job, you should read through this chapter; it can help you determine if your finances and skills are in shape to begin consulting immediately, or if you should consider taking another short-term job to improve your situation before you begin. If you start consulting capriciously, your chances of success will be greatly reduced unless you have an unusual amount of financial stamina. When I left my job, I was lucky enough to be plugged into a sales network, and I was able to take a customer with me.

Now that you've decided to become a consultant, going to your humdrum job will be far more exciting. You'll be an industrial spy from the company of You, recruiting contacts, acquiring information, and building inexorably toward that time when you can break out on your own.

Establishing Contacts

Perhaps the most important thing you can do before you leave your job is start finding contacts in the local industry. Your personal network of contacts will be your richest source of work when you begin consulting, so it's obvious that you should know as many people as possible when you begin. When I left my job, I actually had a day planner filled with about 200 business cards of local professionals in networking and related fields. The week I left, I called nearly every one of them to tell them that I had just established my own consulting firm, what sort of work I was in the market for, and that I paid a 5 percent finder's fee on the labor I performed. Without a doubt, this tactic was the most important thing I did when I started consulting.

Some types of contacts are worth more than others. Here is the breakdown:

Salespeople   Who are working for large network systems distributors or manufacturers and selling direct are at the top of the contact list. These people are all looking for "side jobs" that they can make money on, and when they hear that you pay commission, they'll keep your plate full. Chapter 8, *The Other Kind of Networking*, discusses this marketing tactic in detail.

Consultants   Who are pursuing related but not competing fields, such as cabling, are the second most important. These folks often run into situations they need help with, and if they know you're available, they'll call you in to help.

End customers   Who are potentially waiting for networking help are useful to know about, but since they'll usually provide only one or two contracts at most, they aren't as important as those who actively seek work. You may call a hundred end customers before you find one that needs networking help, but work is work.

Salaried employees   Who are working for other companies are not all that valuable as contacts because they don't get a lot of rotation among various companies. You might want to keep their cards in case you need to know something specific, but you probably don't need to bother calling to tell them you are in business for yourself.

NOTE   Most of my work comes through personal contacts now, especially through a few good ones. One of my best contacts is a former coworker who now runs his own cabling company. Since he's in companies all the time putting in physical cable plants before the network goes in, he hands out my business card all the time, and I constantly get calls from companies he's put me in touch with. Our relationship is actually reciprocal—I use his services for all my physical plant subcontracts.

Here are some ideas to help you establish a large group of contacts. It's important to make a lot of contacts while you're still employed in the industry because you become extremely isolated once you work for yourself. Salespeople no longer come knocking, and you don't have outside consultants hovering around. Try these tactics to expand your base of contacts before you leave your job:

Collect business cards   To acquire a base to start from when you leave. Pretend they're going to be worth something someday (imagine the value of Bill Gates' rookie card today…). You don't even really have to know the person, since they likely won't remember you when you call anyway. I'm not suggesting you steal business cards from your coworkers, but…Okay, yes, I'm recommending you steal business cards from your coworkers. Tell your coworkers that you collect business cards as a hobby, so if they're going to toss some, send them your way.

Make industrial contacts   To help establish your reputation once you leave. To get exposure to these contacts outside your company, attend industrial trade shows, seminars, and other outside business functions. You can usually get free trade show "expo only" passes by sending in registration cards from computer or network magazines, or by filling out a survey card at the show. In any case, most industrial shows are inexpensive for floor access.

Insert yourself into conversations   To get yourself introduced to outside consultants or the employees of other customers when they are around your office.

Volunteer for assignments   To gain exposure to outside consultants and service providers. Work abounds when something needs to be designed or installed, and volunteers are usually appreciated. The individuals who perform the design and building of network systems are extremely important to your marketing campaign.

Go to lunch with the salespeople from other companies   To establish useful future contacts. When salesmen show up, they're often hard-pressed to find someone to take to lunch, especially if they're annoying. Do it anyway. No matter how annoying a salesperson might be, if they're making their commission in sales, they're in front of a tremendous number of customers, some of whom will inevitably need networking help.

Essentially, you should try to get to know as many salespeople and consultants as possible in your local area and industry before you leave your company. The more people who are aware of your new firm, the more salespeople you have working for you to help find work.

Adjusting Finances

Nothing will kill your consulting career faster than running out of money. If you are forced to take a full-time job before your consulting career has had a chance to blossom, it'll probably be years before you have the chance to try again.

Once you begin consulting, your source of regular income will go away. You'll likely watch your savings slip away, finally get that first contract, and then end up living for a month on credit cards before you get paid. Many consultants damage their credit ratings when they start consulting and dig themselves into debt; you should expect to max your credit cards as well, but don't let that damage your credit rating. You should be able to at least cover your minimum payments on everything for a few months. If absolutely necessary, consider a second mortgage or loan secured against the value of your car to keep those minimum payments current.

If you damage your credit rating, you will be unable to purchase networking hardware. Purchasing network hardware requires either a credit card with a hefty limit (for purchasing over the Internet) or a credit account with a distributor, neither of which are securable with bad credit. Don't think that incorporating will get around this: a business with no credit rating is a business with a bad credit rating. Every vendor will ask for a personal guarantee in the form of a co-signature when your business starts out, so it will always come down to your personal credit.

Before you begin consulting, take a look at the worst-case financial scenario you're willing to accept. Is making a go of consulting worth declaring bankruptcy? Is it worth damaging your credit rating? Is it worth using up your savings? Determine the level of risk that you are comfortable with, and then create a backup plan for finding a job fast once you've reached that point.

Be prepared for the consequences, as well: if you finance your attempt at consulting on credit cards and it fails, you would wind up with thousands of dollars of revolving credit debt that will add hundreds of dollars to your expenses once you start working again.

To prepare for consulting, I recommend having a war chest of three months' expenses saved up. Notice that I said expenses, not salary. You're probably going to be living on a serious budget, so get ready to hunker down (hey, there's another strange word that spell checks!) and live simply for about a year.

There are two ways to prepare:

➤ Decrease your expenses

➤ Increase your buying power

The idea behind my recommendations here is to work toward a debt-free, low-expense lifestyle for the time when you quit your job, and then use the financial vehicles you've created to extend the amount of time you can work without being paid.

Decrease Your Expenses

The best way to get your consulting career off to a successful start is to decrease your expenses. You should consider trimming everything in your budget that isn't absolutely necessary so that you have the maximum run time on the money you'll save. Everyone's financial situation is different; don't think that every one of these recommendations will apply to you.

Pay off all your revolving credit debt   Don't even consider quitting your job until you've taken care of your credit card debt. If you begin while you still have to make monthly payments, you'll likely ruin your credit rating once you start consulting. Revolving credit debt can quickly siphon off your monthly paycheck, one dollar at a time. If you have to get a debt consolidation loan to pay it off, do so. But avoid doing anything that will damage your credit rating—you'll need credit when you consult.

Most banks, especially smaller banks and credit unions, will provide a debt consolidation loan. Ask your banker what they will do for you. They will usually want to attach an asset like your house or a car to the loan, which is okay. It's an easy process, much like applying for a credit card.

Be wary of high-interest unsecured signature loans: you aren't going to get anywhere by consolidating unless the interest rate and monthly payments go down. Secured loans, which have much lower interest rates, are the way to go because they reduce your interest payments.

Refinance your home (if you have one)   This will lower the monthly payment. Although it will lengthen your term, you can always pay down your principal when your consulting career is successful. At the moment, you need to lower your recurring expenses. Consider either refinancing or taking out a second mortgage to pay down all your short-term debt. I know common sense says you shouldn't trade short-term debt for long-term debt, but again, you need to reduce your monthly expenditures as much as possible when you start consulting, so this once-in-a-lifetime change is an exception to the rule.

Get out of expensive car payments   Yes, this may mean giving up your baby, but you really should start consulting with a vehicle that's paid off. When I started, I drove a very inexpensive car that was paid off. Consider leasing a vehicle if you won't put too many miles on it. If you're "upside down" on your car payment, it's a good bet that your finances are too strained to consider consulting within the year. Get it paid down before you quit your job. You do need to have a reliable car.

Stop eating out and start eating at home   You should consider stocking a pantry with a few months' food supply in case things really get tight. This may sound silly, but there may come a time when an extra $500 makes all the difference.

Purchase big-ticket necessities while you're still employed   If your stove is on its last legs, get a new one now. Major appliances, cars, and everything else discussed in Chapter 6, *Tools of the Trade*, should be purchased now while you still have the ability to do it—however, they should be paid off before you quit so that the duration you'll have to keep your job once you've decided to quit is the time it takes you to pay off all of the big-ticket items you had to buy on credit.

Pay insurance up for the year   Most insurance policies are sold on a term basis of one year, which can be paid in full at any time to avoid monthly payments. This includes car insurance, homeowners or renters insurance, and health insurance. Although the highly organized and disciplined may think paying anything in advance is silly, if you're anything like me, you don't have enough discipline to eat at home while there's still money in the bank. By taking care of expenses in advance, you know exactly when your money has really run out.

Set aside your mortgage or rent payment for a year   Don't pay your mortgage in advance, as your lender will apply the entire payment to principal and still expect your next month's payment on time. You may be able to pay your rent a year in advance, however. I suggest opening a different account for money you've allocated to pay your mortgage. That way, you'll never touch that money, and you won't have to worry about accidentally coming up short near the end of the year.

Sign up for transferable benefits like a retirement plan and health insurance   If you have stock options, exercise them if you think they'll have value. You probably won't be able to keep options once you leave.

Essentially, you should do everything you can do to prepare for your consulting career before you leave your job.

Increase Your Buying Power

The other way to increase your financial stamina besides reducing your expenditures is by increasing your available capital. There are a number of good ways to do this. Again, needs vary, so consider these suggestions:

Retire   Either do this or negotiate for a golden parachute if you've been at your company more than fifteen years or are close to any sort of retirement benefit. Most large companies now offer a reduced retirement package for terms less than 20 years, and may offer a substantial exit bonus for long-term employees who are laid off. If your company is laying people off, but you aren't on the list, consider offering to take a layoff with an exit bonus. It may mean someone who needs it can keep their job.

Take a second job   Consider a light-duty night or weekend job if you don't have kids. If you can keep this job while you start your consulting career, you'll have a much easier time making the transition. You can even find computer-related night jobs since numerous firms provide 24-hour support and many smaller companies have a night technician to run back-up jobs and perform system upgrades.

Get as much revolving credit as you can   Depending on what your credit rating will support, you can try to get at least two months' worth of expenses as available credit on credit cards. When you do this, you should apply for all the cards simultaneously. The reason for this is because they'll check your credit report for recent credit request activity. If all of your credit requests are received by the credit bureaus in the same month, the activity won't show up. You will need at least two credit cards: one for personal purchases and one for work-related or expense-able purchases. By putting your expenses on a separate card, you can easily calculate them come tax time, and you'll have a record of what those expenses were in the form of your credit card bills. Try to get a card that will itemize expenses into accounting categories.

Get a line of credit established   Use your house as collateral. A line of credit can go a long way toward helping you make money since you'll then be able to resell materials and software, which you can mark up. Talk to your banker about your plans; I was astonished at how willing my bank was to help with an unsecured line of credit once I told them I was starting a small business. If your bank seems recalcitrant, shop around at other banks and switch when you find one willing to work for your business.

Declare the maximum number of tax deductions in the year you will quit working   You'll get more money per paycheck, and since your taxable income will probably be lower overall than it would have been if you'd remained employed, you still won't have to worry about a huge tax burden at the end of the year.

Buy a home now if you intend to any time in the next five years   I know this goes against my advice to lower your expenses, but if you don't buy a house before you quit your job, it'll likely be about three years before a lender will talk to you once you're self-employed. Since you won't have a paycheck when you're a consultant, when you apply for secured credit (home or car loans), you have to furnish your tax returns. Lenders typically want to see at least two years worth of tax returns in order to consider you. This means that once you begin consulting, it's difficult to get a mortgage or a car loan until you've been profitable for at least two years; that is assuming that you haven't otherwise tarnished your credit with late payments or defaults. Owning a home will improve your credit situation and provide you with a source of emergency money through a second mortgage if you need it.

File for unemployment when you leave your job   Unemployment isn't much, but every little bit helps. Even though you intend to consult, you aren't actually working until you get your first contract, so there's no reason why you shouldn't avail yourself of your unemployment benefits. This means you'll have to arrange to be laid off or fired, because if you quit you'll be ineligible for unemployment. If your company won't lay you off, try coming to work nude until they fire you. Better yet, stop working completely and spend your time telling everyone what you really think until you do get fired. Or begin looking for contracts on the company dime—that usually pisses people off as well. (I'm kidding, of course—don't burn bridges unless you have to).

The idea here is to make as much money as possible available to you for as long as possible. This will extend the amount of time you can look for contracts before you have to give up. Running out of money up front is the most common reason why consultants fail.

During the course of your consulting, if you find that you have run into a dry spell, consider registering with a brokerage to find temporary work. Watch out, though—brokerages are more addictive than sleeping late. If you really plan on making a go of independent consulting, use brokerages only as the last resort before full-time employment.

Obtaining Skills and Certifications

There's no good way to measure your own technical skill against others without attempting some sort of industrial certification like the MCSE or CNE—and (having written quite a few MCSE study guides) even those don't prove much other than that you're good at taking tests. I know exceptionally qualified network consultants who've failed MCP exams because they don't know Microsoft's vision of reality, and I've gotten e-mail from readers who brag that they scored very well on the NT Server exam without doing anything except reading my books. You tell me—which individual is more qualified to consult?

That said, your clients will probably ask if you're certified by the proper authority on whatever product it is you're supporting for them. Saying no usually puts a damper on the discussion (and of course, they can call a phone number and check, so don't lie), so for the small amount that it takes to become certified, you should make sure you are. Passing or failing the exams can also help you determine if you've got the basic technical skills you'll need to consult.

Think to yourself: am I talented enough to design, install, and service a new network without help? You probably already know the answer to this question, and unless you're deluded, your gut reaction to that question is probably right. This answer is also the answer to whether or not you should consider consulting at this time.

Here are some more questions to ask yourself. When was the last time you failed to solve a problem at work? Did that failure occur because you couldn't figure out what was wrong, or did it occur because you didn't have the time or budget to fix the problem? Do you have continuing problems with the systems you manage at work that you don't know how to solve? Are you frustrated at work, or do you feel like the master of your domain?

If your work systems are humming along on their own and you've got plenty of time to work on corollary duties like user support, you're probably qualified to start consulting now. If, on the other hand, you find yourself endlessly chasing down the same sorts of problems and you are consistently working late, if you feel like you're under the gun because your systems aren't performing like they should be, you may want to spend more time in the corporate environment figuring out sustainable management policies before you begin implementing systems for other people.

Some people actually detest the certification system so much that they refuse to even attempt to get certified. Whatever your personal feelings about certification may be, if your customers ask if you're certified, don't launch into a tirade about how stupid you think certification is, or how evil Microsoft, Novell, or Red Hat (yes, there are people who think Red Hat is evil) is, or how certification doesn't prove anything. Those arguments all sound like excuses. From a marketing perspective, the only correct answer is to say that you are certified in the area of expertise demanded by the job, or perhaps that no standard certification exists. Before you say this, swallow your pride and get at least one significant industrial certification.

TIP Sybex publishes certification study guides (often the only thing you'll need to prepare for your exams) covering every important industrial certification there is. Check out **www.sybex.com** for their complete catalog.

Steal Expertise

Even if you hate your job, you shouldn't shoot yourself in the foot by quitting before you're ready. Squeeze your current job for everything you can get out of it before you quit. Here's a list of ways you can milk your company for experience and training before you quit:

Get certified on the company dime Most companies will pay for an employee's certification exams (about $600, another $400 for books and other course materials for MCSE, similar for a CNE) and training materials if you ask. Books are cheap for a company, but growing a library can be expensive for an individual. Some companies will demand that you stay on for a specific period of time when they pay for certifications. It's up to you whether that time will be worth it or not.

Volunteer for the really hard jobs   Every time a problem crops up, propose how a specific technology could be used to solve it. Then volunteer to implement the solution. Remote employees need access to company data? Volunteer to set up a VPN. Salespeople want to enter quotes from their customer's computers? Sounds like an e-commerce Web site waiting to happen. Even if you're "stepping on toes," few coworkers will want to take on high-profile and risky assignments. Even junior technicians will find themselves working very high-level projects if their boss wants to distance himself from possible failure. The idea here is to start acting like a consultant now by creating demand for the things you want to learn about and then learning what you need to know to solve the problem. As an employee, you've got far wider failure latitude than you will have as a consultant, so learn end-to-end project management now. Don't worry about failure—hey, you're going to quit anyway, right? Better to learn how to deal with failure while you're still getting paid.

Practice your communication skills   Document your activities when you troubleshoot systems. Write user's manuals. Survey and completely document your existing network. Make your e-mail communications more professional and less casual. Stop swearing. Stop gossiping. Stop treating members of the opposite sex like members of the opposite sex.

Use your budget to purchase training equipment   Convince people that a custom-built multiprocessor RAID machine would solve the database delay problems, then build that system. Push the idea of converting the company backbone from 100Base-T to Gigabit Ethernet, then implement the change. Convince management that they should convert from Novell to NT, or NT to Unix, or Unix to Novell—from whatever you know to whatever you want to learn. Upgrade the network from Ethernet to Fast Ethernet, or from Token Ring to FDDI.

Of course, people may notice the new, more motivated you—and an astute boss may even suspect what you're up to. It doesn't matter—they'll still work you for what they can get out of you before you go. Starting to act like a consultant now is a win-win situation for you and your company.

Some people think they're too far down the organizational hierarchy for these tactics to work for them. My personal experience says that that's poppycock. Let's digress for another self-serving, egotistical pep talk about me, shall we? Those of you who hate this stuff can feel free to skip to the next section.

My career as a network integrator began as a seaman in the navy. The only lower ranks are reserved for people in boot camp and technical school. There's probably no lower-ranking worker in a more rigidly controlled hierarchy anywhere in the working world. In spite of this, through a combination of volunteering, suggesting, and a strong desire to avoid cleaning toilets, I was able to go from no networking experience at all to building and maintaining the navy's prototype shipboard fiber-optic local area networks in a surprisingly short time.

I started by volunteering to fix PCs around my ship. I'd been trained as an Electronic Warfare operator, which, while technical, has nothing to do with personal computers. Very few sailors had computer experience back then, so someone willing to attempt to fix problems had a free hand at it. Although I'd been a hacker in high school, had designed and wire-wrapped simple eight-bit computers in my digital electronics class, and was a proficient Pascal and assembly language programmer, I'd never worked on IBM PC-compatible computers before I joined the Navy. But having some electronics background and an understanding of computer theory put me in the right place to learn to fix the PCs onboard my ship. After fixing a few, I found that word spread quickly among the problem-plagued computer users. PC repair became an unofficial corollary duty of mine.

When a ship I was temporarily assigned to attempted to put the first shipboard local area network together, the contractors who installed the hardware could not get the network running. I volunteered to take a crack at it, and studied the manuals that came with the network operating system (Novell) until I knew my way around the server pretty well. Once I discovered the problem and fixed it (improper card bindings on the server and bad driver bindings on the clients), the network came up, and my job went from chipping paint and scrubbing toilets to maintaining networks.

When I left my temporary assignment on that ship, I sought out the second-in-command on my own ship and explained the merits of local area networking to him. During one meeting, a significantly higher-ranking individual who wanted to be in charge of the network disagreed with me about my proposed network architecture, proposing instead a silly dial-up bulletin board system that would use the ship's telephone system. When it became clear that my design would be adopted, that individual actually lunged across the table at me spewing obscenities and had to be restrained and removed. The experience left me somewhat shaken and more aware of the politics that surround any highly visible project.

After putting a network on my own ship, my work in the Navy became network management exclusively. My low rank meant very little after that. After assisting a few other ships in building their own networks, I left the Navy to work for the contractor who installed the fiber-optic cable plant on my ship.

At my new job, I pretty much wound up starting over. I had no business or corporate experience, and I wound up taking the job at a considerably lower salary than I should have, and with no defined responsibilities. The company's engineers rightly disliked my lack of formal education and my single track of experience, so I was excluded from all the reindeer games (unless I wanted to pull cable). This left me in the office most of the time while they worked on-site, managing projects. I felt somewhat bewildered by the state of affairs, but I didn't know what to do about it. I spent more time having lunch with cable salesmen than actually working because I was the only person in the office with time to go.

That actually wound up being a tremendous benefit. A salesman had identified a potential customer who needed a network put in, and because I was available, he asked me to come talk to them since I knew integration and he didn't. When we got there, I discussed the various technology options with the customer. I sold them on the idea of an optical fiber cable plant when they had been considering just copper. The salesman was ecstatic (at the time, fiber was about 10 times as much as copper), but when I explained my victory to the engineers back at the office, they nearly bit my head off. It seems that neither they nor anyone they'd ever heard of had installed fiber to every desk in an office—they had installed quite a bit of long-haul outdoor plant and backbone fiber, but they had never bid this quantity of fiber on a single job. It wasn't even clear what sort of fiber should be used. The job would be mine to manage, install, test, and document because they wanted nothing to do with it.

So I went home and pored over the customer's office prints, measuring everything detail. I went to the customer's office and measured out every one of 500 cable runs individually. I analyzed my company's bidding documents to determine how many man-hours the engineers had bid similar types of jobs, and then applied those metrics to the measurements I'd taken. The engineers at the office had rules of thumb and standard measurements they knew from experience—I had neither, so I went the long, hard road and obsessed over every detail. I pored over catalogs to identify the right types of cable and connectors, specifying types our company had never before used—another source of exasperation for the engineers.

N O T E "Rule of thumb" means using your thumb as a ruler—the last segment of most adults' thumbs is just about an inch long. Other urban legends concerning the origin of this phrase are incorrect and have no basis in historical fact.

When the time came to run the job, I asked for 10 people for three weeks. I got five—four installers the engineers didn't want to work with themselves, and one foreman they trusted to keep an eye on me.

We went to work. Everything went pretty smoothly when we pulled cable, although I was forced to fire an installer because he was completely worthless. Another new hire turned out to be very motivated, however, and more than made up for the sloth of the other installer.

When we began to terminate fiber runs, it became clear that we wouldn't have enough time if we followed the traditional method prescribed by the manufacturer. The foreman and I came up with a new method of quick-cooling the heated connectors, and after proving the method with optical time-domain reflectometers (which would reveal even the slightest adverse effect on the fiber), we went to work. The method cut 50 percent off the termination time. The foreman and I worked three days straight at the end of the job to terminate over 2000 optical fibers—by the time we were finished, we were averaging just 30 seconds per connector for a complete termination. The manufacturer's specification would have taken about five minutes each.

When all was said and done, the job took 20 man-hours less time than I'd bid, left 300 feet of cable remnants (out of 30,000 feet) and about a dozen spare connectors. The engineers at the office analyzed my bid documents, invoices for job materials, time cards, expenses, and finally the job profit for days before declaring the job a success. Once they did, however, I had proven myself worthy to work with them, and, in fact, became a specialist in fiber-to-the-desk jobs. Within one year after finishing that job, my salary doubled to be in line with what the engineers made.

I'm sure there are companies out there so rigidly hierarchical that the opportunity to move into information systems would be difficult—but no matter what your situation, you should let your supervisor know that that's where your interests lie. Watch the positions your company advertises in the newspaper, and apply for the IS-related ones. You have a pretty good chance of getting such jobs because most companies would much rather hire from within. Companies prefer to promote because they're getting a "known good" worker—somebody they already know, rather than risking a new hire who might be more of a liability than a benefit to the company.

Stealth Consulting

As much as my personal story of struggle in the face of endless toil might warm the cockles of your heart (where exactly are the cockles, anyway? Why can MS-Word spell check cockles?), some of you are undoubtedly stranded in the opposite situation—there's too much expertise in your company for you to get a leg up.

If your company has more geeks than a Dead concert has hippies and you're low on the totem pole looking up with envy, you might have a hard time getting relevant experience. Here are some tips that might help:

Camouflage yourself as a geek. This might consist of wearing T-shirts with incomprehensible slogans like "Bandwidth: Demand IT!" from companies you've never heard of, or papering your cubicle with Dilbert cartoons. Buy a 3Com Palm organizer and whip it out at every opportunity.

Volunteer The "V" word again. Act as a liaison between your department and IT. Convince your coworkers to come to you first with problems, which you'll often be able to solve. If you can't fix the problem, have them go through the normal help desk channels. Propose system upgrades that everyone else avoids (like that conversion to DHCP from fixed IP addresses) to your boss, and then offer to help implement. The more of a pain in the ass you are to the IT department, the more likely they are to transfer you in (so that they can then make your life difficult).

Talk the Talk Speak the same jargon as everyone else in the IT department. Mutual respect among geeks is built on the jargon file, so if you don't know what I mean by the jargon file, figure it out. You'll need to know. Don't think this means you should salt all your conversation with jargon, however—do it only when you're interfacing with systems people. Avoid being wrong at all costs—make sure you know what you say you know, and qualify uncertainty by saying you're uncertain when you don't know for sure. Failing to solve a difficult problem isn't the same as being wrong.

Walk the Walk Make sure you know your skills and you can back up what you say. Failing at a difficult task is okay, but if you can't succeed at anything, you're in the wrong business. If you constantly bite off more than you can chew and wind up causing other people more work, you'll find yourself out of work sooner than you might like. You've got to crawl before you can walk—don't go proposing e-commerce solutions until you understand how the underlying technology works. If you find you've volunteered for something you don't know how to accomplish, see if you can find help online, through user's groups, or even by getting the budget to hire a consultant. Managing an implementation is nearly as good as implementing it yourself, if you can get away with it.

Do It Yourself Worst case, buy your own two computers and set up a network at home. You can download a free evaluation edition of most IT software directly off the Web. Firewalls, operating systems, database management systems—it's all there, free for the learning. If you can't get relevant experience at work, get it at home. Microsoft sells evaluation editions of Windows NT and nearly all their back-office tools for the cost of the CD and shipping. Can't get a copy of NT? Then learn Linux. Computers are cheap. Eval software is free. There goes your last excuse.

Although it may take time, remember that your rank or position at your current job doesn't matter when you become a consultant. You don't have to be the IT director or the CTO before you can quit to consult. You just have to know network administration inside and out. Nobody is going to follow you around and whisper "That guy didn't know anything about computers two years ago, and now he's passing himself off as a NetWare expert."—not even if that's the truth. The only thing that matters once you become a consultant is that you can deliver working solutions to the customer's IT problems.

Anyone in a technical job can learn everything they need to know to consult before they quit their job, irrespective of their position or responsibilities at work.

Conclusion

There are numerous ways you can use your current job to help your future consulting career get off to a running start. Your job now is a lifeline to the industry that you can squeeze for expertise, marketing contacts, and financial benefits. Plan now to use these resources to your benefit when you start your business.

Tools of the Trade 6

*"No problem, Bob, I'll get my people on it. Hey, I gotta run—
I really need to get into this meeting..."*

Ah, now for the fun part—the Toys! This chapter profiles everything you need to have to progress from geek to übergeek. This chapter is based entirely on my experience—although you'll find a lot of specific brand recommendations, nobody has paid a promotional fee or even given me equipment to talk about their stuff—this is just the stuff I use myself.

This chapter does not represent a comprehensive survey of the administrative tools market—any such attempt would be out-of-date as soon as it was printed, and would involve serious effort on my part. I can assure you that I've received a copy of nearly every unsolicited invitation to download software since the concept of unsolicited e-mail first formed in the devious mind of some half geek/half marketer mutation five years ago. So I've seen, if not everything, everything worth seeing.

In the years that I've been a consultant, I've also bought a lot of crap. At first (being an American man), I strongly resisted the idea of standing in a return line, so I stoically accepted my bad purchase as my fault. As the box of junk flowed over in my office, my wife put her foot down and forced me to learn to return. I now return about a quarter of the equipment I buy, which allows me the freedom to experiment without wasting money. Get used to returning equipment that doesn't meet your expectations—you may be doing a lot of it.

Setting Up an Office

Setting up a home office consists of dedicating a space in your home, outfitting that space with the requisite furniture, and fattening up your computer with upgrades and software.

Setting up a home office is the first step toward starting your business. Don't consider starting your consulting practice by renting a professional office because the rent will drain your limited finances; if you feel you must eventually have an office away from home, do so when your income supports it. You should not incur any recurring expenses you can avoid when you start out. Build your office in your home.

Making an Office Environment

When I started consulting, I took over an extra room in the back of the house we rented and transformed it into my first home office. This room had apparently been built as a family room, but since it was just my wife and me at the time, we didn't really need it.

I didn't have money for a desk, so I bought three folding picnic tables at Home Depot and lined one corner of the room with them. I set up my desktop computer (which my former employer let me have when they couldn't afford my final paycheck), my Macintosh, my test server, and my printer on those tables. This left enough room to work on computers when I needed to, and there was still some space left over for other desktop peripherals. The tables worked so well that I continued to use them even when my income supported getting whatever I wanted. I didn't exchange them for a desk until we moved, and even then, when I ran out of space, I bought another table of the same type and set it up the same way.

When my wife and I bought a house, we probably bought one that was a little too small because of its location. It has only two bedrooms, which at the time seemed fine, but we still haven't unpacked everything because we don't have anywhere to put it all.

I converted the second bedroom into an office by removing the built-in closet drawers and shelves and installing a piece of butcher-block countertop in the remaining nook to create a built-in desk. It works great, and with my picnic table next to it, I've got plenty of room for everything. We use the room as a guest room as well, so it has a foldout couch along with all my shelving for books.

You need a dedicated room for your office for tax purposes. About as close as you can reasonably come to sharing purposes is if you let it double as a guest room, but be aware that doing this may cause you tax problems if you make a deduction for the room. If you intend to take the home-office deduction, the room is supposed to be dedicated.

After you have picked out the room that will be yours, you could consider taking a trip to Office Depot (or a similar office supply store) to look for a chair, but before you do, read about my experiences. When I first set up my office, I bought a really cheap chair (cheap is a relative term: for me, $50 is a cheap chair) at Office Depot. That didn't last long; after about a month of backaches, I went back and bought a medium-priced chair ($150). That worked for about two years, but I still noticed considerable fatigue at the end of the day, so I finally went to an ergonomic chair store and splurged on a really good chair ($500). I advise you to skip the agony and go straight for a good chair. You'll be sitting in it more than you think. An uncomfortable chair creates distractions and causes your mind to drift. You'll be a lot more effective if your back isn't telling you to get up all the time.

Working at home all the time can be difficult for many people. With no coworkers around to bounce ideas off of (or rubber bands or paper wads), you may find yourself getting fatigued very quickly. If you are like me, you might find yourself distracted by your own boredom; this might not be totally because of the change in environs, though; I had the same problem working in a cubicle or an office that was too closed in. I have two solutions to the boredom problem: first, I try to work on two or more projects at the same time. When my brain gets tired of one, rather than stop working, I switch to another. If I need to get out of the house, I do a site visit to a customer on retainer. Or sometimes, I just head down to the beach and chill out for an hour or two. Frequent breaks, a walk around the block, or even a good window will help you stay focused and free of mental fatigue when you work at home.

The other tactic I use when I have to stay focused on a single task is to work in public. This usually means taking my laptop down to a coffee shop or to the home of a consultant friend. For some reason, working with other people around allows me to stay focused better. Everyone is unique, so I can't say this will work for you—if you find it more distracting to work in public, then by all means stay home. You'll have to try a few different things to find out what works for you.

If you decide you have to have an office (or if you can't find the room to make an office at home), there might be a few other options out there. For instance, consider the fact that I have had two customers offer me the use of their facilities at no cost. They would provide a cubicle, desk, chair, phone, fax and copy services, and all the other amenities of a normal office (including coworkers) so that I could work out of their offices. Their generosity is, of course, driven by their desire to keep a network integrator on-site. Of course, you usually can't work this arrangement until you have a relationship with the customer, so don't bring it up when you're trying to sell the job. If I wanted to make a presentation, some of my clients have even offered me the use of their conference rooms and projection equipment. If and when you broach this topic with a customer, you may consider offering them a discount on your retainer to make it worth it for them. The majority of your customers would have no problem with this arrangement as long as they have the space and your appearance doesn't cause them any marketing problems (see Chapter 4 for things they might have a problem with).

Choosing Computers

After you have gotten all the furniture for your office set up and in its proper place, you can start looking for computers. You probably already have one, but you will need two computers: a desktop server and a laptop mobile client that travels well. I build my own desktop machines since I'm very picky about components. I recommend that you do the same, because you need to stay current on computer hardware technology and problems. Problems you run into before your clients see them are problems you never need to let them see. By making sure your own equipment is leading edge, you can work out problems in advance, thus keeping you from looking stupid when you can't get a computer working at a customer's site. I don't recommend building machines for your clients unless you really like performing warranty service repairs.

Desktop Server Components

Build the best machine you can afford. My server evolves continually; at the moment it consists of the following:

Pentium III-600 microprocessor running in an Abit BF-6 motherboard, with 256MB RAM   You'll need plenty of processor power for evaluating server software for your clients—and to make sure your computer isn't the bottleneck when you have a serious deadline.

Promise FASTTRAK66 UDMA-66 RAID 0+1 controller for disk access I use four 7500 RMP IBM 27GB UDMA-66 disks, which means my server boots NT and logs on in less than 30 seconds. A lot of disk space is also especially important, because you should run multiple installations of your operating system. You don't want to test software on the same installation that you rely on for your business needs. I learned this lesson the hard way a few years back when I installed AltaVista Firewall on my personal machine and wound up having to restore from tape because it locked the machine down. I use the RAID controller because it's important to keep up with RAID technology—many industrial machines use RAID controllers (albeit of a slightly different variety), so you should be familiar with how they work and how they fail.

_n_Vidia GeForce 256 3D accelerator video adapter   I purchased this to evaluate a client's 3D CAD software. You'll find that you need to occasionally purchase hardware similar to that of your clients so you can keep track of their operational characteristics.

Smart and Friendly 8× CDRW   I use this to make installation CDs and to provide permanent copies of the documentation and user's manuals to my customers. Avoid the temptation to rip copies of your software for clients or your client's software for your own purposes.

OnStream Echo 30GB UDMA-33 tape backup controller   Never work without a good backup mechanism. I hate tape, but I still haven't found a way to avoid it. You should be using a tape backup software similar to that of your clients (probably Seagate Backup Exec), so you know exactly how to operate it in emergency situations.

LS-120 superfloppy   I use this for transferring files between my various computers whenever I don't have the network up. These drives are bootable and can emulate the A: drive for NT installations with the right motherboard. Most importantly, they are more sensitive than regular floppy drives and can frequently read data off of damaged floppies when a regular floppy drive can't. I've saved files for two customers with this device. They are always extremely grateful, and since it's easy, I don't have to charge for it.

HP 6100 series scanner   I use this for imaging all my paperwork. I don't store paper; I store images in a compressed format on my hard disk. I basically just dump everything in folders by fiscal year, so when I'm looking for something I don't have so much to wade through. With good image cataloging software, finding stuff is easier than digging through a filing cabinet. Once the year closes, I burn the paperwork images to CD and store that.

Castlewood ORB 2.2 GB removable hard drive   I use this to store downloaded evaluation software and other stuff I may need to travel with that isn't convenient to put on a CD-ROM. Although I use removable media in the past, I have found that it's not as useful as a CD-ROM burner, so I wouldn't spend the money on it unless you had a specific need.

Tektronix Phaser 740 color laser printer   I use this to create full-color business cards, letterhead, documentation, and user's manuals. This printer is the least expensive color laser printer on the market, easy to work with, fast, and most importantly, it creates beautiful output that exceeds the quality of documents produced by all but the most esoteric printing devices. A good color laser printer will go farther than any other single component in making your company look professional. Having gone the color inkjet and monochrome laser printer routes, I highly recommend spending more on a color laser as soon as you can afford it. The only problem with this printer is its enormous size—it weighs in at about 100 lbs. and is nearly as large as a dishwasher.

Microsoft natural keyboard   This allows me to type about 20 percent faster than a normal flat keyboard and helps reduce wrist fatigue. Having written about 5000 book pages in the last three years, keyboard quality is a serious issue for me.

Microsoft IntelliMouse with the IntelliEye optical tracking feature   The IntelliEye mouse is solid state and works on nearly any surface (except gloss white), so it's great for travel. It looks and works just like a regular mouse, except it emits a laser beam from the bottom when you pick it up. I've tried just about every mouse and keyboard option on the planet, from trackballs (which wind up hurting my wrists after repetitive use) to pen pads (which cause arm fatigue) to keyboards with built-in pointers (which are annoyingly imprecise). I keep going back to regular mice eventually, because they are accurate and cause the least fatigue problems for me.

The entire setup would cost less than $8000 to put together today, except for the monitor, which is a ViewSonic P815 21" that weighed in at a hefty $1000 by itself. A good 17" monitor can be had for less than $300, though, which should be perfectly sufficient for most people. I find I need a lot of "room" on my computer's desktop, which a larger monitor provides. Having used larger monitors for years now, I have a hard time going back to 14" and 15" monitors.

You probably won't need more than 128MB RAM, but you'll need more disk space than ever, so get the biggest reasonably priced disks you can, and buy two—you'll need to mirror. Also, make sure your tape backup capacity is larger than your disks. If you have to change tapes, you'll shut off the backup service because the constant tape changing annoys you.

Eight thousand dollars might sound like a lot of money, but as the start-up capital expense for a business, it's practically nothing. The money you spend on your office is an investment in your future ability to work, so while you shouldn't go hog-wild, you also shouldn't think of your office tools as frivolous expenses either. Don't go for the lowest cost equipment, go for the best value—those tools that provide a reasonable balance between functionality and price.

Choosing Your Laptop

Your laptop need not be expensive; any Pentium II or better will do. Go for an active matrix screen, though, or you'll regret it—the alternative, the passive matrix screen, is hard to view at different angles, and therefore, you won't be able to use it for customer presentations. Your laptop also doesn't have to have a huge hard disk since you'll do most of your work off of your server's disks when you're at home. I'd advise you to get at least 64MB in a laptop, though, to keep disk swapping down. You should be able to get an adequate laptop for no more than $1500 new, or $2500 if you splurge. Make sure you get a laptop with CardBus and USB ports; you'll need them both since fast Ethernet adapters require CardBus. It would be rare not to find CardBus in a new computer, but a lot of used computers don't actually have CardBus slots.

NOTE I use Windows NT Server (or Windows 2000 Server) on my computer (since I have to write about it), but NT Workstation (or Windows 2000 Professional) is probably more appropriate for most people. I use Windows 98 on my laptop ($90, usually bundled), but I expect to switch to Windows 2000 as soon as I trust it and the drivers for all my hardware are available.

Troubleshooting All Systems

If you aren't that good at building and fixing computers, now is the time to build these skills. When you run your own practice, there won't be anyone else around to help you fix things, and unfortunately, about 30 percent of the problems you run into will be hardware problems with computers that you will need to be able to troubleshoot and fix. The best way to get good at building computers is to build and maintain your own. An easy way to get good quickly is by taking a weekend job at a computer chop shop (there are probably plenty of these in your town) where they sell custom configured computers. Your OS installation experience will get you the job, and in just a few weeks you'll know everything there is to know about the current state of PC hardware.

I suggest that you buy a used Macintosh ($500) somewhere and learn how to use and repair it. Every time I think these things are finally slipping away from the corporate world, Apple makes some stunning turnaround and suddenly they're cropping up like dandelions in a lawn of PCs again. Don't get me wrong; Macintoshes have a more elegant hardware design than PCs, and the MacOS is more stable than Windows 95 and 98. But it is a little annoying to have an alien architecture cropping up here and there because you have to maintain a separate set of trivial facts to work on Macs. You won't be an übergeek until you can fix any and all computers though, so go get one. You'll find they aren't as evil as you thought once you get to know them. You'll also find that your Mac skills help when working on Suns and other Unix workstations; Macs are arguably more closely related to them in hardware than PCs.

Selecting Useful Software

The software in this section is the software I use all the time—if not every day, nearly every day. You should have similarly performing software for each of these categories.

Microsoft Office

I use Microsoft Office, mostly because that's what my customers use and I need to be able to configure it. This will most likely be the case with you, too, at least until the sword of justice prevails upon Microsoft and their hegemony is broken. I'm playing with StarOffice (Sun's free office package) just in case…

I get the professional edition because it comes with Microsoft Access, which I find to be convenient for whipping up little databases for things like support issues (although I've recently begun using Outlook for that sort of thing).

I use Excel for generating bids and pricing, and I use Word to generate proposals based on a standard template.

Organizational Software

I use Microsoft Outlook because it's the best organizational system I've found. The facts that it syncs well with my Palm computer and comes with Office Pro are nice bonuses.

Outlook is handy for a lot more than just e-mail. Some other less well-known features that I use all the time are the calendar and task manager functions. You can also create custom forms with their own folders for things like keeping track of customer service requests.

Accounting

I use QuickBooks to manage my accounting, which works well for small service-based businesses that don't need to deal with inventory. QuickBooks Pro even handles payroll if you decide to add employees. QuickBooks is easy to use even if you aren't accustomed to accounting software, and it will be useful until your business does about $5 million a year in sales. Quick-Books also has rudimentary multiuser functionality, but that's not very important for the self-employed. Small business customers who use Quick-Books will usually use the multiuser functionality, so you should be familiar with it. Back up your accounting information often, because all file sharing–based accounting systems can corrupt files if one of the client computers crashes while running the software.

For larger businesses or businesses that require inventory functionality, I recommend MAS-90. It's a bit quirky, but MAS-90 is a "real" accounting system in that it requires true posting and performs double-ended bookkeeping, neither of which are actually performed by QuickBooks. MAS-90 is also scalable; it comes in a simple, multiuser form similar to QuickBooks, a truc client/server edition, and it will soon be released in a SQL Server edition for larger enterprises. MAS-90 is appropriate for businesses in the $1- to $100-million-dollar annual revenue range.

Technical Drawings

There's only one way to go for technical drawings: Visio Professional. Visio Pro (the edition for network diagrams) is so easy to use compared to traditional CAD software that it blows away the competition. With Visio, I can lay out an entire network diagram in about as much time as it takes me to figure the network out. The drag-and-drop interface and the wealth of included symbols, as well as its ability to connect to an equipment database make it the obvious choice for network diagramming.

I wouldn't suggest bothering to try to use a typical drawing or CAD program to create network diagrams; any competition using Visio will outclass the perceived quality of your documentation immediately.

Diagnostics

I subscribe to the old school of computer and network diagnostics; I prefer to use simple tools and superior gray matter to figure out what's wrong. A typical troubleshooting session for me usually involves just the operating system and the software that comes with it. If I need to verify the physical plant when truly bizarre network problems crop up, though, I'm not above borrowing a category 5 cable scanner or an optical time-domain reflectometer from some of my friends in the cabling business. If you don't know anyone who can help you out here, Electro Rent can rent you this otherwise very expensive equipment. You should transfer the expense to your customer if you need to rent diagnostic equipment.

For suspected data-link layer problems (network adapters, hubs, and bridges), the cheapest way to test is to swap in known-good equipment. This may mean borrowing equipment from other portions of the network or purchasing new equipment and returning it if you're wrong (and you haven't broken it).

Network layer problems are best troubleshot with the venerable Unix command-line tools like ping, tracert, and telnet. For really hairy network layer problems, use a network monitor. If you're routing through an NT machine, you can use the NT Network monitor that comes with NT Server. Otherwise, consider using the unlimited version that comes with SMS Server, or something like Sniffer Basic (Formerly NetXRay) from Network General. These monitors tend to cost about $1000 apiece, so you'd have to really need them to make them worth the cost.

For Internet connectivity troubleshooting, I've never found anything better than WS-Ping Pro Pack. Yes, it's a stupid name, but it's a really awesome piece of software. It performs pings, trace routes, Windows browsing, port scanning, name lookups, and all the other things you used to have to do at the command prompt. Best of all, it's less than $50, and you can download it today from www.ipswitch.com.

For troubleshooting over the Internet at the application layer, I use the telnet terminal built into NT. Most application layer Unix services like NNTP, POP3, SMTP, and HTTP will accept connections from text-based telnet clients so that you can test for connectivity right to the remote application when you're having trouble getting a client to connect to a server.

Computer Administration Software

Administrative tools are those tools you use to configure and maintain computers.

Drive Image

Drive Image is my favorite hard-disk imaging software. Hard-disk imaging software allows you to copy one hard disk to another. This is invaluable when setting up many similarly configured machines, such as a client roll-out for a new network. Basically, you configure one computer completely, and then you simply copy its hard disk to all the other computers. One reboot and they're up and running. *NT Server 4 24seven* (from Sybex Inc., by yours truly) provides complete details about how to run a massive client roll-out using this software.

Symantec's Norton Ghost is the more traditional imaging package, but it fails on file system errors it detects and will not copy the disk. This is problematic because changes to the NTFS file system, like those introduced in Service Pack 3 and Windows 2000, can keep this package from copying a hard disk. Drive Image is my preferred package because it reports the error but copies the image anyway.

Partition Commander

Partition Commander (or the competing PartitionMagic, if you prefer) allows you to repartition hard disks with running operating systems and data on them without disturbing the existing installation. This is especially handy for things like resizing the multiple hard-disk partitions that come on a number of new Dell computers when you only want one, or resizing your NTFS system partition to use the entire disk. Some recent versions of the software require a FAT partition in which to install their extra features; for that reason, I'm sticking with my older version that boots from a floppy.

Operating Systems

I carry all my software with me in a CD case in the trunk of my car. This ensures that if someone steals my car, I'll lose all my software as well. Actually, I do it because of the number of times I've thought "Damn, I could get this errant partition off if I just had my RedHat boot CD."

Clients cannot be expected to keep their software in any coherent order. I've lost many hours asking people to find their Windows 98 CD in order to install some feature or fix they need, so now I just carry my own. Never rely on your customer to perform any task, especially if it needs to be done in order for you to get paid, even something as simple as finding a piece of software. I make sure I've got copies of the following operating systems with me at all times:

➤ RedHat Linux

➤ Windows 95 and 98

➤ Windows NT Workstation

➤ Windows NT Server

➤ Latest Service Packs/TechNet

WARNING Never install software for a customer unless they have a valid license for the software. If your customer is ever prosecuted for software piracy, they'll play stupid and claim their consultant gavo it to them, so they figured it was okay.

VNC

VNC (Virtual Network Computing) is the most convenient remote administration program ever written. Imagine pcAnywhere that's fast, free, and runs across Unix, Macintosh, and Windows platforms. Yes, you will be able to control a Mac from a PC, a PC from a Unix or Linux machine, and a Linux machine from a Mac. Best of all, it's free and small, so it's a fast download.

Memorize the following URL: www.uk.research.att.com. This site has the binaries for every version, so you can install VNC on any Internet-connected computer at any time.

VNC comes as a server and as a client (or viewer). The server serves its desktop image and accepts keystrokes and mouse movements. The viewer displays the desktop image and transmits keystrokes and mouse movements to the server. This allows you to run the viewer to control any computer running the VNC server. The server can be run as an application (I recommend this mode for security reasons), which must be explicitly started by a local user, or as a service that is always available.

When I know the problem is simple, I use VNC to handle tech support calls for users' desktops. When a user calls with a problem, I have them launch VNC on their computer, and then I pull up the viewer from my office and begin remotely correcting their problem. This works for any software problem above the network layer—as long as TCP/IP is running, you'll be able to attach with VNC.

You will run into problems with networks that use private internal addressing and network address translation on the firewall. Essentially, there's no way to reach these computers because they don't have valid Internet addresses. In the past, the only way around this problem was to create a static translation on the firewall to get to the client. As of the latest version, VNC supports a "reverse connection" method that allows the server to establish the connection to the viewer rather than vice versa. This allows the dynamic translation in the firewall for the outbound server computer to provide the channel into the network. It's also much better for security since the person whose machine is being controlled determines which computer gets to control it.

WARNING Never leave VNC running as a service on computers that have Internet access. Although VNC's password protection scheme is a true challenge/response hash, it's no more secure than any other hashed password logon method. VNC will allow complete remote control of your computers, so consider the ramifications of using it very carefully.

MS-DOS Emergency Boot Disk

I always keep an MS-DOS boot disk handy for those times when I need to format and partition a new disk quickly, or when an operating system has crashed and I need to get access to the disk. For NT, this used to be nearly worthless if the computer used the NTFS file system. But the good people at www.winternals.com have created NTFS file system drivers for MS-DOS that will allow you to access your NTFS volumes from a boot floppy to correct problems like newly installed drivers that crash the OS.

WARNING NTFS-DOS will also allow anyone else to read and copy files from your server, so never leave your boot floppies in a server.

Home Networking

You'll need some method to connect your server and your laptop (or other clients) together. I use Raytheon Raylink wireless network adapters, which are also sold as Aviator WebGear adapters. These adapters are now down to about $100 each in sets of two, so for $200, you can get your laptop on the Internet from anywhere on your property at a blazing 2Mbps. Don't be fooled into getting the Diamond HomeFree wireless adapters—in a word, they suck. Their printed range maximum is 150 feet (vs. 1500 feet for the Raylink/Aviators), and their practical maximum is around 50 feet. Their top speed is only 1MB. Essentially, these adapters are an IrDA infrared transceiver that has a simple radio instead of an optical LED and Photo-transistor pair. They also have a bizarre encryption scheme that makes the setup extremely difficult.

Once you have wireless Web access from your laptop, you'll never go back. I can now work anywhere in the house on whatever I want to work on, which keeps the Home Office dementia at bay.

My server has two network adapters, the wireless, and a fast Ethernet wired adapter that attaches to a small hub for my printer and firewall. I use a Sonicwall 10 user firewall (around $350, including hardware and software), which is so inexpensive that I couldn't build a free Linux-based firewall for less money because the computer to do it would cost more.

Internet Access

I have a cablemodem at the moment for Internet access, which provides upload speeds of 128Kbps and download speeds of 3Mbps (shared among the neighborhood). The upload speed isn't fast enough to serve a general interest Web site, but it's enough for a simple Web presence for your customers. I'm trying to switch to high speed DSL so I can serve a Web site, but my phone lines may not be of high enough quality. Chapter 8 lists reasons why you'll need Internet access (as if you didn't already know).

You will need some sort of high-speed Internet access. I recommend either cablemodems or xDSL service if they're available in your area. Pricing runs around $50/month for each. Other options are PC Direct satellite access, which works over a DSS satellite dish for download and your phone line for upload. You may also consider using regular dialup with channel bonding, which works well in Windows 95, 98, and Windows NT, and is provided nationally by MindSpring. However, you'll require a phone line for each channel, so it can be expensive to get any significant speed. Three lines are roughly equal to ISDN using V.90 modems, depending upon your connection speed. I've had trouble getting more than two lines to work reliably with any ISP, however, so be prepared for frustration if you go this route unless you've also got a RAS server to answer all the phone lines.

Office Phone

I no longer use a dedicated office phone. I used to have a dedicated line, but it was too much hassle because I'm out of the office so much. I now advertise my cellular phone number for all my calls.

Using a cell phone has its problems as well—it frequently drops calls, and it's expensive: I pay an average of $120 per month to support my customers.

I've been mulling over a newly available option: A "real" voicemail system: Symantec TalkWorks Pro version 4. This system supports transferring and forwarding calls. This way, you could have a voicemail system, which runs on your computer, answer the phone and shunt callers into various voicemail boxes. You could then automatically forward high-priority calls to your cell phone. This requires two voice-capable modems and phone lines: one to receive calls, and another to dial when a transfer occurs. You could use your business line as the incoming line, and your fax line to transfer out on (the same software will be managing your faxes).

You can take your phone calls with a professional-sounding voicemail system that runs in your office PCs and allow customers who know the code to transfer directly to your cell phone. Given this new functionality, I'm considering switching back to landlines to reduce the amount of time I'm on the phone. This will also allow me to switch from my cellular provider, AirTouch (whom I detest), to other cellular service providers without changing my business phone number each time. (Although, of course, I'll have to change it back to the landline the first time.)

I haven't tested this myself yet, so I'm reiterating their published specifications rather than my experience. I've used TalkWorks Pro 3.0, so I'm comfortable with the user interface and with recommending the software.

Fax

I decided that I didn't want to pay for a fax since a modem works just as well and keeps the documents electronically. As it turns out, that's almost true; I did have to buy a scanner for those few times when I had to send actual paper. But I liked the fact that I could store my documents electronically. I use the Windows NT fax service that can be downloaded at no cost from www.microsoft.com. Windows 98 also comes with a fax service. If you use TalkWorks Pro for voicemail, it also supports faxing. Most fax modems come with fax software as well, although you may find it worthwhile to purchase higher quality faxing software.

Recently, I ran into the automated fax service of eFax.com. This company assigns you a phone number from their block of numbers and receives faxes for you. They then e-mail you your incoming faxes. This allows you to eliminate a dedicated fax line ($20 per month). The best part: it's a free service. They do send a junk e-mail about once a month begging you to upgrade to their $3 per month service that allows you to send outbound faxes, but I just use my home line for that since I no longer have to dedicate a line to receiving faxes. Using eFax.com is a great way to eliminate an annoying monthly expense, and their outbound service is probably valuable for most people as well. The only problem is that the fax number isn't in the same area code as your phone number, and is usually long distance. This hasn't presented a problem for me, since my fax volume is low. It may even make your firm look really big, since the numbers on your business card will span states.

Imaging

You will need a scanner, but any $200 scanner will do for faxing and most imaging. There's now very little difference in image quality between the top of the line and the bottom, so it doesn't make a lot of sense to purchase an expensive scanner, in my opinion. I use my scanner about once every six months, so you may decide you don't need one at all if you don't mind running to Kinko's to fax the occasional paper document.

Printing

The image of your company is based partially on the quality of your printed documents. I find this to be so important that I shelled out for a color laser printer (A Tektronix Phaser 740, which I highly recommend).

Before I had the color laser, I had both a monochrome laser and a color inkjet printer. I used the monochrome laser to print large documents that didn't need color (because laser printers are always cheaper than inkjet printers in consumables) and the color printer for network diagrams and cover sheets.

Don't even consider buying a printer with less than 600dpi resolution. Although 300dpi looked fine when printers first came out, businesspeople these days are all used to high-resolution printers, which makes something printed using 300dpi look like a cheaply printed document.

TIP Don't use an inkjet printer to print your cards; the ink rubs off on the fingers of your clients. If you can't laser print them, have them preprinted. Homemade business cards do have serrated edges that even a good printer can't help, but you can rub those off a stack at a time on the corner of a hard surface. Don't worry too much about the edges, though; a good-looking, full-color card you print yourself will also enhance your image in the minds of your customers, even if they know you printed it out, because it means you've mastered the arcane art of aligning printer paper correctly.

Gearing Up

Now for the real toys: equipment you keep on your person. No geek is stylish without an array of personal electronics available at a moment's notice. I carry two indispensable items: a cellular phone and a 3Com Palm computer, one in each front pocket (kidding—of course I wear pocketless T-shirts, so I carry the phone in my left front pocket of my pants and the Palm computer in my back right).

Cellular Phone

Get a cellular phone as your primary business line instead of using a landline. If you're busy, you'll be at customers' sites more often than not, so you'll need to be able to take and receive calls from wherever you are. Modern phones from national providers also work all around the country, so you can hide your travels from your customers because you'll always be available no matter where you are.

I use my phone so much that I buy the maximum plan offered by my service provider. I spend about $120 per month on the phone, which is a lot, but it's only about double what I spent on the landline anyway. I use the service provider's voicemail system, which allows me to take voicemail while I'm on the phone and which sounds like every corporation's voicemail system.

Although I leave my phone on, I rarely take calls that come in immediately. I prefer to have people leave voicemail so that I can prioritize and screen out frivolous calls. Since you don't pay for airtime on calls that go to voicemail, you can reduce the amount of time you spend on the phone this way. My phone has caller ID (available with most digital systems), so I can decide whether or not to answer a call when it comes in. If I don't recognize it, I don't answer.

Get a phone that's small enough to fit in your pants pocket or on a belt clip. If you don't, you won't carry it all the time, and you'll find yourself missing important calls. I use a Motorola StarTAC, which is a bit fragile, but it has the best form factor for pocket carry, in my opinion. Avoid phones with uncovered button pads, as they tend to dial in your pocket or require unlock codes before you can answer. Spend a little extra on your phone to get the features you need.

Forget about pagers. I used to carry one, but they're just not as professional as voicemail. They also don't allow you to prioritize very well if you don't recognize the number. Since you don't know the reason why someone called, you have to call them right back. With voicemail, you can determine how and when you need to respond because you know what's going on.

Forget about answering services. They're more of a pain than they're worth. They don't make you seem professional; they make you seem unreachable. The average business customer expects voicemail these days, not a receptionist.

Palm Computer

I would also suggest that you get a 3Com Palm computer. I know I should be more generic; I keep trying to like Windows CE devices, but I've always wound up returning each generation I buy. Something about dead batteries makes the full-color screen seem dull and lifeless. The disappointing lack of applications for these devices is problematic, as well, and the fact that they seem slow because the OS is way too complex for the processors, etc. Essentially, Windows CE is more than a palmtop can chew right now, but I expect that will someday change.

The Palm computer, on the other hand, is the ideal marriage of appropriate hardware and software. Based on the same processor as early Macintoshes, and with an operating system that was clearly designed by people who worked for Apple in the early days, a Palm is the hand-held equal to the early Macintosh: an elegant harbinger of the industry to come.

Apple's early work with the Newton was very geek-chic, but of little practical value. Newtons were simply too big to carry and (until the last generation) underpowered. They suffered from exactly the same type of problems that CE machines suffer from now.

The Palm computer, on the other hand, is both small enough to fit in your pocket and powerful enough to handle organizational tasks and Game Boy–like recreation. I have the Palm VII, which allows wireless Web and e-mail access from my car (which I find very handy) for about $20 per month at the rate I use it. Another device, The Palm V, is tiny, and is what you should consider if size is a significant issue for you. The Palm IIIe is now under $200, so anyone can afford it. They sync with Outlook, Act!, Lotus Notes, and just about every other contact manager on the planet for contact and task management. They are also the very reason why I'm able to stay organized. Without them I'd be lost.

Two friends of mine swear by the Psion Series 5 organizer, which is about the size of a fat checkbook and opens to reveal a keyboard you can nearly type on. One friend has actually written a considerable amount of fiction on it. I find the interface to be too primitive and lacking in coherency, but they are an option for the übergeek. I had a Psion II back when they were the only thing you could even remotely call a hand-held computer, but back then, they had little practical value. Psions can be programmed directly on the handheld in OPL (Organizer Programming Language) , a version of BASIC with some database functionality similar to the obsolete dBase language. Palms have no built-in programming capability.

Driving in Style

Want a nice car? Want a nice car for free? Read on.

As a consultant, you'll drive a lot. I drive my business vehicle about 35,000 miles per year (which is more than the majority of consultants; you should figure you'll drive between 15,000 and 20,000 unless you live in one of the 10 largest metro areas in the country). The IRS allows you to deduct 31 cents per mile you drive (except a commute to your place of work) for the cost of a business vehicle. This is money you get to keep to pay for the incidental costs of maintaining a business vehicle. You're not allowed to deduct mileage to or from your usual place of work, however, which is one reason I recommend keeping a home office.

Since I don't commute to my place of work, and since I use my business car for business and my personal car for personal travel, I simply deduct all the mileage I accrue on my business vehicle. If you have only one vehicle, or if you mix the use of your vehicle, you'll need to either keep a detailed log of your mileage per trip or make a justifiable percentage estimate of your usage come tax time (that you can back up somehow). It's really not worth the hassle—as soon as you can, keep a vehicle for work alone.

Given those numbers, my average tax deduction for the car is about $11,000 per year. Subtracting $2000 for gas, oil, and tune-up over the course of a year leaves $9000. I consider this $9000 per year to be my budget for owning a vehicle. Dividing that by 12 equal monthly payments yields a monthly payment amount of $750. Now, applying that monthly payment amount and the 7 percent car loan I was able to finagle with a six-year loan. I was able to seat myself in a brand-new luxury car for free, using the money I would have paid to the government if I weren't driving it down the road.

In my first year of consulting (when I drove the Hyundai), I couldn't believe how much the automobile deduction was. That year, I deducted $8000 for a vehicle that was only worth (on a good day) $3000. Of course, the 30,000 miles I put on it were the death of it, but needless to say, I had no problem justifying the used luxury car I bought after it. That car cost me $13,000, and it paid for itself in tax deductions in 18 months.

I recommend getting a lease-returned luxury vehicle as soon as your business starts really moving. It'll improve your image in the minds of your customers, and it's easy to justify once you start working enough to actually pay for it. If you drive less than 15,000 miles per year, consider a lease: it's in the price range you'll be able to deduct, and you won't go over the mile limitation. Use the following formula to determine your car payment budget:

$$[(\text{Annual miles} \times .31) \times 80\%] \div 12$$

Use the result as your maximum car payment for a work vehicle, and you'll be driving for free for as long as you consult. You'll find more detail on this and other cool deductions in Chapter 14, *Accounting and Taxes*.

Conclusion

All the tools and software I've talked about in this chapter amount to about $15,000, which you should consider to be the startup costs of a consulting firm. If you're like me and most other geeks and you've already got a lot of this stuff, your startup costs will be lower. And you shouldn't feel like you have to have everything before you start; since your consulting load will be small when you start, you won't need nearly as many tools to make working more convenient. Feel free to purchase this stuff (and anything else you find that's useful) as you go along.

Establishing Your Business

7

"And then after you've filed your form 6878P, you need to take the ZSR code they give you and file a form 354W with the state and the corresponding form 3645EX with the federal government.... THEN you'll be ready to stand in this line."

Stand in front of your bathroom mirror, look yourself squarely in the eyes, and read this aloud:

"I am a Networking Consultant."

There. You have just established your consulting business.

In the United States, there exists a common-law right to work, which is usually referred to as *sole propriety*. As far as the federal government is concerned, you don't need a license to work, nor do you need to incorporate, nor do you need to talk to a lawyer or do anything else. You can simply begin taking on work, billing for it, and paying income tax.

Unfortunately, that right doesn't necessarily extend to the state or local level. Some states require business licenses for any business activity, and some local governments require them in states that do not. At least one state even requires all businesses to collect sales tax, even for services. Even though most states won't require you to do anything specific to establish yourself as an independent consultant, the fact that some will should be explored. In this chapter, I will discuss the type of state and local restrictions on business you are apt to encounter and will give you my opinion on how to handle these.

I will also go into the numerous other things you could do to establish your business:

➤ You could file a legal alias (company name) for your sole proprietorship so you appear to be a "real" company.

➤ You could incorporate.

➤ You could register trademarks.

➤ You could obtain a reseller's permit.

➤ You must obtain a federal Employer's Identification Number (EIN) if you begin employing people, or create a partnership or incorporate.

➤ You could obtain various types of insurance.

You don't have to do any of these things, and if you decide to, you don't need to do them before you begin consulting. Whether and when you do these things depends largely on your business's ability to do so and the requirements of the state and local government to which you are subject. This chapter covers all these activities in detail.

Starting a Business

An individual who works alone and does business under their own name is a *sole proprietor*. In most states (and in all states with a decent economy), you don't need to do anything to operate as a business under your own name. You may work, charge for your work, and pay your taxes without any government's specific permission. So, if I want to work as "Matthew Strebe, Integrator," I can. That's not to say that they don't have new and different ways to tax you, but we'll get to that later.

This section details the different ways you can establish your business:

➤ As a sole proprietorship

➤ As a partnership or limited liability company

➤ As a corporation (C or S type)

No matter how you decide to start, it's important to remember that you can always change your mind later when your business develops. Don't worry about being locked into a business model that isn't a good fit for you.

The real trick to starting a business is to avoid spending any money until you've actually made some. Don't go into debt by hiring a transactional lawyer to incorporate your business before you know whether or not you can successfully market yourself, and don't go trademarking every logo idea you come up with until you've been using the image property for a while and are comfortable with it.

Sole Proprietorships

Sole proprietorships are companies that operate merely as extensions of the single person (or married couple in community property states like California) who owns them. In most states, you can operate as a contractor using your own name as the business name (or a derivative including your complete name, like "Matthew Strebe Consulting") without any state registration at all.

If you want to register a business name other than your own name, all states require either a business license or a *Doing Business As (DBA)* legal alias, also called a *fictitious name*.

Because you cannot register the same name as someone else in your state, you should research the name (most county registrars have catalogs you can search through) and register it before you spend money on things like trademarks and domain name registrations. If you register a domain name, and then find that someone else has a DBA using that name, they could sue you for the rights to that domain name based on their common law trademark rights of prior use.

Establishing a Name and Registering It

DBAs and fictitious names are simply legal aliases that allow you to open bank accounts in the business's name and cash checks written to that alias. They also serve to establish a common-law (unregistered) trademark, but any other business use of the name may do that as well, depending on existing rights of another's use of the same name. If you choose to use a DBA or fictitious name, you will have to dig through a catalog of names that have been registered in your state to make sure your name hasn't already been taken.

TIP You'll find this catalog at the office of the registrar for fictitious names or business licenses in your city. Internet searches won't yield conclusive results (and there aren't any sites that list business names conclusively), although if the domain name isn't registered (check www.register.com) and no trademarks are registered (check www.uspto.gov), then there's a good chance you'll have no problem in the local area.

After you've determined that the name is not in use in your local area (usually the state), you will fill out a simple form at the registrar's office and file it (usually along with a small fee of less than $50). Fees and forms vary from state to state, but they're not heinous in any case. Your copy of the filed form is your proof of use of the name. You will be able to use this form to open a bank account in the company's name. You will also be required to publish a blurb stating that you're using the name in some publication like a newspaper in order to establish use of the name.

As soon as you register your name, you'll be inundated with direct mail offers from newspapers you've never heard of, and they'll be asking to publish your name; you'll also receive offers from insurance agents, accountants, lawyers, and credit-card merchant service bureaus. It's not wise to leap right into business relationships of any sort until you have at least a little business acumen, so I'd toss most of that stuff and seek out the services you need based on the referrals from people you trust.

Obtaining a Business License

What a *business license* is varies from state to state. In some states, a business license is required to register a name, but it also serves as what is called a *reseller's permit* (or license) in other states. Some states require specific licenses for specific types of businesses but not for others. Check with your state or local government for the exact requirements for business licenses, and make sure they know that you don't intend to resell merchandise (at least not at first) and that you're interested only in service work.

Unfortunately, there's no way for me to tell you exactly whom to contact, because it differs for each state and then again for many municipalities. The local office of the Small Business Administration will be able to point you in the right direction for your municipality, although they will not be able to help you obtain a business license or a fictitious name. Check the blue page government listings in your phone book for listings concerning business licenses or business registration, or check with your state's tax agency. Most states have Web sites for their tax departments; you can find these at www.yahoo.com by clicking Government, then Taxes, then United States, then State Tax Agencies, then the name of your state. Some of these sites are helpful for finding information about starting a business; others are not.

Many clerks assume you already know what they know when you call them, so if you ask about a business license, they'll assume you want what amounts to a reseller's permit. Most likely, you don't really need this information or this permit, and unless you're specific about the fact that you don't intend to be a vendor, you will hear an earful of useless knowledge.

I don't know of any states that specifically license consultants, but many states may extend their requirements for a contractor's license to people who install physical cable plants. That's not the same thing as network equipment installers, but there's enough gray area that you might want to check to see if your state requires a contractor's license, as well. Contractor's licenses are usually based on the safety aspects of construction work, so they shouldn't apply to network consulting.

Partnerships

A *partnership* is essentially the concept of the sole proprietorship extended to multiple people. Partners in a business have a partnership agreement that defines the roles of the participants, but other than that, they act much like a sole proprietorship. The business is merely an extension of the general partners themselves.

My best advice on partnerships is don't bother. There's little reason to start a consulting business with partners when you could just as easily run your own sole proprietorship and then subcontract among other consultants to get work done. By following this method, you'll avoid many of the problems inherent in partnerships, such as the distribution of labor and the problems that revolve around being liable for the actions of your partners.

When you become partners with someone, you're essentially becoming married in the legal sense. Partnerships can go awry for all sorts of reasons that have nothing to do with competence or the character of the partners. Partnerships are really appropriate only when there's some joint product that can't otherwise be created without multiple participants. This is not the case with network integration. And in those cases where multiple equity participation is required to create the product, incorporation is a much better vehicle.

TIP Limited liability companies (LLCs) are a relatively new vehicle to protect "partners" (LLCs have members) from liability in a non-incorporated entity. They don't provide any special tax benefit and are not recognized by the federal government, so the rules that apply to them vary from state to state. My advice on forming as an LLC is the same as my advice on forming as a partnership.

Incorporation

Incorporation is the process of making your business a legal entity separate from yourself. Corporation, a word derived from the Latin word for body and meaning "embodiment," is a legal entity allowed to act much like a sole proprietorship or partnership. A corporation has a bank account, pays taxes, hires people, and can sue and be sued in court. In an abstract sense, a corporation is a fictitious sole proprietor.

Corporations are not some mysterious magical status achievable only by large companies run by rich people. In fact, in most cases, incorporating a business is an easy process you can perform in a single day for a few hundred dollars or less. Incorporation is really just the natural outgrowth of the common-law right to work that has been adapted to the needs of modern capitalism.

A Brief History of Incorporation

Corporations can be jointly owned by any number of people. In fact, the original legal concept of the corporation arose out of the need for joint ownership of small portions of a business.

Renaissance merchants had to form joint ventures in order to carry out expensive trade operations that were difficult to divide up except on a shared basis. Groups of merchants would put together a fund of money to finance a trade mission. They would do this by buying a portion of the trade commodity, or their "share" of the "stock." When that merchandise was sold, each merchant would receive an equal split (a dividend) of the profit resulting from the trade (either money or other trade merchandise). After a while, it became convenient to recognize the continued existence of these shared business relationships beyond single ventures, and the concept of the corporation was born, wherein each shareholder purchased a share of the corporate stock. The British East India Company and the Dutch West Indies Company were two such early incorporations.

An early problem with these corporations was legal liability. With so many owners in the mix, it became difficult to hold the owners of a business personally responsible for the business's actions, especially when the liable activity might be the fault of just one owner or even a non-owner employee. To solve this problem, governments allowed corporations to gain the status of a full legal entity, which basically meant that the liability stopped with the corporation itself and did not affect the owners beyond the possible loss of their investment into the stock of the corporation.

In the 18th century in Europe and the 19th century in the United States, these corporations became so valuable in their own right that a marketplace for the exchange of corporation shares came into being. In this marketplace, merchants could sell portions of their ownership for cash and then buy shares of ownership in other corporations. *Stock exchanges*, as these markets were called, were venues where shares of these publicly traded companies were bought and sold. The shareholders of these stock exchanges (those merchants who had "seats" on the board of exchange) controlled which corporations the exchange would allow to offer their stock. To this day, companies that wish to offer their stock for sale on a public stock exchange must work through a brokerage firm that has a seat on the exchange.

Governments began regulating the exchange of stock in the 19th century, once corporations became so important that the movement of stock actually affected the economy of the country, and once the public exchanges were open to the general (and gullible) public. Early on, most cities had their own stock exchanges where local companies would list their stocks, but this had the disadvantage that potential investors would have to look at exchanges all over the country. Since communication was difficult in the early part of the 20th century, most investors limited their buying to the exchanges in just the largest cities. Since corporations that wished to raise money listed on the exchanges where money was most likely to be had, it didn't take long for the largest exchange of the day to wind up being the only important exchange. In the U.S., this happened to be the exchange in the largest city at the time, New York. While other exchanges survived and while new specialty exchanges thrive, the New York Stock Exchange is still the largest and most important exchange in the world.

C Corporations

Traditional corporations, called *C Corporations*, do suffer from a tax problem as a result of the way modern income taxes work. Businesses pay income tax on the profit they make. The portion of that profit that is distributed to owners (the dividend) becomes part of that owner's yearly income, where it is again taxed as part of the shareholder's individual income tax. In other words, corporate profit is taxed twice. In large corporations, this isn't much of an issue because ownership is so diluted—large corporations have millions of shareholder owners. For small business owners, however, it's a huge problem: if you're distributing profits to just one or two owners, taxing it twice can reduce its value so much that it would be stupid to incorporate.

Since most businesses start as small businesses, the double tax problem became a disincentive to incorporate, which in turn made it hard for small businesses to receive private investment since the company couldn't be shared easily. Thus, the double tax problem became a barrier to the growth of small businesses.

S Corporations

To solve this problem, the *S Corporation*, or S Corp, was created. S Corps do not pay income tax on their profits; rather, all profits or losses are completely distributed to the owners at the end of each year. This way, they are only taxed as part of each shareholder's personal income tax.

To prevent large (especially publicly traded) corporations from receiving this benefit, there are numerous size and activity restrictions on S Corporations. The directors of an S Corp can convert it to a C Corp at the beginning of the tax year if they decide they need to. The IRS can also reclassify an S Corp as a C Corp if it operates outside the restrictions placed on S Corporations. S Corporations are currently limited to 75 shareholders (although legislation is pushed through constantly by lobbies trying to raise this limit, so it may be 150 by the time you read this), and they cannot be publicly traded for that reason.

How Corporations Operate

Corporations are run by a board of directors, which is either composed of or elected by the shareholders, as determined by the company's corporate charter. The chairman, who is usually the largest shareholder, leads the board of directors. The board of directors sets the course for the operation of the company and hires the executive officers, including the Chief Executive Officer (CEO), who is the person directly responsible for the management of the company on a daily basis. Beyond this point, the details of corporations vary according to their individual charters. Any business, whether incorporated or not, may have a President, who is usually the founder, the largest shareholder, or the general manager. A corporation can exist as well with only one person, though three positions must be filled; that is, you can be the President, Secretary, and Treasurer, all at one time.

Benefits of Incorporation

The status corporations enjoy as a separate legal entity from their owners provides two primary benefits:

> ➤ Corporations are taxed differently than individuals.

> ➤ Shareholders of corporations are not liable for the activities of the corporation.

The ramifications of these two benefits are explored in the next few sections.

Starting a corporation isn't hard, but because of government regulation, it's not as easy as standing in front of a mirror and shouting motivational statements at yourself because some silly book told you to. You will have to file articles of incorporation (as well as a few other miscellaneous filings for things like name registration, and so forth) with the Secretary of State in the state in which your business incorporates.

Traditionally, to incorporate a business, you would either have an accountant or a lawyer who specialized in transaction law handle the form filing for you. This isn't necessary anymore. Now, you can simply pick up an "incorporation workbook" at most major bookstores; it will include all the appropriate forms, advice, and necessary agencies for every state. These books usually also come with the requisite forms for reseller's permits, state and federal tax ID numbers, and all the other minutiae required to incorporate your business.

TIP My accountant recommends going the workbook route for S Corporations. If you decide you have to start as a C Corporation (which is the wrong way unless you've got hundreds of people interested in investing, or if tax reasons compel you), you should probably have a transactional lawyer or a tax accountant set the business up for you.

Understanding Taxes and Regulation

Just because you have the right to work doesn't mean that the government has given up its right to tax you. Usually, this taxation is in the form of simple personal income tax, but in at least one state (Connecticut), you may be required to charge sales tax for "contracting" services, and therefore, you would need to have a tax identification number.

Federal Income Tax

The basic tax that all income-earning legal entities (people, corporations, and trusts) pay is a tax on income. The percentage of income that you must pay varies from 15 percent to 39.6 percent in personal income tax, depending upon how much money you make.

For corporations, "income" is usually interpreted to mean "profit," that is, the money remaining after the costs of doing business are expensed against earnings. C Corporations pay a 13 percent federal tax on profits, while S Corporations must distribute their profit at the end of the year to the shareholders so that this profit can then be taxed at the shareholder's personal income tax amount.

Self-Employment Tax

The so-called self-employment tax is the separate fixed entitlements like Medicare and Social Security that are normally "split" between the employee and the employer (each pays 7.65 percent of the employee's net income). Actually, the split is just political cockamamie (hey, that spell checks!)— employees are paying it whether they see it in their paychecks or not because it's pegged to their salary—employers just figure it on top of salary as a cost of employment. Why the government chose to "show" employees half of these entitlements in their paycheck stubs is hard to fathom.

In any case, if you had any doubt that the split was cockamamie before, consider the self-employment tax. In this situation, because consultants are both the employer and the employee, they get to pay both ends of the tax: the 7.65 percent normally paid by the employer and the 7.65 percent normally paid by the employee. You will pay 15.3 percent of your net income in self-employment tax.

The trick to self-employment tax is to avoid as much of it as possible by incorporating once your consulting income exceeds what you would be paid as a network integrator in your area if you were an employee. By incorporating as an S Corp, you become an employee of the S Corp, so you will pay yourself a salary. You will still owe the equivalent of self-employment on that salary at the 15.3% rate, but the corporation will pay the other half and may treat that payment as an expense deduction. The remainder of the company's profits can then be distributed to you as the equivalent of dividends, which are subject to income tax but not subject to self-employment tax. Chapter 14 explains this tactic in detail.

State Taxes and Licenses

Nearly all states levy some sort of taxes on businesses; in fact, most levy many. Typical taxes include the following:

Income Tax   Taxes the profit that a business makes.

Sales Tax   Directly taxes the price at which goods are sold.

Property Tax   Annually taxes the tangible property (usually real estate and vehicles) owned by a business.

Income and Revenue Tax

Most states operate just like the federal government in that they charge income tax and may charge for entitlements like health coverage, unemployment insurance, and so forth. Usually, figuring these taxes is easy since most states parrot the U.S. Government tax code. Most of the time, they just require you to apply the state's tax tables to your federal filing numbers.

Generally, the only states that don't charge income tax are those with a natural resource, like Oil, Gambling, or Plenty of Retired People, because the income derived from the resource obviates the need and because the state would like to attract more people to it. Other states are apparently full because they seem to be actively trying to push both people and businesses out with heinous tax requirements.

There is no way to avoid paying income tax except not to work for compensation. You can minimize your income tax liability by moving to a state or country that doesn't charge it, but that's a little more extreme than most people are willing to consider, and most likely, you will still end up paying some sort of federal income tax.

Some states have actual revenue taxes, which are a tax on the gross income of a business before expenses, but those states tend to have really crappy economies that businesses tend to avoid, for some reason.

Each state has different taxation requirements and requirements for business licensing. I had intended to include a detailed list of all the requirements for each state when I set out to write this book, but the fact that many municipalities charge taxes differently from their states made the whole thing quite pointless. Even if I told you what the state requirements were, I couldn't possibly list all the possible requirements for your county or city government, so you'd still have to call and find out for yourself.

Unfortunately, there's no better way to figure out what tax and license requirements apply to you than to call your state's Department of Revenue/ Taxation or to visit their Web site. Check out Web sites for the various states at dir.yahoo.com/Government/U_S__Government/Taxes/State_Tax_Agencies/ (make sure to type two underscores after the "S" in U_S__Government).

These sites will also provide you with the requirements for obtaining a business license, as well, if one is required for the operation of any business. Most states require only sales tax from retail vendors, but some states and local governments license all types of businesses.

ALASKA'S PERMANENT FUND

Alaska is unique in that it has what many people consider to be a reverse-tax in the form of its Permanent Fund. The Permanent Fund was originally the royalty Alaska received from its oil properties, 50 percent of which was returned annually to the population. Now diversified, the fund acts as more of broad-spectrum mutual fund that is heavily invested in corporate stocks—in fact, it's among the 100 largest funds of any kind in the world. The 1999 dividend for every resident of Alaska was nearly $2000. It almost makes me want to move, except that I couldn't bear to live in a place where there aren't any Fry's Electronics stores.

Sales Tax

Sales tax is the tax most states charge on the sales transactions within their borders. The rate at which the merchandise is taxed usually falls between 5 and 10 percent of the total value of the merchandise. In most cases, labor is not taxed (except that the laborer pays tax on their income, as mentioned earlier). Some exceptions to this include the fact that at least one state (Connecticut) also charges sales tax on services, and a few states (usually those with natural resources, or those that make their money from income tax) don't charge a sales tax at all.

When a business (like a grocery store, for example) collects tax on the items you purchase, that business is then required to remit that collected tax to the government. If you decide to sell material directly (without performing a service), then you will have to charge, collect, and remit sales tax. Paying sales tax for a business consists of determining your periodic sales tax liability (usually quarterly, but sometimes monthly or annually), and mailing a check for that amount to your state's tax authority. When you get your reseller's permit, you'll be given a book of complete instructions detailing exactly how and when to pay sales tax on the goods you've sold. Most state tax boards are so aggressive in the collection of sales tax that they make the IRS look downright neighborly by comparison. Because sales tax is a trust tax that is never your property, if you fall behind in the payment of sales tax, you are putting your business and yourself (whether you're incorporated or not) in serious jeopardy.

The trick to avoiding problems with sales tax is not to have a reseller's permit. It is my strong recommendation to avoid the whole issue by not acting as a retail vendor. If you don't have a resale license, there's no possible way for a state tax agency to find you accountable for sales tax fraud. On the other hand, if you do have a resale license, you will find that sales tax boards will clamp a lien on your business faster than any other government agency if you don't pay up. They have the power to hold the owners of a corporation personally liable for the sales tax. Sales tax liens cannot be discharged in bankruptcy (personal or business), so they will follow you around until they're paid off. The same is true for employee withholding taxes (trust fund taxes), which is a great reason to avoid having employees.

As long as you pay sales tax on the items you purchase for your service customers when you buy them, you do not need to charge sales tax when you sell the item to a customer. In most states, sales tax need only be paid once in the chain of distribution. Some states have specific exceptions for equipment provided as part of a service contract and not billed for separately; others simply don't address the issue of reselling tax-paid equipment. In any case, if you don't have a reseller's permit, there's no way for you to be held accountable for not charging sales tax, even if the laws in your state are unclear on the subject.

If you're really nervous about the idea of not paying sales tax on whatever markup you add to the equipment you pass through to your vendors, then don't mark it up. There's no case where you can be held accountable if you charge your customer the exact price you paid for an item. You can then simply charge a "handling fee" as a separate line item on your invoice to cover the service of identifying, purchasing, and delivering the item. Using this tactic, you can evade even the strictest interpretation of resale and thus the entire sales tax issue. Your customers won't mind a modest fee to save them the hassle of acquiring equipment—in fact, many of my customers have me purchase equipment for them because it's still cheaper than getting it on their own since many have no facility to buy over the Web.

There is one problem with not being a reseller: many large distributors, notably Ingram Micro and TechData, won't talk to you unless you have a reseller's permit. Since these companies are the top-level distributors for nearly everything network related, this used to present a serious problem for independent consultants, especially those not within driving distance of a Fry's Electronics. Now, thanks to the miracle of the Internet, there are literally thousands of online resellers that simply act as Web front-ends for these distributors. They charge tax, shipping, credit card charges, and a modest markup on goods sold, but they purchase in such volume that you're likely to get a better price from them (including their markup and credit card fees) than you would have gotten from Ingram Micro anyway.

Check out www.shopper.com for a searchable comparison engine that will link you to every significant online vendor in existence. This engine will compare prices and sort them in price order, thus performing your comparison-shopping for you. When I use this engine, I then scan the list in price order until I find a nearby out-of-state vendor; this way I can avoid paying any sales tax.

I also highly recommend www.cdw.com, one of the largest mail-order network equipment dealers, because they can ship next-day delivery on orders taken up until midnight the night before. Many other vendors may not post your order until the next day, and then they might not actually ship your product until the following day for a two-day turnaround.

N O T E I've had only one negative experience purchasing equipment online from companies I'd never heard of, and that involved an unexpected two-week delay due to a systems crash.

Property Tax

Like individuals, businesses in most states are charged an annual tax on property, and sometimes on major equipment like vehicles. The property tax rate is usually about 1 percent of the total value of the property per year. Vehicle taxes vary so widely by state that there's no point in discussing them here. Most consulting businesses will not own tangible real estate, so this tax isn't much of an issue.

Talk to your accountant about the pros and cons of having your incorporated business buy your company vehicle. The business can then depreciate the car as a business expense. If you purchase the car privately , the business can reimburse you, and write-off the reimbursement as a business expense, and the reimbursement to you is not income to you.

You may find that your local government does not tax businesses for owning vehicles but does tax individuals. Or you may find that car insurance is considerably higher for businesses than it is for individuals. Your accountant will probably have to calculate out both options completely to determine the total cost of ownership of each method to select the less expensive option in your area.

Finding the Right Insurance

You don't need any insurance to operate a business.

That said, there are a few insurances you'd be stupid not to have, there are a few insurances most people like to have, and there are a few forms of insurance customers may require you to have if you want to work for them. Other types of insurance are just silly financial vehicles sold to people with severe risk-aversion disorders.

Business Insurance

Businesses have a different set of insurance requirements than individuals primarily because they're exposed to a much higher risk of being sued than individuals are. Individuals are typically only sued in tort cases, in which someone gets hit by your car or falls down your stairs. Business lawsuits arise most frequently from contractual disagreements, and for that reason, they're fairly common.

General Liability

General liability (G&L) is basically insurance acquired to protect against being sued for tort. G&L protects you or your company from lawsuits employees might bring against you for typical "slip and fall" accidents (personal injury) or other "risk of doing" business occurrences, like employee misconduct that results in a lawsuit that doesn't involve a contract. G&L is usually pretty inexpensive (usually less than $1000 per year for consultants).

G&L usually has specific exclusions for professional malpractice (when you've messed something up, or at least, your customer believes you have, and they're suing you for it). You can get G&L policies that cover this, but they're considerably more expensive.

When you have G&L and you are sued, you simply call your insurance provider and sign the power of attorney over to them so that they can defend or settle the case. Chapter 15, *The Law*, has more details about general liability insurance.

Do you need G&L insurance? That depends on how likely you think you are to be sued. I tend to think that well-written contracts can avoid the problem, so I don't carry G&L myself. My lawyer is a big believer in G&L insurance, however, as he sees people being sued every day, and he points out that it's cheap enough that most businesses should have it if for no other reason than to defend against tort.

Errors and Omissions

Errors and Omissions (E&O) is basically malpractice insurance for professionals and companies—it's insurance against being sued for contractual disputes. It insures you against the cost of being sued if you mess up. As such, it's hideously expensive (usually about $5000/year, if you can find it).

Since I don't suck at networking, I prefer to use incorporation as my shield against personal liability for professional acts. If my company is sued, the worst case is that my corporation could be sued for its assets. Since your company shouldn't have much in the way of assets, and since a properly operated corporation protects its owners from personal liability, your maximum loss will be whatever income you haven't paid out or distributed and whatever assets your corporation owns, such as your computer and perhaps your business vehicle. For most single consultants, that doesn't amount to much and it's certainly not irreplaceable.

If you suck at networking or if you've been sued numerous times before, you might find E&O insurance to be valuable.

Performance Bonds

Sometimes, medium-sized business customers require performance bonds, which are essentially units of individual project insurance, from all contractors who work for them, especially when construction is involved. Bonds are hard to come by—usually, you have to have assets to put up as collateral to secure a bond.

My best advice is either to talk your customer out of requiring a performance bond (by explaining that they're nearly impossible for individual consultants to obtain) or to pass on the contract. The only way you or any other consultant will qualify for a performance bond is to attach a major asset like your home to the bond. The last thing you need is to lose your house because you couldn't complete a job. Keep in mind that companies that require bonds are also highly likely to try to exercise them by suing you.

When I worked with a contracting company, we were usually required to bond jobs that were larger than $100,000, especially if we were working for a general contractor. Since as a consultant you will be working for companies that have no construction experience, they will most likely not even know about performance bonds. I've never had a customer require one since I started consulting.

Equipment Insurance

You can get insurance for literally anything these days, business chattel included. The equipment in your home office is probably not covered by your homeowners insurance if you identify it as "work equipment." Whether the computer sitting in your home (that you use for both business and pleasure) is a "work" asset or a personal asset is a gray area in the eyes of your insurance company—but I'd certainly try to get them to cover it anyway.

In any case, if you're really worried about the cost of your equipment, you can get equipment insurance (sometimes called "Inland Marine" insurance because the whole idea of insuring equipment came from the shipping industry). I think it's a complete waste of money however, since office equipment is relatively cheap and easy to replace these days and the odds of anything coverable (this insurance usually only covers acts of nature, not theft or intentional destruction because you're pissed at it) happening to it are remote.

Employee Insurance

If you have employees, you must carry two types of insurance: workers' compensation, which is insurance that compensates workers (hence the name) if they become injured while working; and unemployment insurance, which compensates your employees if they're laid off (but not fired).

Being self employed, even if your business is incorporated, you don't need either insurance—in fact, you can't file for either if you're the owner of the company in the vast majority of cases.

So, the law here is simple: if you have non-owner employees, you must have both types of insurance in most states. Otherwise, you don't need either. If you need this insurance, contact your state tax authority. Many states operate both types of insurances themselves rather than letting public insurance companies handle them.

Personal Insurance

Personal insurance comprises those insurance vehicles written against you personally. For instance, now that you are self-employed, you must individually purchase the employee benefits you had when you worked for someone else.

Health Insurance

Health insurance is the most common employee benefit you'll lose when you're self-employed. Most people, myself included, consider this insurance to be too valuable not to have, but unfortunately, it's somewhat expensive when purchased outside of a group plan.

I purchase health coverage through Kaiser Permanente (a hospital-owning insurance provider that requires you to use their facilities) here in California. The cost is a reasonable $250 per month for my wife and me. There are no forms to fill out, no people you have to call before going in, and they have a highly computerized patient record system. They have facilities all over our area, so we've been happy with them.

Most people don't live in areas where old-fashioned, hospital-owning insurers exist, so they have to purchase health insurance from the more common HMO. HMOs are far more likely to question procedures than hospital group plans, and in my opinion, they provide a lower quality of customer service for insurance issues. The care provided varies dramatically among organizations, so check out a consumer magazine or other comparative survey before you join a plan.

Many HMOs are responding to the surge in self-employment by offering reasonable non-group insurance coverage. You should be able to find quality health coverage for your entire family for less than $500 a month at the absolute most. If you can't, get an insurance agent to find it for you. If your insurance costs are higher than that, you may consider one of the new tax-free medical savings plans. These allow you to contribute to a personally managed investment fund to be used only for medical expenses.

Life and Disability Insurance

Life insurance is always a good idea if you are the primary breadwinner in your family, at least until your mortgage is paid off. This is especially important for the self-employed, since your income varies considerably.

Most insurers advise buying enough term life insurance to pay off all your debt and provide for the education of all your dependents at a minimum. I buy $500,000 of term insurance, for which I pay about $25 per month. Life insurance for a younger person is about the cheapest form of insurance you can get. You can get disability riders on most life insurance policies that will invoke the policy if you are disabled. The definition of disabled varies considerably from policy to policy, so be sure you understand the definition of your specific policy if disability insurance is important to you. I would not buy a disability policy that wasn't attached to a life insurance policy since death is actually more likely than permanent disability these days and since the coverage is usually more expensive if purchased separately.

Once you're home is paid off, there's not much point in having life insurance since you won't be leaving any significant debt to worry about and since, in the worst case, the value of the home can support your family until other means become available. Oddly, the time when most people finish paying off their house coincides with the age at which term insurance starts to get really expensive.

Whole life coverage is life insurance you contribute to for your whole life. (I know, that's not what they mean by whole, but it's funny.) Usually the premiums are level throughout your lifetime or until the policy is paid out, because the policy has no term. The policy cost is far higher when you're young than a term policy, but far lower when you're older (and more likely to die). Whole life is considered by many to be an investment vehicle, since once the policy is paid for, it can be borrowed against. In my opinion, buying a low-yield life insurance policy as an investment is silly—if you want to invest, invest. I stick with low-cost term insurance, and I'll be dropping life insurance completely once I have a house paid off.

Car Insurance

Car insurance is nothing new—you've probably got it now and that won't change when you become a consultant. What will change is how much you drive. When I filed for car insurance, the agent asked me how far I drove to and from work. I quite honestly answered that since I was self employed, I had a home office and I didn't commute. The agent happily plugged in "0," and I got a pretty good rate. It didn't occur to me until later that the insurance company wanted to know how many miles I'd be putting on my car in a usual day—which is about 100. I still haven't bothered to call and tell them, but you should probably be clear about what you do during the day when you get insurance.

Also be aware of the fact that businesses are usually charged a much higher rate for car insurance than individuals, which may make it more expensive to insure if you purchase "a company car" through your corporation. Talk to your insurance agent to determine what the exact ramifications will be in your case.

Conclusion

You don't have to worry about filling out a lot of forms and obtaining permits to do business as a consultant in most states. Check with your local Small Business Administration office or state tax authority to be sure, but in most states, all you need to do to operate as a business using your own name is begin working.

Most consultants start out as sole proprietors. They only incorporate once they start making enough money to be really heavily taxed. Corporations are taxed differently than sole proprietorships and can shield their owners against certain legal liabilities. Incorporating as an S Corporation has specific tax benefits for small businesses.

In most states, your business taxes will be accounted for when you pay your personal income tax. If you sell equipment directly, you may need to collect and remit sales tax, but that can usually be avoided by simply paying tax on the equipment before you resell it.

Certain types of insurance are important for individuals. Consider getting general liability insurance for your business, health insurance for your family, and life insurance for yourself. If you have employees, you must also get workers' compensation and unemployment insurance for them. Most people don't find insurance policies other than the ones mentioned here to be worth the premiums.

The Other Kind of Networking

*"Actually, sir, I don't think any of my friends
need data network services."*

Marketing is the most inscrutable and the second most important part of any business. Marketing is so difficult that many operational businesses never actually do it that well (case in point: Microsoft). The importance of marketing is obvious. Your network consulting business will fail for one of only three reasons:

➤ You suck at networking.

➤ You suck at marketing.

➤ You smell funny.

Now, assuming of course that you've mastered most of the social skills they teach in kindergarten and that you have the requisite technical skill to solve your customer's problems, the only reason your business might fail is poor marketing.

Network integration is in such high demand right now (and for the foreseeable future) that if anyone (with networking skills) anywhere can't find work, it's their own fault. I no longer perform any sort of active marketing, yet I still turn down more work than I take on because I'm already working far more than I want to. This is the case among every networking consultant I know who is competent.

So basically, you only need to have two skills to begin consulting: networking and networking. You need to be able to build networks of computers, and be able to build a network of commissioned salespeople.

Of course, I'm assuming that you intend to start your business in an area that has a commercial base of businesses. If you live in Enumclaw, Washington or Paeonia, Colorado, you should probably buy a really good car, because you'll be driving a long way to find work. But anyone within driving distance of 100,000 people should have no problem running a network integration consulting business. (I know a guy in Paeonia who supplements his consulting by running an ISP for the local folk, though, so with just a little creativity you can make it happen in the country, as well.)

Marketing, as inscrutable as it might be for mass-produced commodities and services, is fairly simple for custom services like network integration.

There are only two types of marketing:

Passive marketing   Wherein you advertise and wait for customers to come to you.

Active marketing   Wherein you or your agents contact customers directly and present your services.

Of the two, only one type actually works for network consulting: active marketing. No form of traditional passive marketing is effective for consulting.

I actually spend quite a bit of time in this chapter talking about all types of advertising in an effort to explain exactly which things work and which don't. Hopefully, it'll keep you from spending tens of thousands of dollars to put your face atop every cab in your metro area only to find that it has made you the butt of jokes at cocktail parties.

Analyzing the Market

Most serious business owners would analyze the market saturation for the service they intend to provide before starting a business. This way, they ensure that enough demand exists to satisfy the amount of revenue they want to make.

The network integration market is so wide open that this really isn't necessary, however. Unless you live in San Jose, California (the heart of Silicon Valley), network integrators will be few and far between. I live in San Diego, which is among the 10 most highly saturated cities in the nation for high-tech professionals, and there are still not enough network integrators to go around. I'm very selective about the clients I'll take on. I've probably only run into three or four network consultants in the years I've worked here whom I didn't already know.

Also, remember how highly specialized computer professionals are. I perform integration work for two companies that develop software; programmers are oddly ignorant of computer and networking hardware, and bizarrely reluctant to learn anything about it. They tend to prefer to stay firmly in the abstract world of programming languages. I have another customer who employs a large number of physicists. Literally half of the people on the payroll have Ph.D.s in hard science—the equation-filled whiteboards in this company look like they're straight out of a "Far Side" cartoon. Yet these brilliant minds are wholly unable or unwilling to read the software manuals that come with the tools they use.

Every company with more than 10 employees in the industrialized world would benefit from the services of a skilled network integrator. The demand for network integration services will exceed the demand for financial or corporate legal services very shortly, so there's plenty of work to go around.

Essentially, you're not going to need much help with marketing except to get your name out in your area. That's not easy when you're just getting started (and it's not easy to take back when you're trying to quit. The next few sections talk about different marketing tactics, most of which don't work that well for consultants but which are important to know about if simply to avoid.

Passive Marketing

Any sort of marketing that involves advertising yourself and then waiting for customers to come find you is passive marketing. There are many different types of passive marketing, and you're probably already familiar with all of them.

Most forms of passive advertising are a waste of time because the audience to whom you wish to market is small—just business executives—and passive marketing hits the broad audience of the public at large and is, therefore, very expensive.

The Phone Book

Phone-book advertising will garner about one call per year. That call will be from some kook who's looking to build a network in his home/pyramid/cave. I've never gotten useful work from a phone-book ad, and neither has any consultant I know. Phone books are basically targeted toward home consumers who don't have the money to spend on home networking and who will require far more technical support than the average business consumer.

Residential work is the pits—don't even consider trying it. Every time I help someone out with their home computer, they seem to think they've got an open line to call me for support any time they can't get their kid's Reader

Rabbit CD-ROM working. I haven't been able to get my mom off my back since I gave her a computer. On the other hand, she does call a lot more often. Verdict: help only those home users you care to hear from.

Don't waste your money on a phone book ad. The people it brings in are not appropriate customers for a consultant, and businesses don't consult the phone book when they're looking for technical help.

Newspaper

Newspaper ads are also mostly worthless for the same reason as the phone book—they target home consumers. Running a noticeable ad in a daily paper with any large circulation is also fairly expensive (usually between $1500 and $10,000 per day), and rarely draws any useful response.

Even those publications targeted specifically toward computer users won't yield much result. San Diego has one of the country's best weekly pulp magazines for computer users, and ads in it for consulting and networking are not effective. Why? Because only geeks and wanna-be geeks read it. It's perfect for computer storeowners, but it's not a business-to-business publication.

Your target market is the owners, managers, and financial controllers of regional, small- to medium-sized businesses. If you were going to advertise in any mass-market medium, it should be a periodical that caters to this group of people. You are not marketing to geeks. What does this group read? They read *The Economist*, *Newsweek*, *Red Herring*, and other weekly news magazines. If you can afford to advertise there ($50,000 per ad per issue and up), you don't need my help.

Billboards

Yep, also a waste of time and very expensive. Although billboards do reach a wide audience (everyone gets trapped in traffic), the prices for well-placed billboards are very high. Basically any place you've seen an advertisement for beer is out of your budget.

Benches

Benches are the low-rent form of billboard advertisement, a realm populated by real-estate agents, bail-bondsmen, and the purveyors of remedies for being overweight (which oddly never involves simply spending less money on food…(I'm fat, so I can joke about it (I'm also a programmer, so I can nest parentheses indefinitely))). Bench ads, while inexpensive, are also fairly ineffective except when advertising a product or service that appeals to a significant portion of the population.

Cabs

Taxi advertisements are targeted squarely toward travelers, so they consist mostly of ads for hotels, rental car companies, and other pursuits of a less savory nature engaged in by people who are away from their home. This form of advertisement doesn't reach your target audience.

Cars

Cars are a different matter. If you use a van, truck, SUV, or a car with a large flat area (that's getting rare these days) as your business vehicle, you may want to consider painting your logo, motto, and phone number on the side. Although this form of advertisement is also fairly ineffective, it has the advantage of at least being free of recurring cost. In my opinion, it also makes you appear more serious about your business, more professional, and more like a large company to your customers.

Press Releases

Press releases are also a waste of time for consultants; in most cases, periodicals won't consider publishing press releases for small businesses unless they offer a new and unique service and product. You don't, so don't bother wasting your time faxing press releases to everyone.

Magazines

It costs far too much to advertise in magazines. Your year's salary would pay for a single, full-page regional ad in a national magazine. Enough said.

Radio/Television

Radio and television are even worse than magazines because of the high rates they charge for advertising and because they are ephemeral. Single-shot ads in either medium are also highly ineffective; the reason you keep seeing and hearing the same ads repeatedly is because advertisers know that repetition works. You don't have the kind of money it would take for a useful marketing campaign in these mediums.

Direct Mail

Direct mail, mailing letters directly to prospective clients, is expensive, time-consuming, and ineffective. My own personal study of 1000 pieces of direct mail sent out (at a cost of $320 in postage and another $100 in printer cartridges) yielded the following stunning results: not a single reply. It's easier to simply write a check to the post office and save the wear and tear on your tongue.

Mass E-Mailing

Junk e-mail is extraordinarily ineffective. On average, only about 1 in 1000 mass e-mails garners a response and they rarely make sense for regional businesses since you can't get lists that categorize e-mail addresses by locality. And that's not saying anything about the fact that people hate getting junk e-mail.

The difference between mass e-mailing and direct mail is that mass e-mailing costs you very little. Assuming you found some poor company who hadn't properly secured their SMTP server (you have to exploit someone with a high-bandwidth connection to perform mass e-mailing effectively), you could transmit 100,000 e-mails at no cost.

The exceptionally low cost of mass e-mailing is what makes its low response rate worthwhile for some types of businesses. Although only 1 in 1,000 receives a response, you can get 100 responses from a single batch mailing. For purveyors of products, especially products that can be delivered via the Internet, this is acceptable.

For purveyors of services (like you), it still doesn't work. Firstly, scavenging a list of 100,000 e-mail addresses in your area is nearly impossible. Those who sell lists steal e-mail address from the headers of e-mail messages that flow through their own SMTP relays, from AOL, and from other easily hacked service providers. These addresses contain no information that identifies the geographic origin of the e-mail address, so you'll never find a list provider that can get you 100,000 e-mail addresses in your area. Mass e-mailing to everyone in the country might yield 100 responses, but the odds that even one of them would be within your service radius are very slight.

Broadcast Faxing

Broadcast faxing is just as ineffective as mass e-mailing, but it also pisses people off because you're spending their paper to advertise to them. It's also illegal in many states.

Internet

Web sites are a good idea, but not as a marketing tool to attract new customers. They are more appropriate as a method to keep existing customers hooked on your services.

You should have a Web site, but don't consider it a form of passive advertisement. You can't rely upon search engines to bring in new customers because whatever search terms a user types in that would include your site will also include millions of others, and your site won't be listed until page 5000. A Web site alone does not really constitute mass media advertising. Without an ad campaign, a Web site alone is about as useful as a billboard in your bedroom. Nobody's going to see it. You could put money behind a banner advertising campaign on a search engine, but that costs about as much as a full-page national magazine ad. Ad banners are not an effective form of advertisement for a small service business because they are hideously expensive. I'll talk more about your Web site in the section on public image.

Mailing lists for your already established customers are not the same as junk e-mail. You should run a mailing list to keep your customers informed of security issues with software they run, new viruses, services you provide, etc. In the text of the message, always include a link to an area on your Web site that will allow them to easily unsubscribe in case they don't appreciate it. Mass e-mailings are a great "low maintenance" way to stay in touch with current and former customers without the seeming neediness of a phone call or personal e-mail.

Active Marketing

Active marketing describes those marketing efforts where you or your agents talk directly to customers to establish a consulting relationship.

Active marketing doesn't have to be as annoying as Amway, vacation condo sales pitches, and incessant phone calls from the *San Diego Union Tribune* (yes, I'm grinding axes here). By creating a virtual sales force (explained in the next section on networking) who will approach your customers in a variety of contexts, and by qualifying the people you talk to before you call them, you can make sure you're always talking to people who are relieved to have finally found someone who can solve their problems.

Networking

Networking is the marketing term for "putting the word out" among your acquaintances. Basically, networking involves meeting a lot of people, impressing them socially, and then telling them what you do and that you're looking for work. It's pretty easy once you get the hang of it. Chapter 3 discussed how I'd gotten a job through a contact—that's a precise example of network marketing.

Networking might seem passive at first glance, but you aren't advertising to customers, you're creating a network of people you know to act as salespeople who will speak directly with customers. This virtual sales force will give your number to customers and usually leave it up to them to call you.

The tough part of networking is starting. I was lucky—I left my former job with a complete network that has kept me working ever since. If you can manage this, I recommend it. Chapter 5 explains how to do this.

How do you jumpstart a network if you weren't in a position to steal one from your former employer? It's not all that difficult.

1. Identify high-value contacts.
2. Call to introduce yourself.
3. Complement their enormous egos.
4. Invite them to lunch.
5. Leave a stack of business cards.
6. Make sure they know you pay a commission.

Most salespeople would be tickled pink to have somebody buy them lunch for a change, so it's really not hard to introduce yourself to them. Here's a typical cold introduction (i.e., introducing yourself) to a salesperson (salespeople have to listen long enough to figure out whether there's a sale in the conversation, so they can't just hang up like others might):

Salesperson: Hello, this is Laura speaking, how may I help you?

Me: Hi Laura, my name is Matthew Strebe, and I'm starting a network-consulting firm in the area. I provide network services to small and medium sized businesses. Do you have much exposure to businesses of that size? [Key: Finish with a question to keep the conversation moving.]

Salesperson: Well, yes, I do, but I'm still not sure how I can help you. We don't need any network consulting here.

Me: Actually, I was thinking that if you ran into a customer who needed some assistance with network integration, you could pass on my business card. I pay a 5 percent finder's fee to people who bring work in to me, so a lot of people in the industry use me as a way to help their customers solve networking problems. [Key: Mention what's in it for them (the commission) right off the bat.]

Salesperson: Oh, well, I probably do have a number of customers who could use some networking help.

Me: I tell you what: let me buy you lunch, and I'll explain what it is that I do. I'll then give you a few business cards for you to hand out at your discretion to your customers who you think might need my help. Is there a convenient time for you this week? [Key: Worst case, at least they get a free lunch.]

Salesperson: Well, I'm free on Friday.

Me: Great. Shall we meet at 1:00 P.M. at Chang's? I like to avoid the crowd. [Key: Choose a nice restaurant to present a professional appearance.]

Salesperson: One o'clock is great for me. I look forward to meeting you, Matthew.

Me: Great! Well, I'll see you on Friday. Bye! [Key: Always finish with a friendly and enthusiastic tone.]

Once salespeople know that they'll get a solid commission for simply handing out your business card to a person who contracted with you, they will turn you down only if their primary job actually prevents them from performing any other sales work. Heck, half of them will do it anyway. A 5 percent commission on sales is a very small price to pay to keep your plate full.

Once you've got a few customers, make sure they know you're looking to take on additional work. The employees of your current customers are probably the second most likely way you'll find work. One client of mine changes jobs fairly frequently—and he always manages to get me work at his new job. I've worked for his last three employers as a consultant.

Finally, make sure the other service providers for your customers know that you are looking for work. Accountants, bookkeepers, lawyers, and other business-to-business professionals have a tremendous amount of exposure to various businesses, and they're looking for people to help them find work, as well. Professional consultants who work in other industries are a tremendous marketing asset.

Beware the Sales Consultant

Never, ever, ever get into a situation where you pay a salesperson anything but commission. Never pay a retainer, an hourly wage, a salary, or enter into any contractual agreements with a salesperson in advance of them bringing in work.

Absolutely every time I've seen a salesperson paid in advance, the employer has felt ripped off when the work hasn't come in. Nobody can promise sales results, and you can't afford to pay people for trying. Salespeople understand that their industry works on commission, and legitimate salespeople understand that when they work for small businesses, they make their money on commission alone. Good salespeople have no problem with this because they always make enough commission. Poor salespeople go from job to job, wrangling advances, retainers, and wages so they can look for work that they ultimately never find.

Time after time, I've seen small businesses and professionals sold into a deal where they pay a salesperson (usually in the guise of a "marketing consultant") to look for work for them. Generally, the salesperson has a "hot deal" they're working at the moment, and they just need a retainer "so they can concentrate on just this one deal" to clinch it. Time goes by, the salesperson will report that the customer just needs a little more work, etc. If you offer to meet with the client, the salesperson will make excuses about why the customer can't be met, and ultimately, when they've frustrated you completely, they'll say that the customer went with somebody else because the competition used some unethical practice to lure them. They then simply move on to the next sucker and sell their snake oil again.

Commission is a necessary evil in the world of sales. The purpose of commission is to reward good salespeople while convincing poor salespeople that they can't make enough money in sales for it to be worth the trouble. It's the environmental pressure that allows the survival of only the fittest of salespeople.

A good salesperson might wrestle you for a 10 percent commission—that's a different story altogether. That salesperson is certain of their ability as a salesperson and is simply trying to sweeten the deal for themselves. I'd much rather pay a higher commission than any sort of payment in advance of results.

Cold Calling

Cold calling, calling businesspeople randomly from a list or from the phone book and fishing for opportunities to work, doesn't work. Nobody wants to receive unsolicited phone calls, and they're likely to simply hang up. Even if they listened to you, trying to push your services on people randomly really sucks. I've never met a consultant who reported to me that cold calling ever worked for them.

Although I've never done a scientific survey, I do know of a small networking firm that employed a professional cold caller one day a week (at $33/hr.) who made an average of about 100 cold calls per day. After eight months, they let him go because they hadn't gotten as much work in as they'd spent paying him.

Warm Calling

Warm calling, calling people whom you know are interested in hiring network services, works extremely well. These people already have an identified problem, a budget to solve it, and are actively searching for solutions. Your call to them will be a welcome relief.

How do you find this gold mine of work? The solution is also exceptionally easy: the classified help wanted ads. Even though people say they're looking to hire network administrators, they'd be ecstatic to find a solution without hiring somebody on. Don't look for help desk or technical support work, however. These jobs are low-paying telephone support for major manufacturers. Look specifically for network administration work.

Even when companies think they're really looking for a permanent employee, I've offered to "fill in" until they hire somebody permanently.

This way, I tell them, they can take the time to find the right person rather than just get somebody in to fix immediate problems. Nearly every company I've used this tactic on has accepted. Most often, days, then weeks, then months go by and the idea of hiring a network person is simply forgotten because the network problems have gone away.

Don't let your conscience bother you because you are looking at want ads. If the idea of competing against jobless network integrators tugs at your heartstrings, just give them a copy of this book.

Developing Your Public Image

Your public image is the impression you project in the minds of your prospective customers. It encompasses everything from the clothes you wear and the things you say to the tools you use and the manner in which you present your business.

Obviously, you need to look professional. You should present yourself in a manner similar to any professional service company, using similar strategies that are scaled down for a consultant's budget.

Image Properties

You're probably already thinking about what you're going to name your company, or agonizing about your inability to come up with a good name. Don't worry about it. Whether or not you have any name, logo, motto, or mission statement is entirely up to you and won't make that much difference in your business initially.

Later on, when your business has grown, image properties, things like trademarks, logos, slogans, etc., serve to create an anchor in the minds of your customers to which they can attach your business's activities in general. Every business starts with a default name, though: the name of the owner.

Company Name

Do you need a company name? No. Your Name & Associates, or Your Name & Co. or simple Your Name is just fine.

On the other hand, a company name won't hurt, and it will help to separate your consulting, both in your mind and in the mind of your customers, from you, the person. For example, I consider my writing and consulting to be two different ventures, so when I think and discuss my consulting business, I think of it by its company name.

When I named my company (Netropolis), I did a DNS search and verified that the name was available. Like an idiot, I didn't register it. Months later, someone else did, and they've never used it. They've offered to sell it to me for $30,000, though. I've regretted that ever since. So I've renamed my business Consulting Network Integration Corporation (Connetic) because I could register the domain name.

Unless you're already in love with a name, choose a name by searching the WHOIS database at `networksolutions.com` to make sure you can get the domain name. As soon as you find a fitting name that's available, register the domain name. Nothing will make your business look more professional in IT consulting than having your e-mail address be `yourname @yourcompany.com`.

Logo or Style

Like a name, you don't need a logo, but a good one will help your company look more professional. Logos don't have to be sophisticated—in fact, the simpler your logo is, the better off you'll be. Often, simply stylizing your company name in a fixed manner with a fixed font is a better idea. Think of the major software vendors:

Microsoft   Stylized name

IBM   Stylized initials

Sun   Simple logo with stylized name

Apple   Simple logo with stylized name

A logo's only purpose is to be an immediately recognizable symbol of your company. The simpler it is, the more powerful it is because it's more easily recognized.

Motto or Slogan

With mottos or slogans, you're probably starting to tread into the "shouldn't do it" category because good ones are difficult to come up with and bad ones abound. The purpose of a motto is to cast the company as clever, intelligent, and possessing a vision beyond simply making money. Mottos should compel the customer to do business with the company.

Here is my uneducated opinion on a few popular mottos:

Nike's "Just do it"   Excellent. It's powerful, motivational, and targets the urge to use the product (running shoes).

Microsoft's "Where do you want to go today?"   Bad. It's light on meaning, does not compel, and is unclear about how the product could actually help get you anywhere. Basically, people don't think of the product (software) as helping them to go to some different "place."

Apple's "Think Different"   Fair. It does play to the egos of the customer base by casting the product (computers) with an elitist mystique. Unfortunately, it's grammatically incorrect and just a minor twist on IBM's older and much more powerful "Think" motto.

Connetic's "We Hook You Up"   Good. It explains what the company does (connects computers) and has a double meaning that they solve your problems, all while casting the company in a younger, hipper context. (Okay, I know critiquing my own motto isn't really fair.)

Avoid mottos that are drab, like "Providing IT Solutions to Small Business," if your business name explains what the company does. Explaining what a company does is the purpose of a mission statement if you're going to have one, not a motto or a slogan. If your company name doesn't have anything to do with the industry, then a simple descriptor might be necessary for people to understand what you do.

Mission/Vision Statement

Mission and/or vision statements are necessary only if you intend to get ISO 9000 certified (a complete waste of time for a service business), or if you attempt to sell your company to someone else (also a complete waste of time for service businesses). ISO 9000 certification is a certification offered by the International Standards Organization. It certifies to your customers that your business operates using a regular, procedural methodology that is explained in detail and is not dependent upon the specialized knowledge of specific individuals. Obviously, none of that applies to a one-person consulting firm—in fact, it's just the opposite. Selling a service business (the other reason to hype qualifications) is nearly impossible. If your practice is based entirely on your skill, you have nothing to sell if you aren't in the picture.

If you feel you must fill space on your brochure with something, go ahead and make a mission statement, but avoid these words: customer, exceed, expectations, number-one or premier, quality, succeed, driven, or any other word you'd see on a poster at Successories (that store in the mall with the posters of waves, trees, etc., each captioned with a motivational statement). Every business intends to succeed, pays lip service to quality, hopes to satisfy customers and meet or exceed expectations, and so forth. If that's all you've got to say, skip it.

If, on the other hand, you have something truly different to say, or if your goal is something other than making money (for example, total global domination or charity), a prominent mission statement is in order.

Brochures

Brochures explain your services and products to your customers; they also provide a forum in which common questions can be answered in advance. I've never had a brochure, but I know a lot of people who rely on them for their public image.

Brochures can make you look more professional (assuming the brochure doesn't look like you whipped it out with Print Shop), and they do make a good piece of follow-up mail after you've met with someone.

Brochures should include all of your contact information, a bulleted list of the services you provide (the five or six most important, not the 400 things you know how to do), references (for important jobs or for customers you've worked with), and answers to questions you are frequently asked. Keep it to a single tri-fold 8.5×11 piece of glossy paper, and make sure it's full color. Don't print it out on your inkjet printer; have it printed professionally or use a high-resolution color laser printer. Pass the graphic design by somebody who understands graphic design; better yet, find a brochure you think is effective from another industry and blatantly plagiarize the design (of course, scanning it and actually using art would be a violation of copyright, so just stick with borrowing the format and layout).

Don't go crazy paying a graphic designer thousands of dollars to do a brochure for you. My former employer did that, spending over $16,000 to put together what amounted to a very cheesy, overly colorful portfolio cover that was light on information and heavy on canned graphics. Keep it simple and to the point by doing it yourself.

Web Site

Web sites are really most useful in marketing if they function as if they are an electronic brochure. They allow your customers to explore your capabilities on their own time. If you perform Web-related business, they also allow you to showcase your talent in system design. I use my Web site as a troubleshooting tool, as well—I have quick links to software I'm likely to need to download for troubleshooting purposes; I also have links to troubleshooting FAQs that might be useful for both myself and my customers.

A relatively simple Web site could include a service request form for customers and a link so your customer can send an emergency page to your alphanumeric text paging or cellular service. Both of these functions can be handled in pure HTML using the `mailto` protocol. I'm currently building a Web site help desk for my customers (my Web site is now `connetic` `.net`); it will include MPEG screen capture movies of the common tasks I perform for them (such as configuring e-mail or changing passwords). If you also have a help desk portion of your Web site, your customers can add a link to it on their desktops; that way, they're always just one click away from getting their problem solved, hopefully without requiring a call out to you. These sorts of services also make paying your monthly retainer fee seem extremely valuable.

Now that you can see some of the benefits of having a Web site, here are a few Web site dos and don'ts:

➤ Don't make it look like you put your Web site up in a half-hour and haven't touched it since.

➤ Do put all your contact information on your Web site. You'll find that your customers forget your phone number far faster than they forget your Web site address, so they'll use it to keep track of you.

➤ Don't pay your 12-year-old sibling/child to do it for you. Do it yourself.

➤ Do spend a little money on a decent Web site software program like NetObjects Fusion. I know, professional designers don't like it because it creates all sorts of bizarre HTML, but for self-designed Web sites, there isn't a faster way to put basic content up coherently.

➤ Don't spend a ton of money to have a site designed. Do it yourself. If you don't know anything about Web development, learn at least enough to handle your site yourself so that you can advise your customers when they ask you about it. Also, learning to do it yourself will help keep it from growing stale because you will know how to update it and you won't have to wait around for someone else to do it.

➤ Do post success stories, recommendations, and praise from customers, non-proprietary network designs that are unique or unusual, etc. Never underestimate the power of self-promotion and don't equate promoting your own business interests with egotism.

➤ Do present useful information, such as links to useful downloads for your target audience.

➤ Don't post software, whitepapers, or any other material you didn't write yourself on your site. Links to it are fine, but you should be aware that a body of law is being created that may make it illegal to open information you don't own in a frame that is bounded by your Web site. The reasoning behind this is because this could create confusion in the mind of the viewer as to who owns the copyright. Be safe. Use links only.

➤ Do get your own real domain name. Ideally, this would be the name of your business or a close derivative. If your company name is gone, consider registering in a different country to get it. Some people consider this cheesy, but if you can't use yourname.com, people won't find your site without knowing the link anyway. Plus, with your own domain name, your e-mail address can be me@mycompany.com, instead of me@aol.com.

➤ Do establish your own server, either co-located at an ISP or at the end of your own DSL, ISDN, or cablemodem service. Having your own server will allow you to manage your own mail accounts, quickly make files available via FTP, and a run data-driven, dynamic Web site based on Java, ASP, or Mod-Perl server-side content generators.

Your Web site can become your secondary purveyor of public image. A high-quality Web site can do more to convince a customer that you know what you're doing than all the talk and technical documentation in the world.

The converse is also true: customers will run as if ablaze from a cheesy Web site that conveys inattention to detail, technical errors, and the disorganization indicative of a cluttered mind. If you can't put together a good Web site yourself, it's better not to have one at all.

Business Cards

Business cards are hard to do wrong. As long as they have your logo, name, address, phone number, and e-mail address, they're fine. Have them pre-printed in small lots (your information will change far more frequently than you think it will, if you're anything like me) or print them with a color laser printer on demand. Chapter 6 has ideas about how to home print your own business cards.

Uniforms

Because I'm a fan of casual dress, I like uniforms. I print T-shirts with my company name and logo on them so that I can wear Levi's and T-shirts to work without looking unprofessional. Chapter 4 provides ideas about how to use uniforms with your business.

Conclusion

I've found only two types of marketing that work for small consulting practices: networking in the industry and warm-calling companies you've identified from help wanted ads who are looking for networking staff.

Networking among your associates should be completely automatic. Everyone you talk to should be aware that you are looking for contracts and that you pay a finder's fee.

Unfortunately, you can't start your practice with a network in place. Your best bet when you aren't getting work in through your network is to scan the local classifieds for companies that are looking for network staff and call them to offer interim consulting services.

Contracts:
Write Now or Pay Later

"The contract doesn't specify the species of cabling technician."

For the most part, consulting is the same thing as contracting. The term consultant is usually used to describe a contractor who provides expert advice and highly skilled labor, where as the term contractor applies to anyone who works on a contract basis irrespective of their level of expertise. Essentially, consultants are contractors without tool belts.

Contractors, including consultants, use contracts to formalize their business arrangements. A contract is a formalized oath or promise to do something. That's all it is. Business contracts are reciprocal—they include two (or infrequently more) parties who each promise to do something. In the abstract sense, contracts are simply two-way promises, or a promise in exchange for a promise. You promise to perform certain work, and your client promises to pay you a certain amount for that work. Any agreement to perform work constitutes a contract. As a consultant, you will use contracts as your method of defining the exact work you will do for an exact amount of compensation. By clearly spelling out everything that will occur in advance, you stand a far higher chance of satisfying your customer because both parties will know what is expected of them. In the worst case, you'll also stand a far better chance of successfully pursuing a client in court if it becomes unavoidable; you'll also avoid liability if you are the pursuee.

There are two legally recognized types of contracts: oral contracts and written contracts. Both are legally binding, but oral contracts (or "handshake" contracts) are far more difficult to pursue in court because both parties to the contract have to agree upon what was said before the contract can be enforced, if they can not come to an agreement, the Court supplies the interpretation of what was meant, and both parties will have to pay their lawyers a sum of money to help the judge find those words. Since it's usually difficult to get a plaintiff to agree to something that would then bind them legally, oral contracts are pretty much worth the paper they're printed on.

Problematic Oral Contracts

Many consultants think that contracts are the tools of people who are trying to get away with something, or that contracts would be unnecessary in a perfect world where everyone is honest, or that if something goes to court, the contract is meaningless anyway. These consultants feel that a handshake and a promise are sufficient to complete their work.

That's bull if you ask me. In no other industry will you find considerable work done without a contract; for instance, I can't submit this manuscript late without an addendum to my book contract. Consultants who work without contracts are like people who drive without insurance—sure, it works fine for a long time, but when something goes wrong, you're left with no recourse and can be completely wiped out.

Even in a world where everyone is honest and above-board, misunderstandings abound. Jargon may be unclear to one party, or one of the parties may feel as though they're being perfectly detailed when the other party sees only vague requirements. Writing contracts has less to do with the presumption of upfront dishonesty than with the clear definition of the expectations of both parties.

I've never met a consultant who works without written contracts that hasn't on occasion been dissatisfied with end results of a job. Either they felt like they had been screwed by a client who didn't pay them as much as they felt their work was worth, or they felt that their client demanded excessive work to complete the job. These consultants manage to complain about these clients, and at the same time, they defend their practice of working on a handshake. They don't seem to realize that the ambiguity that produces the problems they have experienced is an unavoidable symptom of an oral contract.

I've even had consultants tell me to pay them whatever I thought their work was worth. Nothing is sillier or more offensive to a client than providing them with the opportunity to either offend or overpay you. Never ever put your clients in this position. Be clear and upfront about your pricing in all situations.

Save yourself a ton of grief by learning to write precise and appropriate contracts. You don't need a lawyer to help you, and you don't need some sixteen-page everything-and-the-kitchen-sink legal template upon which to base your contracts. On the other hand, having a lawyer write, or review, is sometimes good insurance. The validity of a contract and how well it is written, is largely unknown until it is tested, which can be years later, after the contract is signed and the services performed. Most wise attorneys carry malpractice insurance, the benefit of which you could receive if you paid them for their services, and which you wouldn't if you didn't. The rest of this chapter will teach you everything you need to know to write your own contracts from scratch for most consulting occasions.

NOTE Although you don't need a lawyer, as I stated previously, keep in mind that the recommendations for contracting terms in this chapter come from Marc S. Bragg, Esquire. They are general in nature and have not been adapted to the requirements of any specific case, so once you've written your standard consulting contracts, be sure you pass them by a competent trial lawyer. Transactional lawyers are great for helping you start a business, but trial lawyers know what will stand up in court and what won't.

Writing Successful Contracts

Written contracts are simply reciprocal promises written down and witnessed with a signature by both parties. Such contracts have one primary purpose: to record the reciprocal promise made between the parties to the contract. This way, if the promises are unfulfilled, that record of the promises can be entered into evidence in a lawsuit; even if this is done, however, using clarity and avoiding different interpretations in your contract are key.

There is no defined format or specific procedure you must use to write contracts; however, there are common parts of a contract. There are also generally recognized methods that can be used to write contracts; the goal of these is to eliminate the uncertainty of language. Writing a contract isn't difficult—this section will show you how to do it.

Written contracts are usually broken down into the following parts:

Definition of parties   To clearly identify the participants in the contract.

Scope of work   To clearly identify the work to be performed.

Proof of completion   To clearly identify when the first promise is complete.

Terms of payment To clearly identify what is expected in return for the scope of work.

Specification of rights To establish how disputes concerning the contract will be resolved.

Each of these sections is discussed in detail in the following sections.

Define the Contract Participants

It's important to define exactly whom the contract is between. This might seem fairly trivial, but it is important because an easy way to escape a contractual liability is to claim the contract doesn't involve you. If there's no identification of parties, this can happen. Generally, something akin to the following is sufficient:

This document is a contract by and between MyCo, 1234 Street, City, ST 99999 and MyClientCo, 123 Headquarters Way, City, ST 99999, for the provision of the services specified "herein." (Don't try to write like a lawyer, try to avoid using lawyerese. Remember, clarity is the key.)

TIP A great book on writing, for all purposes, is *The Elements of Style*, by Strunk & White, 3d ed.

Define the Scope of Work

The primary purpose of a contract is to state what needs to be done. This is usually called the scope of work, and it embodies the promise of the contractor.

The level of detail at which you define the scope of work is up to you and the client, but it should be sufficient to allow no ambiguity in the finished product. For example, "I will build you a network." is pretty ambiguous and leaves broad room for interpretation. However, "I will build you the network specified by the attached design prints using the equipment specified in the attached bill of materials, and I will configure it as detailed in the attached configuration document." is completely clear and unambiguous when included with the associated attachments.

Rather than simply supplying a paragraph of intent, as above, scopes of work are usually composed of a list of bulleted items, as in the list below. I use an Access database to help write my contracts. I have set it up so that it automatically lists every activity in the scope of work. Consider the following example list from a contract:

➤ Install a 16-port Fast Ethernet Hub and cross-connect it for eight locations.

➤ Install Windows NT Workstation for 100 workstations.

➤ Install a network adapter, connect to the network, and configure driver software for 100 workstations.

➤ Configure a TCP/IP network protocol for 100 workstations.

➤ Configure an attachment to a network file and print server for 100 workstations.

➤ Set the security policy for 100 workstations.

➤ Install Windows NT Server 4 as the Primary Domain Controller for one server.

➤ Install Windows NT Server 4 as the Backup Domain Controller for two servers.

➤ Configure the server backup software and test for three servers.

➤ Configure the printer drivers and print services for 10 printers.

After I have planned out this list, Access generates a report automatically. Notice that the order of the list is not important—the contract need not specify the order in which you will perform the work. While the report is being created, it selects what I call "the elements of labor" from a table that has my per-item charges to perform each service item. Whether you write your contracts by hand or automatically generate them, I recommend this level of detail because it's completely unambiguous and is not subject to a loose interpretation.

Avoid Dependency

When you write your scope of work, make certain that none of your work depends upon work performance by the client, or, if you cannot avoid dependency, make sure that the client's responsibility to perform that work is detailed in the scope of work as well. These "dependencies" are known as "conditions" in the contract. If your scope of work requires that users return a use-case survey, for instance, you would write the scope of work as follows:

My company shall

➤ Provide use-case forms to each user.

➤ Collect use-case forms and compile them into a set of requirements.

Your company shall

➤ Complete each requested use-case form in its entirety.

I cannot overemphasize how important it is to either make sure your work does not depend on work done by your client, or to define the complete responsibility of both parties in your contract. I once put myself in the position of being unable to complete a contract for a client because the IT director saw me, and all other outside consultants, as a threat (as well he should have—I was partially there to evaluate his incompetence). He simply waited for the point in the contract when I had to rely upon his staff to implement changes to the system and then ordered them not to help me. I was left high and dry—I literally could not complete my contract, but because the contract did not specifically define any responsibility on the part of the client, I had no recourse. I also couldn't bill according to the contract until all work was complete. In the end, I submitted a bill for the 50 percent I figured I'd been able to complete, which the client paid without comment. Had I clearly defined their responsibility to assist, I could have use the contract to force the IT director's hand.

That situation brings up an important point: contracts aren't nearly as much about suing and winning in court as they are about resolving these sorts of issues before you get to court. A well-written contract can be used to push recalcitrant employees. Not everyone at your client companies has the same motivations, and there really are some freaks out there who view any intrusion onto their turf as a threat, so they will work against you. It's not your fault; it's just their attitude. Don't be intimidated by these people—they aren't the ones you work for, they aren't the ones paying you, and since you don't have to work with them forever, you can be direct and forceful when you need to be.

It's also important to remember for whom you work when you consult: you work for the company, as directed by its president. You don't work for the IT manager, or the person who brought you in, or anyone else. Most companies are rife with political situations like the one I described above, and as an outside consultant, you will frequently be put in the middle of tense situations between battling managers. With solid contracts, you can protect your interests.

Manage Expectations

By specifying the details of the job execution in the contract, you are managing the expectations the client has about what you will accomplish. This, in turn, leads to a far higher likelihood that the client will be happy with the work you've done.

When I first started consulting, I wrote pretty vague contracts, and not surprisingly, my clients always seems a little skittish when I told them I was finished. I spent a lot of time running around after the contracted work was finished training each employee to use the system because they were nervous about the new system and didn't really know what they had.

Now, of course, I specify group training sessions in my contract (which I charge for as well), and I always end my contracts with a questions-and-answers meeting with all of the end users. While a contract can specify exactly when you're done, I've found that some sort of ritual involving all the users really helps to give them closure and feel as though the job is complete. For larger contracts with important clients, I throw dinner parties for the managers at a restaurant, or beach parties or picnic/barbeques for everyone at the end of the contract. This practice not only provides closure, but it leaves everyone feeling happy about you as a person. That happiness in turn makes them feel satisfied with your work product.

Define the Proof of Completion

A very important part of contracting that is usually left out of the written contracts (especially boilerplate contracts you get from software or from a lawyer) is the definition of proof of completion.

Defining when you are actually done is extremely important when you work on a fixed price basis. This is because the client is motivated to get you to work as much as possible under the auspices of that fixed price. This means that if you don't define exactly when you're finished, you'll wind up working quite a bit more than you intended to for the same fixed price. This isn't an issue with hourly work, because the motivations are opposite: you are motivated to work as much as possible, and the client is motivated to get you off the clock.

Because the definition of completion is really the only sticky part of firm, fixed-price contracting, it's a much better model in my opinion. As usual, with good contracting, this problem is easily solved.

Definition of completion is simply a list of test cases; once these are successfully accomplished, they function as proof that the product is performing according to the customer's expectations. You don't have to write a test case for every little detail; rather, write the most sweeping test cases possible to validate large portions of the system. Usually, the test cases will be the reciprocal of the user requirements. For example, if the users wanted Internet e-mail and Web access, as well as file and print service, then your test cases might be similar to the following:

1. Transmit an e-mail message from a client station to a public Internet address, and show that the reply message from the public Internet address is correctly received.

2. Store a file on the file server from one client station and retrieve it on another.

3. Open anywebsite.com in a Web browser on a client machine, and print the home page from a client station to a specific network printer.

These three test cases validate the user requirements, so they are sufficient to prove that the network works.

Leave space for a user to sign off next to each test case, and don't have the same user sign off every test case if you feel there might be a problem with billing. Once you have a complete set of test signoffs, you can bill the client.

Specify Payment

Payment is the second half of the reciprocal promise: in return for the scope of work, the receiving party will pay. As part of a reciprocal promise, the payment terms should be just as specific as the scope of work if necessary. Payment terms should specify the following:

➤ Exactly how much is to be paid

➤ Exactly when the contract is to be paid

➤ Exactly who is required to pay (usually the other party to the contract)

➤ Exactly to whom payment is to be made

You can get as crazy as you want with breaking down a contract into payment points on milestones or dates, as long as it is both completely clear to both parties and is independent of anything but the scope of work.

Typical payment terms are structured as follows:

➤ Small contracts without equipment are usually billed 100 percent upon completion.

➤ Contracts with equipment usually specify equipment costs up front or upon delivery, with labor to be billed upon completion.

➤ Large or long contracts are usually broken down into subcontract payment milestones.

➤ Contracts with considerable risk (like a client with financial problems, or when you'll have to hire outside expertise) might specify a certain percentage of labor costs up-front.

You can specify anything you can get a client to agree to, but these are the sorts of terms your client should be used to, and therefore, they will most likely not be averse to them.

Payment terms in a contract might be written like this:

Total Project cost: $56,700

The total project cost shall be paid according to the following payment schedule:

➤ Equipment costs due upon acceptance: $32,540

➤ Equipment handling fees due upon delivery: $3,254

➤ Balance due upon successful test signoff: $20,906

All payments are due upon successful completion of the test criteria.

Specify General Terms

The specification of general terms is what you normally see when you buy a boilerplate contract—the entire boilerplate document is specification of generic terms which have tested well in court and which will protect or reserve your rights. Boilerplates don't define the meat of a contract: the scope of work, payment terms, and test criteria.

The specification of terms is critical in the legal sense, but it has no purpose until you get into a litigious situation, so it's the least important part of a working contract.

I've already talked about how to specify job-related terms, like the parties involved in the contract, the scope of work, proof of completion, and payment terms. These terms are what you will usually write yourself. Generic terms are terms you can pretty much "cut and paste" into any contract to beef up your legal position in the event of a lawsuit. Many of these terms may not apply to a specific case, so don't just always include them all. Think about the protection you need and make your contracts specific. This will help you avoid making customers nervous with overly litigious sounding contracts.

Here are some typical general terms, which your contracts should include:

➤ Default

➤ Warranties and Representations

➤ Release

➤ Limitation of Liability

➤ Confidentiality and Ownership of Intellectual Property

➤ Modification

➤ Dispute Resolution

➤ Force Majeure

➤ No Partnership

➤ Assignment

➤ Claim Limitation

➤ Attorneys' Fees

➤ Consent and Waiver

➤ Governing Law

➤ Entire Agreement

➤ Severability

These terms will all be detailed here. Specific terms written by Marc S. Bragg are included in the sample contract at the conclusion of this chapter.

TIP Remember to talk to your own lawyer about the terms you need to protect your specific interests, and keep in mind that your terms shouldn't be one-sided: contracts are designed to protect both parties. If your clients see a particularly heinous term hidden in your contract, they may decide not to go with you without ever telling you why.

Default

A default clause is intended to indicate what the obligations of the parties are in the event that one party or the other defaults, or fails to perform, their part of the contract. Usually, you would specify that if you don't get paid, all your contractual obligations are nullified and that you can't be held accountable for anything.

You'll also want to put in language to the effect that your client must notify you in writing if they believe you are in default, and that they must give you some period of time to remedy the fault before their contractual obligation to pay you ends.

Warranties and Representations

This term is intended to "replace" any verbal claims you may have made about the work you perform with a general statement that states that you can't be held accountable for any claims not written in the contract. Most states have different laws regarding warranties, so the effect of this term varies widely. Check with a lawyer in your area for more information about your state.

Release and Indemnificaiton

This term is intended to shield you from a lawsuit by a third party (other than your client) for the work you performed on the contract—in other words, if they get sued, they can't sue you or allow you to be sued, they have to spend their resources to defend you.

Many companies find this language scary, and unless you already have a solid relationship, they may not hire you because it appears that you are shifting so much of the risk to their shoulders. One way to avoid this problem is to carry good insurance and be sure the coverage extends to your limits of liability.

Limitation of Liability

This term is intended to limit the amount of damages you can be held accountable for to the amount of money you've made. In other words, you can't be sued to recover damages beyond the actual cost the client incurred to retain you, no matter what happened. For example, if you accidentally set the building on fire while installing a hub, you can only be sued for what you charged for your labor and the hub, not for the cost of the building.

Some states do not allow this limitation, so check with a local attorney for details.

Confidentiality

This term clarifies the fact that both parties expect the agreement to be entered into privately, and that both parties will respect the propriety of the other by not divulging any information relating to the project to a third party. For many contracts, this term is unnecessary; for others, it is indispensable. It's always good to have, just in case.

Ownership of Intellectual Property

If the contract contains intellectual property (like a software system, a book or manual, or complex designs that a competitor could use), then you should include a specific term that clearly defines who owns the license to the software. You can create any sort of licensing mechanism you want, but generally the licenses are worded so either you retain all rights or you transfer them all to the purchasing party.

Modifications

This simple term states that the agreement can only be modified in writing, which prevents a written contract from transforming back into an oral agreement.

Dispute Resolution

This term defines exactly how a dispute in the interpretation of the agreement will be resolved. Assuming that both parties are earnestly attempting to get the job done, you'll want to keep things as inexpensive as possible, which means you'll specify binding arbitration. You will also usually want to specify your own venue so the burden of travel will be on the other party.

Force Majure

This term specifies that you can't be held accountable for events that are beyond your control that impact the performance of work. For example, if a pipe burst in the ceiling over a server that you had installed during the execution of a contract, you aren't liable for replacing or even repairing the server.

No Partnership

This term absolutely prevents the contract from being interpreted as a partnership, which could make you liable for the activities of the other party or allow them to obligate you.

Assignment

This term prevents the contract from being transferred to another party. Although I've never heard of this happening, it's technically possible to simply assign a responsibility to someone else if one party enters into a contract with that third party.

Subcontracting is actually a form of assignment, so you'll want to protect your ability to bring in subcontractors.

Claim Limitation

This term limits the amount of time that a suit could be brought against you after the completion of the contract. Essentially, it defines the point at which you no longer need to worry about work you've done coming back to bite you.

Attorneys' Fees

This term specifies that the losing party (the one found liable) must shoulder all the costs of bringing legal action. This has the effect of reducing frivolous suits and protecting innocent parties from harassment by lawyer's fees.

Consents and Waivers

This term indicates that just because you haven't pursued a small issue, you haven't given up your right to pursue it or similar issues later. For example, just because you didn't make an issue of it the first time a customer paid you late doesn't mean that you give up the right to make an issue of it later.

Governing Law or Jurisdiction

This term specifies the governing law (which state or nation) shall be used to interpret the contract, and the default venue.

Entire Agreement

This term specifies that the contract specifies the entire agreement on behalf of both parties—that nothing else, written or oral, was promised.

Severability

This term specifies that if an included term is not legally enforceable, then the remainder of the contract is still intact and is not rendered void. This prevents a party from using a loophole or a technicality to squirm out of a contract.

Conclusion

I can't think of a better way to conclude this chapter than to present a sample contract, so here it is. Usually, a contract would be preceded by a cover page with your logo and contact information.

Parties

This document is a contract by and between Connetic, a California Corporation (hereafter referred to as The Consultant), and Digital Widgets, a Delaware Corporation (hereafter referred to as The Client), for the provision of the services specified herein.

Authorized agent of Connetic:

Matthew Strebe

_____ Signed this Date: _____

Authorized agent of Digital Widgets:

Henry J. Tillman

_____ Signed this Date: _____

Scope of Work

The following represents the complete and total services required by this contract:

➤ Install a 16-port Fast Ethernet Hub and cross-connect for eight locations.

➤ Install Windows NT Workstation for 100 workstations.

➤ Install a network adapter, connect to the network, and configure driver software for 100 workstations.

➤ Configure a TCP/IP network protocol and an SMTP/POP e-mail client for 100 workstations.

➤ Configure an attachment to a network file and print server for 100 workstations.

➤ Set the security policy for 100 workstations.

➤ Install Windows NT Server 4 as the Primary Domain Controller for one server.

➤ Install Windows NT Server 4 as the Backup Domain Controller for one server.

➤ Install RedHat Linux 6 as an SMTP/POP mail server for one server.

➤ Configure the server backup software and test it for three servers.

➤ Configure the printer drivers and print services for 10 printers.

Bill Of Material

The following is the complete list of material that shall be provided by The Consultant. The Client shall provide any additional material required to complete the scope of work.

QTY	ITEM
100	Fast Ethernet Network Adapters
3	Powerful Servers
2	Windows NT Server 4
1	RedHat Linux 6 CD-ROM

100	NT Server Client Access Licenses
100	NT Workstation 4
8	16 Port Fast Ethernet Hubs

Proof of Completion

The contractual obligations of The Consultant shall be considered complete upon the successful completion of the following test cases, as witnessed by legitimate agents for The Client:

1. Transmit an e-mail message from a client station to a public Internet address, and show that the reply message from the public Internet address is correctly received.

   Completion witnessed by: _____ On: ___/___/___

2. Store a file on the file server from one client station and retrieve it on another.

   Completion witnessed by: _____ On: ___/___/___

3. Open anywebsite.com in a Web browser on a client machine and print the home page from a client station to a specific network printer.

   Completion witnessed by: _____ On: ___/___/___

4. Complete a backup to tape with verify of the machines identified as servers.

   Completion witnessed by: _____ On: ___/___/___

Payment Terms

The Client shall pay The Consultant according to the following payment schedule:

➤ Equipment costs due upon acceptance: $32,540

➤ Equipment handling fees due upon delivery: $3,254

➤ Balance due upon successful test signoff: $20,906

All payments are due upon success completion of the test criteria.

General Terms

NOTE Square brackets indicate notes to the reader that should be adapted to a specific case rather than actual legal text.

Default   "Default" shall mean [non-payment according to terms of Agreement]In the event of Default on the part of The Client, The Consultant may cease all further performance under this Agreement and shall not be liable for any losses or damage suffered by The Client as a result of The Consultant's cessation of services. After such Default, The Consultant shall not be obligated to provide any additional Services unless mutually agreed to in writing between the Parties. In the event The Client believes The Consultant is in default or breach of this Agreement, The Client shall provide The Consultant with timely written notice of the default or breach and expressly identify the nature of the default or breach in that notice. Further, The Consultant shall have [a reasonable amount of time in the circumstances, which will vary between contracts] ten (10) days to cure ("Cure Period") that default or breach, failing which, this Agreement shall automatically terminate without any further obligation by one party to the other. Notwithstanding the above, The Consultant shall be entitled to full payment for all services and equipment provided to The Client as of the expiration of the Cure Period.

Warranties and Representations   The Consultant does not make and hereby disclaims, and The Client hereby waives, any representations or warranties, arising by law or otherwise, regarding the Services described in this Agreement, or any portion thereof, including, without limitation, implied warranties of merchantability, fitness for a particular purpose, non-infringement, or arising from course of dealing, course of performance or usage in trade. Without limiting the foregoing, The Consultant specifically does not warrant the Services described herein (a) against failure of performance including, without limitation, any failure due to computer hardware or communication systems, or (b) any economic or other benefit that The Client might obtain through its participation in this Agreement. [This section can, of course, be modified to make specific warranties or representations if required, but they should be very narrowly tailored. The effect of this disclaimer is different in different states, and with respect to providing services to consumers or to commercial ventures.] With respect to any Equipment supplied, only the manufacturer's warranty, if any, shall apply to any repair or maintenance, unless expressly set forth to the contrary in this Agreement.

Release and Indemnification   The Client hereby releases and agrees to hold harmless, defend and indemnify The Consultant, from any and all claims, actions, proceedings, suits, liabilities, damages (actual, consequential, or incidental), settlements, penalties, fines, costs or expenses (including without limitation, reasonable attorney's fees and other litigation expenses) of every kind, whether known or unknown, incurred by The Client arising out of this Agreement.

Limitation of Liability   In no event shall The Consultant be liable, in contract, warranty, or tort (including negligence whether active, passive or imputed), product liability, strict liabilty, or any other theory for any indirect, incidental, special, punitive or consequential damages arising out of the use or inability to use the Services or performance of any related services, even if The Consultant has been advised of the possibility of such damages. To the maximum extent permitted by applicable law, in no event shall the aggregate liability of The Consultant whether in contract, warranty, tort (including negligence whether active, passive or imputed), product liability, strict liability, or any other theory for any indirect, incidental, special, punitive or consequential damages arising out of the use or inability to use the Services or performance of any related services, exceed the amount The Client actually paid to The Consultant for the Services. The Client hereby releases The Consultant from any and all obligations, liabilities, and claim in excess of this limitation. [Some states do not allow this limitation.]

Confidentiality [if necessary]   Each Party agrees that the Confidential Information of the other Party will be held in confidence to the same extent and the same manner as each party protects its own Confidential Information, but each Party agrees that in no event will less than reasonable care be used. Each Party shall, however, be permitted to disclose relevant aspects of such Confidential Information to its officers or employees on a need-to-know basis, provided they have undertaken to protect the Confidential Information to the same extent as required under this Agreement. "Confidential Information" means each Party's trade secrets, financial information, formulas, specifications, programs, instructions, technical know-how, methods of operation, testing benchmarks, any other information identified by a Party as Confidential Information, and any other information that should reasonably be understood to be confidential or proprietary. The Confidential Information referred to in this Section shall not apply in the following cases: If it was already known to the other party, if it was disclosed without obligation to keep the information confidential, if it was publicly known or became publicly known through no-fault of the receiving party, if it was independently developed by the receiving party without use of the other Party's Confidential Information, or if it is required to be disclosed by a court of competent jurisdiction and in that case, the disclosing party shall be granted a reasonable opportunity to obtain a protective order.

Ownership of Intellectual Property[if necessary]   Each Party reserves all of its right, title, and interest in its intellectual property rights (including without limitation, copyright, trademark, patent, and trade secrets except as specifically set forth in this Section. [This Section depends on terms and scope of work].

> **The Consultant Grant** [Use this language when you give up rights to the work you produce.]   By submitting any information or materials authored by The Consultant to The Client (Licensed Materials) The Consultant hereby grants The Client a non-exclusive, worldwide, royalty-free, irrevocable, and sublicensable right to exercise all copyright and rights of publicity over the Licensed Materials, in any existing or future applications as are necessary to use the Services.

> **The Client Grant** [Use this language when you retain the rights to the work you produce.]   The Client grants The Consultant a license to commercially use or resell any Licensed Materials developed, authored or created by The Consultant that have not been identified by The Client as Confidential Information.

Modifications   All modifications to this Agreement must be in writing and signed by all Parties.

Dispute Resolution   Except for any breach of this Agreement entitling either Party to injunctive relief, if any dispute occurs between the Parties arising out of or relating to this Agreement, or its execution or performance, it will be submitted to arbitration. The arbitration will be binding, and conducted by one arbitrator in accordance with the commercial arbitration rules of the American Arbitration Association then in effect. The arbitration will be held, and the award will be deemed made in [your county and state] and may be entered in any court having jurisdiction.

Force Majure   The Consultant shall be excused from performance to the extent that performance is prevented, delayed, or obstructed by causes beyond The Consultant's reasonable control, including delays in performance by The Client, acts of Nature (fire, storm, floods, earthquakes, etc.), civil disturbances, disruption of telecommunications, power or essential services.

No Partnership   Nothing contained in this Agreement is intended to constitute the Parties as partners or joint venturers in the legal sense. Neither party intends that a partnership, joint venture or similar relationship be formed by this Agreement or any performance hereunder. Neither Party shall have any express or implied right or authority to assume or create any obligations on behalf of, or in the name of, the other or to bind the other to any contract, agreement or undertaking with any third party.

Assignment   Neither of the Parties may sell, transfer, assign or otherwise dispose of any of its rights or obligations under this Agreement to any person without the express written consent of the other party, except that The Consultant may, in its sole discretion, hire or subcontract out portions or all of the Services to be provided hereunder.

Claim Limitation   The Client agrees, regardless of any statute or law to the contrary, that any claim or cause of action arising out of or relating to this Agreement must be filed within one (1) year after such claim of action arose or be forever barred.

Attorneys' Fees   If any Party brings an action arising out of this Agreement, the prevailing party shall be entitled to an award of reasonable attorneys' fees, and any court costs incurred in such action or proceeding, in addition to any other damages or relief awarded.

Consents and Waivers   The failure of any Party at any time or times to require performance of any provision hereof shall in no manner affect its right at a later time to enforce the same, unless the same is waived in writing. No waiver by a Party of any condition or any breach of any term, covenant, representation, or warranty contained in this Agreement shall be effective unless in writing, and no waiver of any one or more instances shall be deemed to be a further or continuing waiver of any such condition or breach in other instances.

Governing Law and Jurisdiction   This Agreement shall be governed by and construed in accordance with the laws of the State of [your state] applicable to agreements made and entirely to be performed within such state, without regard to its conflict of laws rules. The Client hereby irrevocably and unconditionally submits to the exclusive jurisdiction of any state or federal court sitting in [your state] over any suit, actin or proceeding arising out of or relating to this Agreement.

Entire Agreement   The terms set forth in this Agreement are intended by the Parties as a final, complete and exclusive expression of their agreement with respect to the Services contemplated by this Agreement and may not be contradicted, explained or supplemented by evidence of any prior agreement, any contemporaneous oral agreement, or any consistent additional terms. There are no restrictions, promises, representations, warranties, covenants, or undertakings, other than those expressly set forth or referred to herein. This Agreement is not intended to confer upon any person other than the Parties hereto any rights or remedies hereunder.

Severability   Should any term or provision hereof be deemed invalid, void or unenforceable either in its entirety or in a particular application, the remainder of this Agreement shall nonetheless remain in full force and effect, and, if the subject term or provision is deemed to be invalid, void or unenforceable only with respect to a particular application, such term or provision shall remain in full force and effect with respect to all other applications.

10
Fair Is What Everyone Agrees To

"I think a pure optical-fiber infrastructure makes the perfect statement, and it looks great with the mahogany ceiling tiles."

Pricing is considered by many to be a black art: an inscrutable divination best left to industry insiders who publish lists of pricing based on statistical surveys. You can't be trusted to set your own rates because if you charge too little, you won't be happy; if you charge too much, your customer won't be satisfied.

That opinion is basically garbage, because it applies principles of supply-side labor provisioning to a demand-side problem: industrial rate setting is appropriate only in a *supply-side* economy—when the supply of skilled workers outstrips the demand for them. In situations in which the demand for a skilled worker outstrips the supply (a *demand-side* economy), each worker can, and should, charge as much as they possibly can for the service they provide. Network integration is in tremendous demand, and despite the number of MCSE candidates circulating about, according to the federal government, the demand won't be filled for at least the next decade.

You aren't in business to do anybody any favors; you're in business to support yourself and your family. Naturally, this means you should make as much money as you possibly can without doing anything illegal.

The correct price is one that you and your customer both agree to and are happy with. Ideally, every contract would be a negotiation between you and your customer to set the price for the work performed. Obviously, you need a starting point for bidding, however, so your experience (and mine) can be used to set your initial rates until you begin to modify them to moderate the amount of work you do.

Never position yourself as a cut-rate budget integrator. The less you charge, the less your customers will respect you. I've known customers to reject bids outright from other consulting firms because the hourly rate was too low. The customer felt that either there must be some serious problem with the way the other company operated, or that the company would extend the amount of time they worked to make up for the low rate.

Conversely, you should avoid pricing yourself as a prima donna or a soothsayer (see Chapter 1). Charging exorbitant hourly rates (above $200/hr.) will put you under tremendous time pressure because the customer will constantly be worried about how much they pay you.

In this chapter, I will share my secrets on the pricing methods that, in my experience, provide excellent income and leave my customers feeling like they are getting a tremendous value for their money. I'll also cover common mistakes consultants make when they set their prices, which you can avoid.

Pricing Methods

One thing most new consultants worry about is how to price their services. Most often, this comes down to attempting to determine what their hourly rate should be, since most professional services are sold on an hourly basis.

I'm philosophically opposed to the hourly rate as anything but a rule of thumb for fixed price contracting. By this I mean that rather than charging a set hourly rate no matter how many hours you're on the job, you should use an hourly rate only to determine what the labor portion of a fixed price contract should be. To this day, I've never billed a client for hours. I work exclusively on a firm, fixed-price basis or on a retained basis for all of my clients, and I always have. Using this methodology, I make more money than any consultant I've ever met for the time I spend, I spend less time working than most consultants, I'm motivated to put systems in place that increase reliability and reduce support problems, my customers are more satisfied, and I've never had a billing dispute with a client.

Hourly Rates

Hourly rates are a pox upon consulting. They put a cap on how much money you can make, they scare clients because they're open-ended money pits, and they create motivational problems for both parties in the transaction. I'll cover the reasons I think this throughout the remainder of this chapter. The only reason I'm spending time to talk about them is that they are epidemic in the network consulting market—for some reason, most people seem to think that consultants have to charge on an hourly basis, as if there were some federal law or guild rule about it.

The essence of my disdain for hourly rates is simple: clients aren't buying an hour of your time; they're buying a solution. You should be selling them that solution.

When consultants charge by the hour, they are naturally motivated to spend as much time as possible solving the problem. Costs are high, systems are delivered late, new features are difficult or impossible to add, and the soaring cost sours the system for the customer. These problems are endemic in the hourly economy, not with a specific type of consultant or an individual.

In my opinion, hourly rates are appropriate only in emergencies, or when a customer demands that you charge by the hour (a situation I've never even heard rumor of actually occurring). When a new customer calls in a panic, and cannot describe what's actually wrong with enough accuracy to determine how long it will take to fix, you might have to charge an hourly rate. This is because there's not enough information for you to base a firm fixed price on, so you can't make yourself liable for how long it might take to fix a problem. The one time this situation happened to me, I still quoted a firm, fixed price, but it bit me: I wound up overcharging and lost the customer. In this emergency case, I should have used an hourly rate.

Hourly Rates Cap How Much You Can Make

If you sold 2000 billable hours (the number of hours in a year minus two weeks for vacation) at $100 per hour, you'd make $200,000 per year. That probably seems like a lot considering what you make now, but you'll be surprised how much money you can spend when you run your own business. This amount isn't all that much if you figure you'll actually only bill 50 percent of your time (average for a very active network consultant). By selling your hours at this rate, you are putting a realistic cap of $100,000 on your take-home pay. You can make more than that with a regular job these days.

Hourly Rates Scare Clients

Most clients hate hourly rates, but they pay them because there's usually no alternative. Clients don't like hourly rates because there's no telling how much money they are actually going to spend on solving their problem—it could be 10, 100, or even 1000 hours.

Some consultants will offer a time estimate with their bid, but the estimate is just that—an estimate. This doesn't function as a limit, it just tells the customer when to start getting upset because the project is officially late and over budget.

Taking the concept of estimate further, some consultants will actually put a cap on the amount the customer pays. This satisfies the customer, but it leaves the consultant high and dry: this way, the only possibility is that the consultant will make less than or equal to the amount of the cap. Why not just treat the cap as a firm fixed price and charge that much more for the solution? That way, you're guaranteed to make that amount of money, the client is guaranteed to pay that amount of money, and you don't have to sit around in cubicles at their office burning off hours to justify it.

Hourly Rates Create Motivational Problems for Consultants

Hourly rates give consultants precisely the wrong impetus in their work: the natural desire to work slowly and to take as long as possible. This reasoning is obvious; the longer the project takes, the more the consultant gets to bill.

Now, no ethical person sits around and waits for time to go by so that they can charge more, but this hidden source of inertia expresses itself in other ways: a consultant might charge for time spent driving or flying (this is very common, and unethical if you ask me—it's not your client's fault that you live far from them), or they might charge for every moment they are on site, even though they spent over an hour chatting with clients in a non-working manner, smoking, or going to lunch. In their mind, they spent time at the client's site so they should be paid, but it seems unfair because they haven't spent that time delivering a solution.

For these reasons, systems built by the hour are nearly always delivered late and over budget. This, of course, pisses off the client, which results in discord and the client feeling that they've been taken advantage of.

The federal government learned this lesson the hard way. Because overbilling and delays caused by contractors that charged by the hour were so epidemic in the sixties and seventies, the government will now no longer contract on anything but a firm, fixed-price basis. Everyone should take this lesson to heart. Hourly pricing creates a subconscious barrier to motivation by paying people to waste time.

Hourly Rates Create Motivational Problems for Clients

Paying on an hourly rate motivates clients to get you out of the office as quickly as possible, and might also cause them to ask you to cut corners when you deliver the product. Sure, they're willing to pay you to install a network, but are they willing to pay you for training, documentation, and final testing? Usually not. They just want to get you off the clock as soon as everything is working correctly. This leads to Frankenstein networks that grow like weed gardens because the emphasis has been on getting things done as quickly as possible rather than creating sustainable systems and management policies. These networks are always harder to support and wind up ultimately wasting the time of all users.

Firm, Fixed-Price Contracts

Firm, fixed-price contracts are pacts between a consultant and a client that provide a specific solution for a specific amount of money. The contract defines the entire scope of work and bill of material, as well as the required payment and payment terms. The work is performed according to the contract, and payment is disbursed according to the contract.

Firm, fixed-price contracts are, in my opinion, one of only two effective methods of charging for consulting services. The other is the retained service contract, which is explained in the next section.

Firm, fixed-price contracts are good because they define everything up front: by signing the contract, the client and consultant are agreeing on very specific work that should be done for a specific payment. There's little chance for misunderstanding or chicanery because everything is clearly spelled out.

Some consultants complain that they can't use firm, fixed prices because they don't know how long a problem will take to solve. That argument is stupid. Anyone who doesn't know how long a problem should take to solve is too inexperienced to consult. In other fields, tasks may be less deterministic, but in network integration, if a consultant doesn't know how long it takes, it's because they haven't done it before. That's the consultant's problem, not the client's; in this case, the consultant should eat whatever extra time it takes to learn. If you've done two or three similar contracts, you'll have a good idea.

Some addiction developers (I mean, application developers; see Chapter 1) complain that writing a new contract for each system add-on feature would encumber the process. That's just a form of passive resistance and laziness—printing out a new copy of a form contract and signing your name takes about 15 minutes...

Retainers

A retainer is a fixed recurring (monthly) fee that buys your availability for a customer. Essentially, rather than paying for your time directly, a customer is paying you to be available to fix problems, whatever those problems may be, whenever they occur, and for the duration it takes to fix them.

Retainers are like insurance for your clients. They're paying a set amount per month to guarantee that their systems perform properly, and that it will be repaired whenever it is not. Like insurance, they'll often pay for periods in which they won't need service; conversely, situations will arise in which you will spend a tremendous amount of time on site, but the client's costs won't go up. Because clients like to have dependable costs that can be budgeted, they really like retainers. I like retainers because they allow me to receive income whether I work or not.

At first glance, it might seem that you'd spend a tremendous amount of time on site, and that your income wouldn't go up. In practice, that's up to you. If you implement good sustainable support policies, train users when they make mistakes, and avoid taking on administration duties that soak up a lot of time, you can eventually get to the point where you don't spend much time on site at all. I've had retainer customers who've gone months without needing any support from me at all, and they pay me the entire time because they realize that they'll eventually need me when something goes wrong.

Open-ended service contracts are best handled on a retained basis. You can come up with the fee by statistically determining how much time you spend (on average) supporting a site with a certain number of client work-stations or servers. I have found that by adding up all the client computers (referred to as "seats" in the industry) and servers at the company, I can determine a reasonable monthly retainer rate that I will charge to support whatever problems the client has. My impetus is then to establish systems that save me the most time possible.

Some consultants complain that retainers make clients want them around all the time. While this can happen, it's actually extremely rare. What clients really want is to have all their problems fixed using sustainable methods that don't keep breaking. Once you've got everything working, they certainly don't want you standing around making everyone nervous, but they do still want you available if something goes wrong or for routine administration.

For most customers, you will have to show up enough to seem worth the money. I have gotten into the habit of visiting my retainer customers at least twice a month whether I've been called in for a problem or not. If people don't see you around, they'll eventually forget why they're paying you. It's something of a thin line—you need to visit enough to keep your finger on the pulse of the network, but you don't want to spend too much time hanging around on site. The best bet is to simply schedule a regular weekly or biweekly visit to check tape logs, firewall access, and other indications of potential future problems. I have lost one client because the company controller (accountant) felt she wasn't seeing me around enough to justify the expense. Of course, they replaced me with a consulting firm that charged $90/hr., and their monthly network service bill shot up from the $2400 a month I charged to just over $10,000 a month, on average. Unfortunately for them, when they asked me to come back three months later, my plate was too full to take them back on. It was this experience that convinced me of the need to actually be seen, rather than the ideal of working behind the scenes to keep things running.

The best thing about retainers is that they provide a fixed monthly income you can count on, much like a paycheck. Your goal should be to get enough retainers to pay your monthly bills, like your mortgage and car payment. Once you've got your bills and expenses covered, fixed-price contracts and additional retainers are gravy.

There can be problems with retainers. One of the main ways to get into trouble is by overselling yourself. You can easily get into a situation in which you have too many people to support during busy times. The solution to this problem is either to subcontract additional help or let your least valuable customers go.

Inevitably, you will run into a situation that involves two of your customers having work stoppages due to a network outage simultaneously. The best way to deal with this problem is in your contract: never promise less than a four-hour response time. This gives you time to at least assess both customers' problems individually: one in the morning, and one in the afternoon. If you have more than two customers with simultaneous emergencies, you'll just have to perform network triage: determine who has the most quickly fixable problems and attack them first; then move to the larger, deeper problems. You may piss off a customer in this case, but it's so rare that you shouldn't spend much time worrying about it. It's never actually happened to me.

Another way to deal with the problem of overselling yourself with retainers is to sell various priorities of service. You would charge the most for your premier service, which you sell only to a single customer at a time. You guarantee this customer that no matter what happens, you'll stop what you're doing to deal with their problems. Everyone else gets a lower grade of service for a lower price, with the clear understanding that you may be pulled away to deal with a problem elsewhere.

The Ante: Setting Your Rates

How much should you charge? That depends on a number of factors, but the actual answer is whatever the client will pay. Unfortunately, since that number is not immediately obvious, you have to poke around a bit to find it.

Most fixed-price bidding is based on estimating the amount of time you'll spend and multiplying that by an hourly rate.

Establishing Hourly Rates

Although I don't recommend contracting on an hourly basis, you should establish a table of hourly rates that you use to determine your fixed-price contracts and retainers.

I use an hourly scale to determine my firm, fixed prices for various contracts; I don't reveal what that hourly rate is to the client, however, and I don't break out an itemized menu of prices per task. I consider my pricing information to be proprietary. They can either accept or decline the job at the total price I charge for all work performed.

Here is an example of rates I charge:

WORK CATEGORY	HOURLY BID PRICE
Work I hate	$300
Emergency work	$200
Short job rate	$150 (less than one day)
Standard rate	$100
Long job rate	$62.50 (more than one week of solid work)

Bidding Fixed-Price Contracts

To determine the price for a fixed-price contract, simply figure out how long the contract will take you to perform and multiply that by an hourly rate. Make sure you take into account the time it takes to document and test, and a portion of time to pay for the time you spend bidding the job.

I also use a table of standard times I've developed for how long various tasks usually take me. You can use my task table as a starting point, but you really should develop your own timing chart based on how long you take to perform various functions.

JOB	HOURS
Install NIC, attach client to network	0.5
Install OS, Office, network on client	1
Install OS and standard services on server	4
Install router	1
Install hub, switch	0.5
Install, configure, and test firewall	8
Install and configure mail server	6

NOTE If these numbers seem a little long to you, remember that they include time for documentation and testing.

After you have looked at these charts, you've probably realized that determining your contract price is as simple as counting the equipment, multiplying each category by the time you take per item, multiplying that number by the hourly rate, and then summing all the categories.

As I mentioned in Chapter 9, *Contracts: Write Now or Pay Later*, I have created an Access database that contains all this information. I can create a bid now by simply opening a form, selecting job elements from a pull-down list, and entering a quantity. This part of the contract is simply a report that lists the job elements and quantities, and then presents the sum total cost at the end (for more information on the components of a contract, see Chapter 9). Using this method, creating my entire contract (because my standard terms are built into the report) takes about five minutes and consists mostly of making sure I haven't forgotten anything.

Pricing Retainers

To figure out the price I should charge to secure my retainer services, I typically use $50 per workstation (seat) per month, plus $200 per server per month, plus $200 per WAN or Internet connection. These numbers are somewhat capricious—they aren't based on an hourly rate or even the amount of time I might spend working for a specific customer. I chose these numbers because they provide a very good income for me, and are low enough that my customers can't hire staff for less money.

When you price retainers, you are competing against the cost of adding an employee to do the same work, so you should price your retainers to compete against that metric. A full-time network administrator makes between $30,000 and $70,000, depending upon the area, the administrator's expertise, and the size of the company. I use $50,000 as a nice, round competing figure. At that salary, a network administrator should be able to easily support 100 users in a well-managed network while performing all necessary corollary duties. In a poorly managed network, and administrator may be able to support only 50 users, and in an exceptionally well-managed network with strong remote tools and higher-end computer hardware, an administrator could support as many as 1,000 users.

If I work five days a week handling retainers in networks that I've designed and implemented, I find that I can support a maximum of about 250 seats. Here, I have figured out my maximum average retainer income:

250 seats × $50 = $12,500

5 servers × $200 = $1000

3 WAN links × $200 = $600

Total: $14,100/mo.

This works out to about $170,000 per year. I generally choose not to work that much on retainers; currently, I'm supporting just 90 seats, for a total of about $9,000 in monthly retainer fees (one of the customers is a bit of a pain, so I charge them extra). My other income comes from fixed-price contracts (and book royalties, of course).

I always stipulate simple notification from either party to end my retainers within 30 days. This way, your customers can end the contract if they aren't satisfied with your performance, or you can end the contract if you no longer have time to support the customer. Some customers require quite a bit more hand-holding than they're willing to pay for, so you'll want to be rid of them when you have work to replace this income.

Usually, I will take a customer on a retained basis only if I've designed and installed their network or after I've completed a fixed-price contract to implement various remote management, security, and desktop software standards that I feel are important. For example, before I take on a new client who has serious desktop support problems on a retainer basis, I stipulate, in a fixed-price contract, that they must first move all their desktop computers from Windows 95 to Windows NT Workstation or Windows 2000 Professional, and they must also eliminate any computers that can't effectively run these operating systems. By completing this migration as a fixed-price contract before taking on the retainer, I'm able to solve all existing desktop issues in one fell swoop, and I am able to implement more sustainable support procedures (like preventing users from installing their own software) that will lighten my load when I'm on retainer. In cases where this isn't possible, I double my retainer price. This increase in long-term cost usually convinces reluctant customers to go ahead and implement my recommended changes up front.

Your Poker Face

Okay, so you've written up your bid and you've come up with the price for which you can comfortably do the work. Is that what you should charge?

No. The best way to maximize your income is to figure out what your client will pay, and then charge that. On the other hand, nobody is going to come right out and say "This isn't as high as we were expecting. Pad this by a few thousand dollars and call us back." On the other hand, they very well may look at your proposal, turn pale, and mumble something about calling you back if you've charged far more than they expected.

If your bid price is higher than the customer expected, you'd lose the job. If your bid price is lower than the customer expected, you'd lose the money "left sitting on the table"—that is, the price you could have charged if you'd only known what it was.

By now, you are probably asking yourself "How is an integrator to know beforehand what to charge?" There's no way to know, short of installing numerous small listening devices throughout your client's controller's office. And even that doesn't work very well.

The solution is the three-tiered bid. Whenever you present a bid, present three: a low-priced solution, a medium-priced solution, and a premium solution.

Call (The Medium-Priced Solution)

Start with the medium-priced solution. This is the bid you have already created. It applies to the customer's direct problem, performs the entire scope of work, and charges your regular rate. The medium-priced solution uses the hardware you want to put in place to solve the problem, whatever that hardware may be. It should include such labor items as user training, writing user's manuals, testing and validation, etc.

Pass (The Low-Priced Solution)

Then create the low-priced solution. The low-priced solution is a completely different bid that solves the same problem or a slightly reduced problem.

If you really need the work, the low-priced solution keeps your foot in the door if the customer experiences sticker shock when they see your medium-priced solution. Low-priced solutions also help you to gauge the cash position of the company: those clients who opt for the low-priced solution will require more support, will be more cost conscious along the way, and will be least likely to feel as though they're getting a good deal from any service provider at any cost. For these reasons, I no longer bid low-tier solutions, but I recommend that you do until you're in a position to turn work down. Then, eliminate your low-priced customers one at a time and replace them with new customers who aren't as cash-poor.

Some people think it's unethical, or at least in poor taste, to present a low-priced solution. That thinking is complete hogwash. There's absolutely nothing wrong with matching solutions to a customer's ability to pay. Many companies simply can't afford to spend as much as others, but they still deserve the benefits of networking. Just like there's a place in the car market for Hyundais, there's a place in the network market for the lower-priced network solution.

Here are some ideas for reducing price dramatically without reducing quality (much):

> ➤ Remove work items that aren't absolutely necessary. Examples would be writing user's manuals for the system, performing user training, etc.

> ➤ Replace top-tier hardware (3Com or Cisco, for example) with second-tier hardware (Linksys or NetGear, for example) wherever possible.

This hardware functions just as well and is just as reliable, but it lacks features like SNMP and included management software.

➤ Eliminate high-end network management software (like HP Open-View or Computer Associates Unicenter), and replace it with a lower-priced solution (like Tivoli IT Director[or Attachmate NetWizard)—or, roll your own net management solution with free software like VNC and low-cost roll-out software like Drive Image.

➤ Replace that top-of-the-line computer hardware with last year's top-of-the-line—this usually reduces the price (and performance) by 50 percent. At the moment, a Pentium-III 600 processor alone costs about $500. A Pentium II-450 costs about $150. The difference in performance isn't nearly as extreme as the difference in price.

➤ Use lower-priced software. This may mean bidding a Linux file and print server instead of Windows NT. This can reduce the cost of a network substantially, but long-term support costs will be higher, and the pool of administrators who can work on the system will be lower.

Be sure to let the client know what the ramifications of the low-tier solution are: higher probability of component failure, higher support costs, and lower overall performance. Cash-strapped companies may prefer to pay more in the long run for a lower-priced initial solution, so there's nothing unethical about this as long as you appraise your customer of the consequences.

Raise (The High-Priced Solution)

Always present a premium solution to your customers, even though only a few will go for it. The premium solution allows you to make more money by selling more work and more hardware. Again, this isn't unethical: you're simply providing another option for those customers who have the desire for better solutions and have the money to pay for them. The premium solution keeps you from leaving money on the table—with it, you can soak up just about all the money your client would be willing to pay you.

Ways to add value (that's jargon for squeezing more money) to a contract:

➤ Create a larger scope of work. Instead of just a network, build in voice-over IP, e-mail integrated voicemail, desktop-based instant messaging, server-based faxing, centralized document imaging and document management, and so forth. These higher-end convenience solutions are expensive and unnecessary—just like a Mercedes Benz. For some customers, convenience is worth the money.

➤ Increase security with a better firewall, biometric authentication devices like thumbprint scanners, face recognition, handwriting tablets, voice recognition software, or offer encrypted tunneling over the Internet for remote users.

➤ Install premium network management solutions, like Computer Associates Unicenter or HP OpenView, for larger customers, and Tivoli IT Director or Attachmate NetWizard for smaller customers. These systems are great if you can get them sold in because they reduce your system administration hassles.

➤ Offer high-availability solutions using fail-over servers, clustering, RAID disk arrays, and redundant Internet routing. High availability is expensive, but crucial to many customers.

➤ Offer premium support. This means you'll put this customer ahead of your second- and third-tier customers in an emergency situation, or you'll pay another consultant to respond if, for some reason, you can't—without charging them. You may also give them your cellphone number instead of your voicemail or e-mail address for support. I separate my retainers into three tiers: cell phone, voicemail, and e-mail.

Despite my penchant for sarcasm, offering a premium solution doesn't mean jacking up your hourly rate and ripping off your customers. It means offering solutions that aren't appropriate for cost-conscious customers, but which increase the security, availability, and convenience of the network for those customers for whom cost is not the most important factor.

Consider offering the premium bid as a supplemental "menu of options" to the medium bid. Unlike the low-priced solution, which is always presented as a complete alternative, the premium solution should be presented as packages of options. Examples of bundled packages would be security, availability, and various convenience items. Each option package should be priced separately, so the customer can choose which options they want to pay for. A package would be all the software and equipment to offer network faxing—packages are defined by function, not by application or hardware.

Presenting premium option packages in addition to your medium-priced bid is the biscuit with which you'll soak up all the gravy on the plate. You can pretty much rely on your customer to spend their entire networking budget when you present them with a bunch of cool gizmos they could have on their network. This presentation means quite a bit more work up front during the bid process (it usually takes longer to price out options than it does to create the initial bid), but the first time a customer bites, it's more than worth it. Plus, you get to play with some really fun toys.

When to Hold, When to Fold

Once you are working more than you want to, you no longer need to worry about competing with other consultants or with a customer's preconceived notion of what you should charge. At this point, you can price your services based on the demand for them; essentially, the customers who are willing to pay more for your services are the customers you'll work for.

You don't have to keep your finger on the pulse of every other consultant or read silly industry average tables in computer rags to determine what to charge. Changing your rates is easy if you follow these simple rules:

➤ If you want more work, lower your rates.

➤ If you want less work, raise your rates.

This simple rule takes into account all the market forces that affect you and your customers. If you're not working as much as you want to be working, it could indicate that you don't compete well against other lower-cost consultants, so you should lower your rates to compete better. If you've got too much work on your plate, you are either undercutting other consultants or you are more talented; in either case, you should raise your rates.

Raise and Hold

I use this method to modulate how much work I do. I never turn down work, but if I don't have time to do it, I raise my rates and bid anyway. Just recently I didn't want to take on a new retainer, so I told the client I needed $7000 per month for a one-day-a-week effort. They accepted. I was astonished, but at that price it was worth my time, so I took the contract. To free up time to service this contract, I ended a (much) lower paying contract with another customer by introducing them to another consultant who was looking for more work.

The rule here is to work as much as you want to work, and let the demand for your talents establish how much money you make. Once your plate is full, you should keep looking for work, but raise your rates accordingly. When you get higher paying retainers, eliminate your lowest paying retainers.

Repeat this cycle of raising your bid rates until you no longer get any new retainers, and hold at that point. Using this pricing method, you'll make as much money as it is possible for you to make working the amount you want to work.

This method may sound unfair to customers—I've even had other consultants accuse me of having unethically high rates. This argument has no merit—nobody is putting a gun to the heads of my clients and forcing them to work with me. They pay more for the quality, completeness, and speed with which I solve their problems. They understand this, and so will your clients. You aren't working as a favor for clients, you're working to provide for your family and for yourself. Making as much money as possible allows you to spend more time with your family, and that's what it's all about, as far as I see it.

When to Fold

Although the converse situation (lowering your rates) has never happened to me, I suspect it eventually will. There's nothing wrong with lowering your rates to compete—it doesn't mean you're a failure, or that you're the budget solution, it just means that there are market forces out there forcing you to compete better. You may never know why, but that doesn't matter. You should lower your rates until you win enough bids to fill your time up. Once you're working full time, you've found your starting point, and can begin raising your rates for new clients.

If you find you've had to lower your rates to fill your plate so much that you aren't making enough money to live on, nature is trying to tell you something: network consulting either doesn't work in your market area, or you aren't good enough at it to compete with others in your area, so you should find another job.

How Much Is Enough?

The next question is by how much should you change your rates. The answer to that is how much you want to affect your time. If you need to bring in work in a hurry, you might slash your rates by one-third. If your plate is full and another client comes to you, you might quadruple your normal rate because you don't need or want the work. There's no hard and fast rule to answer this question, but there doesn't need to be. If one increment doesn't seem to be working, you can just keep changing your rates until you find the rates that work for you.

Conclusion

Pricing is not magic. The price you charge should be whatever seems fair to both you and your client. By starting with some average rates, your bidding experiences will quickly tell you whether you need to lower or raise your rates.

Always present lower- and higher-priced options to your clients. This will prevent you from losing bids if you need the work, and it will prevent you from charging less than your client is willing to spend. It is absolutely the best way to make more money, win more bids, and seem more responsive to your customer's needs.

When you've become as busy as you want to be, it's time to raise your rates. Keep raising them until you don't get any more work. If you want to work more, lower your rates, and keep lowering them until your plate is full.

11 Project Management

"Now keep staring and it'll turn 3D."

Once you begin consulting, you'll be responsible for completing entire projects, not just a single portion. This means that unless you're already in a managerial position, you'll need to learn how to manage a project from beginning to end.

The following are the phases of project management:

➤ Requirements planning

➤ System design

➤ Logistics and scheduling

➤ Implementation

➤ Documentation

➤ Test and Delivery

These phases are similar to the phases discussed in Chapter 3, *A Project from Cradle to Grave*, but without the business elements.

Requirements Planning

The first phase of any project is defining what needs to be accomplished. It's always tempting to think you know exactly what needs to be done the second a customer tells you they need a network, but subtle differences in requirements can make sweeping changes to the overall system. Because of this, you need to make sure you talk to everyone who will use the system and record all of their expectations.

A very good, methodical way to collect the complete body of system requirements is called *use-case collection*. Use cases are a fairly recent systems development strategy used mostly in software design; they were espoused by the designers of the Unified Modeling Language (UML). Although UML was designed for software development, it makes a good modeling system for any business system documentation problem. UML is not software; it's a specification for defining documentation (paper or electronic) that will accurately describe the function of a system.

If you're interested in learning the formal methodology, search for UML on amazon.com to find a good text on the subject. For the purposes of system integration, I'm primarily interested in use cases, so that's the only portion I'm actually going to explain.

Collecting Use Cases

Use-case collection is the accumulation of a body of elements of system behavior that describe how a user (or "actor" in UML parlance) will interface (use) the system. Use cases usually take the form of a paragraph, like the following one:

> "The accounting department needs to have full remote access to the accounting system remotely (from their homes) without compromising security."

To begin the process of system design, interview every system user (from CEO to data-entry personnel), and ask them how they need to be able to use the system. The users don't need to worry about how trivial or sweeping their use cases are; it is your job to distill the body of use cases into a requirements document. Users simply need to tell you what they have to be able to do with the system.

After interviewing everyone who will use the system (or in large systems, typical users of each class of user), you will have the material you need to build your requirements document.

Interviews don't have to be performed in person. If an e-mail infrastructure is already in place, it's easiest to simply mass e-mail a use-case form with instructions to everyone. When they all fill it out and return it, you'll have collected your use-case document.

Defining Requirements

Take a look at the use-case example paragraph in the previous section and ask yourself what it really means. "Secure remote access to an accounting system" is a simple sentence, but it already establishes the following basic system requirements:

➤ There must be a network in place.

➤ There must be either a connection to the Internet, dial-up access, or a wide area data link. You will need further clarification either from collecting another use case or by asking for specific clarification, if necessary.

➤ How secure is secure? Does the data have to be encrypted, or is authentication enough? Further clarification is necessary. It may not be possible to provide the required level of security while providing remote access—in this case, conflicting requirements exist.

➤ There must be an accounting system. This is a software package that, once defined, will require some hardware platform. Further definition is required to determine which accounting system is appropriate; however, many accounting systems are already disqualified by the remote access requirement.

As you can see, once the use cases are collected, you will distill them into a set of system requirements that will result in two things: a partial set of requirements and a list of questions.

You will need to interview users again to get answers to all your questions. When you have conflicting use cases (as in the secure remote access to accounting data example), call a meeting of all involved parties, explain the problem, and let the users hash out the combined requirement. This may result in one of the requirements being thrown out, or in additional requirements being accepted to satisfy both groups. Once you've gotten answers to all of your questions, you can complete your design.

Treat each use case independently and distill a complete set of system requirements. Don't worry about repetition in the complete set; you can filter out repeated elements when you've finished distilling each use case.

Once you have the complete set of requirements, group the requirements by obvious aggregations. What determines an obvious aggregation? The jargon. Accounting system is an obvious aggregation, as is remote access, security, and network. Jargon is the use of terms that are industry specific—for example, the term "remote access" doesn't really mean much outside of networking.

Once you've determined the aggregates, start grouping them. Every use case that pertains to accounting should go in the accounting section. Similarly, every use case that pertains to security should go in the security section, and every use case that pertains to remote access belongs in the remote access section. If a requirement crosses groups, put a copy of the requirement in each group. It's quite common to realize you've got another group during the process of sorting use cases. Be flexible and add all the groups you think you might need during this process.

When you're finished, eliminate the redundant requirements within each group. Then take a look at your groups and determine if some aggregate groups are so similar that they should be merged. For example, Internet Access and Remote Access groups might be so closely related that they make sense as a single group. Once you've got a good, coherent breakdown of requirements by group, massage the list of remaining requirements to the same style—for example, one paragraph or section per requirement, and of similar scope or scale.

When you are finished, groups should identify the major physical portions of the network.

System Design

Developing a system design is where your talent as a network integrator comes into play. I can't teach system design in a book about consulting because it is too complex a subject (to learn more about system design, see *NT Server 4 24seven* by Matthew Strebe from Sybex Inc.), but I can tell you what a complete design does. A complete design

➤ Fulfills every final use case. (Some use cases will be thrown out by budgetary constraints or conflicts with more important use cases in the requirements phase.)

➤ Identifies every component of the system, hardware, and software. What constitutes a component? Anything that must be acquired to complete the design.

➤ Specifies exactly how the components are connected. This specification usually takes the form of a diagram showing the components interconnected.

➤ Specifies exactly how the components are configured. Configuration specifications are usually structured as a form filled out with configuration options, or, in more complex systems, as narrative procedures explaining how to configure the component.

➤ Provides a basis for the final system documentation. Your design documentation should be complete enough so that it becomes the basis for the as-built documentation merely by filling in configuration options that weren't important enough to specify in the design, and by correcting those things in the design that were changed in the final documentation.

Many portions of the system design will fall outside your area of responsibility—for example, you likely will not be responsible for configuring the accounting software, but you'll still have to install it and connect it to the network.

Remember, your design and your professionalism are the two things that will sell the job in a competitive situation. Customers will choose the design that comes closest to meeting their full set of requirements, which must be yours if you want the job.

Your design should include a test procedure that will prove that the system is implemented correctly. A test procedure is a simple list of one-line tasks, like "send e-mail from an interior user account, and show that it arrives at a certain Internet address," that proves out complex portions of the system. You can build a list of test cases from the use cases users provided you with in the beginning since it's those use cases that you should have implemented anyway.

Logistics and Scheduling

Once the design is complete, you're ready to schedule the implementation. You'll need to identify suppliers for all the material, purchase or direct the purchasing of the material, and determine when it will be delivered. Once you have delivery dates, you can determine how long it will take for each element of the system to be installed and configured, and how many of these things can be done in parallel.

Because you'll typically be working alone, you don't have to worry much about scheduling a lot of human resources. You may find yourself working with one or more subcontractors, however, so you will have to make sure you know when they'll be available so that you can schedule their portion of the job.

Your customer will want the job completed as quickly as possible, of course. You should avoid promising fast results, though; such promises create expectations in the mind of your customer that you can fulfill only if everything goes according the schedule, which almost never actually happens. Prepare them for at least 25 percent more time than you actually think the job will take.

A lot of people like to use Gantt charting tools like Microsoft Project to make pretty pictures of the implementation schedule. Gantt charts show a horizontal bar on a linear time track for each task. This specifies the duration of the task and how the task relates to other tasks. For example, a connecting line between two tasks indicates that the earlier task must be completed before the later task can begin, as would be the case with these two tasks: "build server" and "install operating system." While these charts look really cool and professional, they're almost useless except as tools to sell the job unless you are religious about updating the project file during the project execution.

The problem with project-scheduling software like Microsoft Project is that it doesn't truly account for all aspects that affect an implementation. It makes projects seem to be behind, when in fact, the project is moving ahead as fast as possible. This is because the project management software isn't well integrated with other sources of information.

For example, when building a project file, you may enter 40 hours of system integration time. Microsoft Project puts up a little bar that spans one work week, and you print this out and provide it to your customers. They now expect the project to be done next Friday, when in fact, you intend to work one day a week for five weeks because you've got other work going on. Since Microsoft Project isn't integrated with Outlook, it doesn't know that your schedule is booked until a certain date, so it creates a project file that, while theoretically accurate, is out of touch with reality.

Every time I've worked on a job that's scheduled with project-management software, the same thing happens. Everyone runs around like a chicken with its head cut off, worried about how far behind the project is running, even though the project is behind only because unreasonable expectations were created by the incorrect use of software during the planning stage.

In my experience, the best way to handle project scheduling is with more typical scheduling software like Microsoft Outlook; by using the group features provided by the Net Folders plug-in, you can share schedule information over the Internet with the other people involved. This way, delays, updates, and the current estimates for completion times are generally available as people update their own personal calendars. This, too, takes discipline, but at least you're using the same tools you use to manage your time anyway, and you can even take your "project" information with you to the site in your Palm device.

Implementation

Implementation is the routine portion of the job you should be familiar with from your previous job—it includes the installation, configuration, and maintenance of hardware and software systems.

During the implementation, there are a number of things you can do to make later phases easy. For example, make sure to record every configuration change you make as you install the system, in both hardware and software. This list of changes from the default configuration will eventually become your documentation. I actually keep a small laptop by my side and write my system documentation as I install the system. This prevents me from forgetting anything; it also allows me to record notes about specific equipment behavior that I might forget if I worked from a more abbreviated set of notes. For small routine jobs, I simply jot down notes on my Palm organizer as I work.

It's likely that you'll make changes to your system design on the fly. Mark these changes on your original design documents so you can produce as-built prints of the system for your documentation package. Appendix B shows the as-built documentation and server configuration for a sample job.

You can also pretest a number of different things to make certain your testing procedure will go smoothly and that you won't be surprised by anything when you test in front of your customer. There's nothing more discouraging than realizing you have to remove a server from a rack and open it back up because you forgot to provide power to the tape drive. Test as you go to make sure you're working in the right order.

Documentation

Documentation should consist of every configuration option you've changed from a default installation. This is needed so that anyone familiar with system installation could use that list to recreate the system. In some cases, this is as simple as writing a list of the options you've set in a Windows NT installation, but it could be as complex as a book of database table scripts, code for stored procedures, and HTML or ASP scripts printed out. The point of installation documentation is to allow anyone to recreate the system from base components.

Good documentation should also include information that makes it easy to use as a reference. Usually, a reference is made up of the same information presented in the installation portion, but it has been abbreviated for reference. This section also usually includes as-built network diagrams, blueprints with cable location lists of servers and the services they provide, client software configuration lists, and so forth. This section allows the system administrators to quickly reference the information they need to maintain the system.

The third section of your documentation should include white papers or narrative technology descriptions for those portions of the system that the typical network administrator might not be familiar with. You may use this section to provide detailed procedures for configuring the system on unusual systems. This portion of the documentation could simply be the user's manuals provided with unusual components. Remember to include all user's manuals, warranty cards, license certificates, driver floppies or CD-ROMs, etc., for components you opened and installed along with your documentation.

Test and Delivery

You must prove that your system performs as the contract states during the test and delivery phase. Essentially, this phase is the time when you simply format the test procedures you created during the design phase so that your customer can initial next to each test element as you or they perform the test procedures. Once the test procedures have been initialed at the bottom, the customer signs the entire document, and you've officially delivered the system. Now you get to bill.

Sign-off is important not because you don't know when you've finished, but to make it blatantly clear to the customer that you are finished and that any further work you perform is outside the scope of the current project. I figured this out the hard way—after nearly every job, I found myself cornered for a week by customers who were uncertain that the job was finished, or who had late-breaking changes they wanted finished. By having a formalized sign-off, they know when you're done and there's no argument about it. You're basically preempting being stuck there until your customer's fear of change subsides.

Conclusion

Proper project management is mandatory when you consult. Not only does good project management show professionalism, it truly helps you create systems that accurate reflect a customer's desires.

On smaller jobs, you may abbreviate the process as appropriate to prevent project management from consuming more time than the actual implementation. For maintenance work, there's no need to use most project management tactics.

12

Clients:
The Good, the Bad,
and the Ugly

"Aha! I knew it!"

Perhaps the best thing about consulting is that you get to choose your employers every time you take a contract. This chapter is about discerning the differences between types of clients. This way, you can decide whether you should work with them, how much you should charge, and if you need to leave a job before it's complete.

Usually, you will work directly for either the general manager or the financial manager. In a small- to medium-sized business, these are the people who decide to hire consultants, and they're also the people who cut the paychecks. Like any boss or employer, these people run the gamut. They may be talented and very cool rich people whom we'd all like to be, or they may be people who display signs of Dilbertian incompetence or act like neurotic cheapskates who consider you to be a bloodsucker who just happens to be vital to their survival.

Nobody likes to fail at or quit any job, but inevitably, there will come a time when, for reasons outside your control, you won't be able to complete a job. Although you should think through the reasons why the job went awry, failing or quitting a single job doesn't mean you've failed at or need to quit consulting.

Whom you work for is up to you. There's no law that says you have to bid a job, accept your successful bid, or keep working on a job on a retained basis unless you've already accepted money. You can quit almost anytime, as long as you're willing to lose the time you've already invested in a job. The only time when you can't quit is after you have billed; if you've done this, you're on the hook until the terms of the contract are complete.

Be careful about whom you consult for, but remember to keep an open mind, as well. While bad clients can cause all sorts of problems, messed up companies are also an excellent source of revenue—let's face it, if your client company was running perfectly, they wouldn't need your help, now would they?

Good Clients

Of course, we'd all like to have good clients. These clients employ only friendly people, they have easy problems, they pay well, and they think you're the greatest service provider on the planet. About half of my clients fit into this category. The following are the characteristics of good clients:

➤ Financially sound

➤ Typical problems

➤ No discernable neurosis in upper management

➤ No actually evil employees

It's easy to tell good clients when you first "meet the company." Good clients can be initially identified by the following:

➤ During your initial meeting, the managers ask a lot of earnest questions about you, networks, and technology.

➤ Healthy plants are present in the office.

➤ The office has good interior design.

➤ There are little folk who mill about and spontaneously break into song.

➤ A lot of new and expensive cars are present in the parking lot (a sure sign of financial stability).

Bad Clients

Nobody would take on bad clients if they could see them coming. The reason you end up dealing with them is because they're always camouflaged as good clients. Many businesses know that they have serious problems, but they've become very good at covering them up. When you shake hands with somebody, you can't tell whether they'll have problems paying you or whether they routinely sacrifice small animals to the god of continued good fortune. These problems, unfortunately, have to be discovered.

The following are the characteristics of bad clients:

➤ Financially unsound

➤ Ethically lacking

➤ Possessed of unsolvable problems or conflicting requirements

➤ Litigious

Although you can't smell bad clients, you may be able to sense early warning signs. Here are some examples:

➤ A client takes an unusually long time to consider work they really need to have done.

➤ A manager actually yells at an employee in front of you.

➤ Healthy animals are present in the office.

➤ Numerous printouts of bizarre motivational statements are taped to the walls, like "Give me Quality or Give me Death!"

➤ Your client actually asks you to lower your prices for them, or they spend a lot of time haggling over inexpensive portions of a contract.

➤ The client stipulates all sorts of unusual legal terms in the contract.

➤ They constantly wipe their hands on their clothing.

➤ Employees pass you folded Post-it notes that read: "Get out while you still can."

➤ Your presentation is frequently interrupted by phone calls in which the manager you're talking to bends completely over the phone and speaks in hushed tones.

➤ Cubicles are wallpapered with "Dilbert" cartoons that have character names lined out and employee names written in.

➤ Handshakes you receive are pasty, cold, and limp.

➤ There are a large number of people at your presentation to whom you are not introduced and who say nothing during it.

➤ Employees smirk when you tell them who you are.

➤ People take Post-it notes back out of the trash and erase them.

NOTE Always write your contracts with an "escape clause" that will let you terminate the contract by simply notifying the client that you're done working with them. Although you won't be able to bill, you can at least wrest yourself away from problem clients without being sued for damages. See Chapter 9 for details on how to write good contracts.

THE CHEAPSKATE

Cheap clients aren't worth working for because they don't just nickel and dime hardware, they try to nickel and dime everyone. They pay as late and as little as they can get away with, they're a constant support hassle because they buy cheap equipment that breaks, and they're the most likely to argue your bill with you.

I had a potential client once who was so cheap that they ordered custom servers without floppy or CD-ROM drives. They then bought a single floppy and CD-ROM that they moved from machine to machine whenever something needed to be installed. This was for servers mind you, not clients.

When they first called me (I was recommended by a current client), they explained their problem to me. I told them I'd take them on, and faxed them a bid with a network diagram attached.

When I got there, I noticed that they had actually run their own network cabling; they had crimping jacks on the ends of each cable rather than installing jacks and faceplates, so they had long cords just dangling out of the walls and ceilings all over the place. This scared me. Then, they had the gall to show me that they had taken my bid design and attempted to implement it on their own—they purchased generic cheap versions of the equipment specified. (I listed Dell servers that ran about $5000 at the time. They paid $1500 each for the inadequate machines they bought.) When they couldn't get the cable up and realized they had the wrong version of NT (they had bought Workstation because it was cheaper), they called me, told me I'd won the bid, and asked me to come in to talk about it.

This potential client also asked leading questions about where they could get a copy of Windows NT without paying what they considered to be an excessive licensing fee. It was clear they wanted me to install a copy of mine on their machine. I suggested Linux to the owner because it was free, and his laughing response was that NT was free, too, if you didn't pay for it. He then made it clear that he expected my labor price to include the server software, but that whether I paid for it or not was up to me. I responded that programmers work hard and deserved to be paid. The owner's retort to that was that only idiots paid for software.

I never went back, and ignored their pleas for further help on my voicemail.

Ugly Clients

Ugly clients are perhaps your best source of income. An ugly client is one who has serious problems but also has a lot of money, so this makes dealing with the problems worth the hassle. Essentially, the managers of these businesses are trying to "throw money at the problem" to make it go away. Consultants, you included, are the traditional receivers of this money.

Charging a lot to solve hard problems isn't unethical; it's capitalism. Again, nobody forces your client to accept your bid price. The extra hassle it takes to deal with difficult clients justifies higher pricing.

THE HIGH MAINTENANCE CLIENT

I have one retained client whom I like working for quite a bit. Unfortunately, there's one person who works there who is extremely high maintenance. Literally 50 percent of my support calls are to support something that has gone wrong with this single user. Of course, he knows absolutely nothing about computers—if a shortcut on his desktop is moved from its normal location, I hear about it. If he tries to load a Web page and the Web server isn't responding as quickly as he thinks it should, I get a service call. No matter how many times I explain what's going on or what he should expect to see, nothing changes. I've even supplied a list of things he should try before calling, but I still get the calls. I've basically had to decide to deal with it or dump the client. So I raised my retainer to cover it.

I take on a lot of ugly clients. Ugly clients have these characteristics:

➤ Financially sound

➤ Hard problems

➤ Strange personalities

➤ Political situations

Here are clues you can use to detect ugly clients early in the process:

➤ The client neither asks many questions, nor seems to care about the cost. They just hire you on the spot.

➤ The offices look like a hurriedly thrown-together shantytown.

➤ There is an even split between brand-new cars and junkers in the parking lot.

➤ The CEO sits you down in front of the IT manager and tells you to "duke it out" at your first meeting.

➤ You notice the presence of a white, powdery substance on the owner's fingers.

THE SERIOUS PROBLEMS CLIENT

One of my retained clients has amazing technical problems. They have an extremely high-growth environment. In personnel alone, they've grown about 200 percent per year. For the last two years, their revenue generation has grown even faster. They've developed their own application software, which works pretty well, but it runs on Unix servers. The client software runs on Windows machines, so they have a very mixed environment. Add to that confusion the fact that nearly every PC was purchased individually when the employee who needed it arrived. Their IT staff is split right down the middle between Unix geeks who don't do Windows, and Windows geeks who don't do Unix. While a hierarchy exists on paper, the two groups act nearly completely independently of each other.

The mixed hardware environment and the rapid growth in the server room have led to a "Frankenstein network" in which every server, hub, and client is unique. Needless to say, class-based support is nearly impossible. Their custom application software comes without user's manuals or effective training, so only a few of the end users know it throughout, and they parcel out nuggets of wisdom to the constant throng of newcomers. I literally see new faces every time I do a site visit.

Problems Pay

The paradoxical thing about ugly customers is that they can be your best customers. Since they know they have hard problems that other consultants before you have likely failed at, they're going to be a little more forgiving than good or bad customers. This also motivates them to pay more for people who make problems go away.

Working against the Team

I am frequently hired to evaluate IT management at companies. This is usually because the company feels that they are not getting the service they deserve, considering the amount of money their internal IT department is being given. These jobs are always really sticky: you work for the finance or upper management departments, but you have to work with the IT people to evaluate them. They know why you're there, and they hate you because of it.

In these situations, I simply put everything on the table: who I am, what I've been hired to do, and that my presence shouldn't be construed as a threat to them if they're a productive part of the team.

THE PROBLEM IT STAFF

Quite frequently, you'll walk into a well-lit server room where the cables are neatly tie-strapped in place, where the machines all hum at the same pitch (because they are all the exact same hardware), and where order seems to rule. Orderly rows of backup tapes, each with laser-printed labels of dates in perfectly ascending order line the top shelves of storage racks, and an aluminum toolkit stands by at the ready, replete with a barcode label you can scan along with your ID to check it out. Invariably, in these places, somebody had to tap in a secret code at the door to let you enter the vaunted server room, and you signed in with a security guard at the front desk and waited for an IT department escort to pick you up.

Everything seems great until you listen to the end users complain about problems endlessly left unresolved (the technician visits the desk, pokes about, declares the problem either fixed or unfixable, and then leaves), services unimplemented ("we're planning a migration to legal IP addresses in the first quarter of 2002"), and closets full of hardware and software packages that nobody installed because they didn't know how.

Much like a communist country, this type of IT staff is very good at certain things like daily procedure, but they lack even the most basic understanding of creative troubleshooting. This is by-the-book (or procedure manual) IT staffing that exists to fulfill a fuzzy mission statement like "we strive to maintain 100 percent uptime for all users in a timely and effective manner" (this is an actual IT department mission statement I've seen). This causes the IT staff to realize that they can show the best results on their personal performance charts by not letting anything change. When something breaks, all they need to do is order a replacement and swap it out. Without fail, expansions to the network are contracted out to people like you and me.

Choosing Sides

Never forget whom you actually work for at a client site: management, the people who cut the checks. You don't work for the IT staff, and you don't work for the employees.

Frequently, in consulting situations in which you've been brought in to fix problems, you'll find that the reason for those problems is the result of bad management practice, either by the executive staff or the IT staff. No matter who is to blame, you work for the executive staff because they're the ones who pay you.

There are no "sides" in a situation where management problems exist, so don't take any. Maintain impartiality. It's really easy to side with users because usually the problems aren't their fault. Nonetheless, you shouldn't let yourself get sucked into your client's office politics. Whatever the problems are, and no matter whom is to blame, your job is simply to fix things.

It can be sticky. I have a situation right now with a client who has a senior manager who is a blithering idiot. Not only does he lack any appreciable talent in any field of endeavor, but he is also dictatorial and abusive towards employees; he blames them for his own lack of management skill. I've literally had to calm crying employees in his wake.

I can't change that situation myself. What I can do is work my hardest to make things run smoothly for his subordinates. I don't gossip with people about his behavior, and I don't talk about him behind his back (except in this book). If the president of the company asks me for my opinion about him, I will present my honest opinion about his work and his character, and I will recommend that he be let go. But I can't approach the company president with this opinion unsolicited.

Don't let yourself get caught gossiping with a tattletale. Keep your opinions about the employees of your clients to yourself.

Crime and Punishment

Never, ever offer to do something illegal to curry favor with a client. In the course of my consulting, I've been asked to do such things as provide unlicensed software, falsify legal statements, shift billings around to hide them, and all manner of other petty little things that a client might want to do to save money.

I never do. In fact, I maintain an image of something of a "goody two-shoes" by gently lecturing on software license law when I'm asked to pirate software; I also suggest alternatives like using open-source software. After the first time it comes up, my clients know not to bother asking me to do anything illegal.

Software Piracy Is Illegal

I'm constantly amazed by customers, even good customers, who don't understand software licensing laws. Although ethical customers don't intentionally pirate software, they're often unaware of times when their usage constitutes accidental software piracy. I've had customers who were completely unaware that they needed to purchase a copy of office pro-[1] grams for every individual computer.

Other customers know outright that they're pirating software and simply don't care. They're convinced that there is no enforcement and that because there's no enforcement, there's no reason to pay for software.

In fact, software-licensing enforcement is rare, but if a customer pisses off an employee, and that employee goes to a software vendor and tells them that the customer is illegally using their software, the customer will most likely have to fend off a lawsuit from the vendor. Disgruntled employees account for the vast majority of software enforcement. Oddly, companies that don't pay for software also tend to have a large number of disgruntled former employees.

If you provide software to a customer illegally, you are the person pirating the software. If you think your unethical customer is going to indemnify you, you're silly. If they get sued, they're going to roll over on you and claim that they paid you to provide the software and that they didn't know it was illegal. Unethical customers will leave you high and dry when problems come to town, so keep your life simple and make sure your customers understand both the licensing terms of the software they use and the fact that you won't assist them in violating those licensing terms.

My rule is simply not to take software into a client's site unless it's loaded onto my laptop. If they need some software, they can buy it and get it delivered. Early in my career, when I traveled with a CD-ROM case of software tools, I'd found employees leafing through it; they'd then asked for copies of my software, as if they were teenagers asking to tape my CDs.

Conclusion

Companies take on the personalities of their upper management, exhibiting much the same range of character, from energetic competence to disorganized incompetence. Up front, it's often difficult to tell whom you're dealing with.

You'll work for a lot of different people as a consultant, many of whom don't share your ethical underpinnings. This doesn't mean you can't work with them; it just means you'll have to spend extra effort making sure their potential liabilities don't become yours.

13 Associations

"No, actually, I didn't realize you could use eyebrow piercing to electrostatically ground yourself."

Once your consulting takes off, you'll quickly find you can't get everything done yourself. When this happened to me (having no tome of all consulting wisdom to turn to), I ran around like a chicken with my head cut off doing more damage control than paying work; I stopped only when my wife suggested hiring someone.

At the time, I was not incorporated and I had no Employer's Identification Number (EIN); the last thing I needed was more complexity. So I asked a friend of mine who had time available (he is a technical writer) to help me out. It was probably the best thing I've done since I started my business, and it was the first step toward improving my quality of life. I now rely upon all sorts of outsourced service providers to make my life simpler and increase the amount of business I can perform.

Of course, it costs money to outsource, but at the point when you're selling all your time for at least $100 per hour, paying someone $25 or $50 per hour to reduce the amount of work you do makes good sense. On the other hand, until you have a full plate, or during those times when you don't, you'll probably choose to perform most of this work yourself because you'll want to save as much as you can. That is the correct and natural way to use outsourced help like consultants and subcontractors.

Subcontractors

Subcontractors are those people whom you pay to assist you in performing a contract. Typically, the following groups make up the pool of subcontractors on which to draw:

- ➤ Consultants
- ➤ Consulting Firms
- ➤ Temporary Employees
- ➤ Contractors

Technically, there's no difference between consulting firms and contractors. The only apparent difference is that people who are members of consulting firms wear suits and don't get their hands dirty; contractors wear jeans and perform useful labor. The business models are otherwise the same.

Consultants are other individuals like you who operate their own businesses and sell some specialty skill. You will employ them whenever you need the skills they offer, or when you have more work to perform than you can handle.

Consultants

You should be associated with at least one other consultant. Try to make sure that your skills overlap and that you can rely upon this person to cover for you when you're busy, and vice versa. Without the help of a reliable associate, you'll have a hard time taking vacations, and you'll have problems scheduling more than three simultaneous retained jobs.

Here is a list of other things consultants can help you with:

➤ Installing unusual operating systems

➤ Installing unusual network applications

➤ Configuring equipment like phone switches, key systems, or routers

➤ Covering for you in your absence

➤ Helping you present the image of a larger firm

Your "backup" consultant doesn't have to be an active consultant. If you know somebody who is regularly employed but has a flexible schedule, or better yet, if you know someone who is self-employed but doesn't work as a consultant, you'll be able to rely upon them without worrying about them competing with you or trying to woo your clients away. I routinely work with self-employed Web developers, technical writers, and employees of other companies. I line them up to cover for me when I'm not available.

I also hire other consultants to handle those portions of a contract that I'm not familiar enough with, in addition to having them cover for me when I'm not available. For example, although I play around with Unix quite a bit, I don't consider myself skilled enough to be certain that I've properly secured a Unix public server; instead, I have a consultant who specializes in Unix test and secure it for me.

Consultants usually have some agreed-upon "interconsultant" rate; this rate should be lower than the lowest price you'll give an end user. For example,

I'll work for another consultant (when I have time) for $50 per hour (on a retained basis) rather than my usual long-term rate of $62.50. This is because the other consultant has handled the bidding and customer handholding, and absorbs the liability (make sure that's understood, of course), so all I have to do is go to the site and get the work done. It's easier for me, and the lower rate reflects that. I expect the same rate to be offered when I call on them. In fact, I work with one consultant on a "comp-time" basis; he and I simply call each other whenever necessary and keep track of the difference in the amount of work we do. At tax time at the end of the year, whichever one of us is behind cuts the other a check for the difference.

WARNING I haven't asked my accountant about the tax liability of working this way, however, so be aware. This method also requires an unusual amount of trust between consultants, so it might not work for everyone.

Consulting Firms

Consulting firms are much like individual consultants in that they can help you with the same types of problems. Unlike individual consultants, however, you may not always know whom you'll be working with, so quality can vary considerably. You may also have problems with a consulting firm aggressively marketing themselves to your customers since the employees of the firm may not be aware or respectful of your relationship with your client. Consulting firms are also more expensive than individual consultants because they have to pay for a lot more overhead. Usually, you will not get an hourly rate lower than about $100 from a consulting firm. They typically charge end users between $150 and $200 dollars per hour, and they generally will only work on an hourly basis—no retainers or fixed price contracts.

Temp Agencies

Temp agencies can help you through the bulk labor portions of a large contract; such workers can perform the following tasks:

➤ Moving computers and network equipment into place

➤ Connecting computers to keyboards, monitors, and mice

➤ Opening and closing computers

➤ Physically installing Plug-and-Play network adapters

➤ Installing network adapter drivers

Hiring temporary labor through a temp agency is very hit-or-miss. You will have to closely supervise all the activities of your temp labor pool; you will be acting more as a foreman or a supervisor while they're working, and most likely, you won't get anything done yourself. You'll also have to inspect all their work very carefully.

In my experience, there are a number of problems with temp labor:

➤ Confusion on the part of the agency about where temps should be sent

➤ The agencies send unreliable employees, especially on short-term assignments

➤ The agencies don't seem to spend much time matching their workers' skill sets to the jobs required of them.

Despite these drawbacks, most temps are very excited about working with computers and with self-employed consultants. Often, you may find that these workers are treating you like a hero because you are a successful, self-employed consultant—these people are essentially unemployed or between jobs, and many may be low-skilled laborers, at that, so seeing someone succeed makes a big impression on them. They will usually be excited to work with you, will attempt to impress you, and will listen adroitly when you tell them what they should do because they want to learn about your job. They will watch every aspect of your behavior with the client, and they will also probably ask you how you got your start, what qualifications you have, and what you think they should do to become like you. You can just tell them to buy a copy of this book.

Using temp labor can be far less expensive than using computer consultants to perform the same work—it doesn't take a $100/hr. consultant to carry computers around. But temp labor is only really effective on especially large jobs that need a large amount of low-skilled work (like placing equipment or connecting components together).

Also, be prepared to give each laborer one of your logo T-shirts to wear while they're on the job site. You don't know what they're going to show up wearing, and you certainly don't want to "scare" your client with a bunch of new faces wandering around lost with expensive equipment. In this case, logo T-shirts can make the perceptive difference between an unorganized mob of workers and an efficient team.

Contractors (Physical Plant)

Perhaps the second most useful business relationship you can cultivate (after another consultant) is one with a physical plant contractor. Physical plant contractors install network cabling—something that about 25 percent of your contracts will require.

Good physical plant contractors perform thorough tests of every cable they install using a Time-Domain Reflectometer (TDR, informally called a cable scanner for copper plants and an OTDR [for optical TDR] for fiber plants), which provides a detailed physical characterization of every cable. This is important, because at 100Mbps, networks can be extremely sensitive to the quality of cabling and cable jacking. Poor cabling will cost you valuable hours of troubleshooting even if it's not your fault, so it's best for you to have a quality cable plant installed up front. Simple "pair–matching" tests that indicate correct wiring won't do because they say nothing of the quality of cables and jacks used or the care taken during the routing of cables—you should demand a full TDR scan of every cable before you go to work.

I recommend simply finding a physical plant contractor that does good work and sticking with them. You'll find this relationship to be reciprocal—you'll use them when you need a physical plant installed, and they'll recommend you when they know of a customer in need of network integration. My physical plant contractor (Connectivity Masters) will even delay billing me until my contract pays out so that I don't have to worry about cash flow during large projects.

You'll find that the majority of your customers will chose the bottom-dollar cable installer because they don't understand the difference between a quality installation and a thrown-together network. To them, a cable is a cable. This is very bad for you because you'll have to go behind them and find all the bad cables when you try to get the network up. This has happened to me so many times that I now hire my physical plant contractor to test unknown cable plants on my dime before I go in. This way, I don't have to worry about hidden problems. I then present a list of the cables that failed and force the original installer to repair them to my satisfaction before I begin working.

TIP If you don't have that kind of a relationship with a contractor, you can rent a cable scanner from an electronics leasing company, like the Electro Rent Corporation, for about $300/mo. You'll save at least that much in time by scanning larger cable plants before you put networks on them.

The better way to ensure the proper installation of cable plants is simply to include the cable plant in your own bid, and inform the customer that you'll handle the installation of it. This allows you to choose the installer you want, and it insures that you won't be wasting time or money trying to repair an inferior plant.

I'm now in the process of training my preferred contractor's installers to install network adapters in computers for me. This way, I'll be able to employ these high-quality skilled workers in a manner that is beneficial to me (they're cheaper than consultants and more reliable than temps) and to them (data-link layer integration is the "next step" for these workers). You'd be wise to cultivate this close relationship with a physical plant contractor yourself.

Outsourcing

As a self-employed businessperson, there are a number of business functions that you can perform on your own—or more wisely, you can outsource. You could, of course, perform your own accounting, create your own image properties, and you could even represent yourself in court—all foolish in ascending order, if you ask me. I specialize in network design, installation, and repair. I don't specialize in graphic design, taxes, or law. Any intelligent person, with study and effort, could probably create a working computer network after a few months. Or they can hire me and get it done in a few days. The same holds true for the things you could do but should outsource:

➤ Accounting and bookkeeping

➤ Legal and corporate work

➤ Graphic and Web design

Keep in mind that I'm not recommending that you begin your business outsourcing these things. Don't pay for anything until your business is making enough money to justify it.

Accounting and Bookkeeping

You will require two types of accounting assistance: general bookkeeping, a recurring monthly task (and the only word with three different double letters in a row) and tax accounting, which occurs after the end of the year and deals with preparing your tax statements and closing the year's books.

Bookkeeping

Anyone can perform their own bookkeeping with modern software like QuickBooks or MYOB (Mind Your Own Business). Luckily, I am married to a professional bookkeeper who won't let me keep my own books, but most of you probably aren't in that same position. The choice of whether or not to keep your own books comes down to one of motivation: will you actually do it? An outside bookkeeper is most useful simply because they will actually perform this noxious and troublesome chore on a regular basis. If you're anything like me, your mass of invoices and receipts would simply pile up until you finally had to deal with them at the end of the year. If you did this, you'd wind up paying penalties for non-payment of your quarterly tax, and you would also spend a month in accounting hell trying to remember what this or that receipt was actually for.

TIP   When you sign your credit card receipts, get in the habit of writing the job number or client name for which you're purchasing the item below the signature line right after you sign. This will make your receipt accounting far easier come tax time.

Bookkeepers are not particularly expensive. Consulting bookkeepers generally charge from $15 to $30 per hour. With the level of business you would be performing, you would need a bookkeeper to come in for only about four hours per month. So for about $100/mo., you get your billing done correctly and on time, and you make your tax accountant's job (if you have one) much easier at the end of the year.

Don't let your home office de-motivate you: if for some reason, you don't want business associates to enter your home, simply put all your accounting materials (invoices, receipts, bills, etc) in a manila envelope and drop it off with your bookkeeper once a month. They'll sort through and file everything for you, enter what needs to be entered, and then they can either store your paperwork for you or they can return it in a file folder, along with a floppy disk that contains your bookkeeping information.

TIP Can't find a bookkeeping consultant? Ask a trustworthy bookkeeper or accountant that works for one of your clients to keep your books at their home on the side. While I think it's unethical to hire people away from your clients, I have no problem with offering side work to them as long as it doesn't interfere with my client's relationship with them. If you choose to do this, be sure to talk to your primary point of contact at your client's business (usually the controller or general manager) before you ask the bookkeeper so that you don't step on any toes. If they have a problem with your plan, try another client. Most clients won't have a problem with this.

Accounting

Nothing will get you into more trouble as a consultant than trying to perform your own tax accounting, unless you're so completely conservative about taxes that you actually want to vastly overpay them. No ancillary function you perform will allow you to save more money than having a good tax accountant.

True story: last year, I used tax accounting software (TurboTax) to do my taxes. After nearly choking on the final amount owed, I gave up and took the whole thing to my tax accountant. His final number was $15,000 less than mine. He billed me for $250. Now, I'm not a stupid person, but after doing everything I thought was reasonable, I'd missed numerous valid deductions; I had also made a couple of errors about how certain portions of my income should be taxed, and I had even missed some taxes I was obliged to pay. My tax accountant fixed all of these problems in short order. His software was much better than mine as well, and it was completely up-to-date.

I don't know how much money you make, but I don't make so much that $15,000 isn't worth bothering with. Once you become a consultant, whether you incorporate or not, your tax liability will become heinous and evil. I was used to filing in a 1040EZ before I started my own business. Now I don't even know all the forms I file, but my tax packet is about an inch thick.

Enough said. Get a good tax accountant. The best way to find one is by asking someone who's self employed who they use (first make sure they are happy with the job their accountant does).

Legal

Other than before you become involved in litigation, there are two times when you should (in my opinion) consult legal counsel: the first is when you establish your business as a corporation (which I recommend, but note that I don't think this is necessary when you establish as a sole proprietorship [See Chapter 7]), and the second is when you are writing the legal terms for your contract. Although this book provides a good template for a contract, there's nothing about it that is specific to your business or your acceptable level of risk. You should talk to a lawyer to help you craft a standard contract that meets all your specific criteria.

You can, of course, buy do-it-yourself software for things like incorporation and other transactional law (writing contracts), but the same problem is present that exists with the advice presented in this book: it's not tailored to your specific case.

Any customer in their right mind will balk at a 16-page contract that has one page specific to their contract and 15 pages of legalese, and rightly so: inordinate attention to legal minutiae is an indication that the party writing the contract (either the consultant or the client) is more likely to take the contract to litigation. Tailor your contracts to fit both the scale and importance of the job. Contracts worth less than $5000 don't warrant much more than a half-page of terms as long as you include limitations of liability and other well-known standard clauses. Contracts worth more than $50,000 rightly deserve fairly lengthy explanations of pre-litigation remedies, rights of parties, and so forth. I recommend having three standard contracts for that reason: low risk/low cost, medium risk/medium cost, and high risk/high cost.

Of course, litigation essentially requires a lawyer unless it's a small claim. Currently, in most states, small claims are claims less than $8000, but check with your local statutes to be certain. Some states do not allow lawyers in small claims court. If you try to sue somebody without a lawyer in a case that's not clear enough for a summary judgment and larger than your state's limit for small claims, you may wind up offending the judge, who will feel that you're wasting everyone's time. While a judge may be more lenient on a defendant, if you have any significant risk, you'd be stupid not to have competent legal counsel represent you.

Lawyer's fees run from about $150 to $350 per hour, depending upon the experience of the lawyer. Expect to pay $200 per hour for competent representation. Over $250 means you're probably paying too much. Legal firms work much like consulting firms: the bigger ones charge more because they have more overhead, but they aren't likely to be any more competent than a solo lawyer or a small legal firm. In fact, if your case is handled by a large firm, it's likely that most of the work you're paying top-dollar for will be performed by low-waged paralegals anyway. Stick with law firms that are the same size as your business, whatever that size is.

WARNING The average case costs about 33 percent of the amount being litigated to pursue in court; hotly contested cases can easily claim the entire value in legal fees.

Design

Most geeks (myself included) feel that because they've mastered Visio Professional and Adobe Illustrator they have all the requisite talent to perform any graphic design task, including the task of coming up with their own logos and brochures.

After numerous attempts (and actual snickers from customers about how cheesy my logo looks), I've given up thinking I have a visually creative bone in my body. Now I'm actively looking for a good graphic designer in whose hands I intend to place my public image properties and my Web site.

I did my design work when my business was new and money was tight. That was appropriate then, but as my business (and income) has grown, I've gotten to the point where the public image of my firm is more important than the one-time cost of a few thousand dollars for professional design work.

Unless you've always been pretty good at art, I suggest you do the same when the size of your business warrants it. Nothing makes a business look cheesy more than poorly done business graphics and unsophisticated brochures. Spend a little extra money and have these important image properties designed by professionals—or don't try to make them look like they're graphically designed. There's nothing wrong with letterhead in a simple typeface, and with using letters rather than brochures. Graphic design is a good example of when it's better not to try than to do it wrong.

Most graphic designers will produce three prototypes of their work (be that logos, brochures, or a sample Web site), from which you can choose the style you like best. They will then usually complete the rest of the work based on that selected design. Typically, they'll have a copywriter (not a person who grants copyrights, a person who writes copy) interview you about your business. They will then write the blurbs that fill your brochure. If you are a competent writer, feel free to write the copy yourself and then have the designer modify it to fit; otherwise, go with the copywriter's text.

Along with logos and brochures, feel free to ask your designer about T-shirts, automotive graphics if you intend to paint your work vehicle, and business cards. Presenting a unified design among all of your business graphics will make your business appear very professional; it can actually swing a customer's opinion if they're antsy about working with an individual who isn't backed up by a firm.

Make sure your graphic designer gives you a digital copy of your logo properties so you can lay out self-printed business cards, brochures, and stationary. I simply use mine to create word and Visio templates for everything; this works well and looks great coming off a color laser printer. The only logo items I outsource are T-shirts, because for some reason cloth tends to jam my printer.

Professional Associations

I am not a member of any professional organization, so I might not be the right person to write this section. Or perhaps that fact makes me the perfect person to write this section. Anyway, my personal opinion is that professional organizations aren't useful for finding work.

Fun and fulfilling, yes. Useful as a marketing tool, no. If you like the fraternity of a professional association, by all means join one. If you think you're going to get a lot of work by hanging out in a clubroom that is filled with other independent network integrators, you're kidding yourself. They all know how to do what you do. While you may certainly find people willing to sub work to you on occasion, you'll find most of them are actively looking to subcontract for others because they're not that good at the marketing aspect of self-employment.

Perhaps if you could get invited into the professional association of a specialty not related to networking (for example, the American Ophthalmological Society), you'd be in network heaven—half of those people probably need help with their computers. Unfortunately, you can't join that club unless you happen to be an ophthalmologist as well as a network consultant.

If there were such a thing as a general professional association of consultants, it would be a good idea to join to find both work and outsourced help, but you would quickly find that most active consultants are computer consultants anyway. There just aren't many Feng Shui (the Oriental art of harmonious interior design) consultants who are good enough to make a living at it. That's not to say that an association with computer consultants isn't useful; it can be—just not for finding work.

Professional organizations can help you get group rates on life, health, and auto insurance, however; this can save you a considerable amount of money. Be sure to run their rates by an independent insurance agent, however; some associations exist as a front to offer group plans, so watch out. As with anything, caveat emptor.

I'm not a big fan of service clubs. My former boss loved them. She was a member of the Chamber of Commerce, the Rotary Club, the San Diego Association of Small Business Owners, the Women in Business club, the Red-Headed Business Owners Association, and the Association of People Between Five and Six Feet Tall. Other than having lunch with everyone and their dog, these associations never did anything for her; but they did seem to be big on asking for help. Not a single dime of revenue came from anyone in these associations. If you like having lunch, these are the clubs for you. If you are looking for a good marketing venue, you'd have better luck standing on the street corner with a sign that reads "Will Integrate for Food."

Trade Shows

Trade shows are important for network integrators, especially the trade show called Networld+Interop. Why? Because trade shows give you the chance to keep up with the state of networking technology and with the people who make that technology happen.

Independent consulting is very insular. As a consultant, you run the risk of getting yourself into a feedback loop in which you only recommend the solutions you already know well. Then, you'll find that you just get more familiar with these solutions and avoid the scary world of the unknown. One day, you'll pick up a computer magazine and realize you don't know anything about anything that they're talking about, and then you'll realize the world has passed you by. Suddenly, your OS/2 and NetWare skills are not competing well in a Linux and NT world.

I have a friend who's been a NetWare consultant for 15 years. A few months ago, he finally decided to take a course on Windows NT. Now he can't stop raving about how fantastic and amazing an operating system it is, and he claims that he'll never install another NetWare server. Having worked with NT for years, I see its wrinkles clearly, but to him, a server operating system that you can run a Web browser on is astounding. He admitted to me that it was stupid for him to go so long before learning about the software. Had he been attending trade shows consistently, he would have watched the floor space for NT-based products spread like a fungus while the NetWare-related floor space shrank like a leaky balloon.

Trade shows allow you to keep your finger on the pulse of networking. In three days, you can walk around the trade show floor and see literally every major piece of networking technology in existence, both hardware and software. There is no better forum for getting an overview of the industry. When you can watch Linux spread from just the SlackWare booth in the corner in '95 to 25 percent of the floor space in '99, it screams "Learn Linux." When you watch Ethernet switch technology hit with a bang and then dwindle in the face of IP routing, it tells you that for some reason, the industry prefers routing to switching, so maybe you ought to figure out exactly why.

Go to Interop every year. It's held in Atlanta in the fall and Las Vegas in the spring. I recommend going to the show in Las Vegas if for no other reason than to remind yourself how cheesy the place really is. And hey, if you stop by the trade-show bookstore, you just might find a guy who looks like a cross between Sasquatch and Meathead from *All in the Family* signing books.

WARNING Don't think that because you find trade shows useful to attend, it would behoove you to rent a booth. Trade shows are for companies with mass-market products, not specialty custom services like network integration. The only service companies you'll find at them are national service bureaus because trade shows are not an appropriate marketing venue for custom services. When the company I used to work for rented a trade-show booth at a local convention hall, it was a disaster because it didn't net a single dime of revenue.

Conclusion

You'll need to make a number of professional associations when you start your business. You'll need to find a good accountant, a bookkeeper, and a lawyer you can trust.

There's no substitute for knowing other good network integrators as well. Network integration is so wide open that there's no real need for competition among consultants. Because of this you'll find yourself both subbing work to and working as a subcontractor for other consultants quite frequently. It makes you look like a large firm (I insist that subcontractors wear my T-shirts on my sites).

Avoid time wasters like service clubs and many professional organizations. If you have a lot of time to waste, they can be fun, but in my experience with them, they tend to just introduce you to a lot of clingy, favor-needing people who never follow through with actual contracts.

Trade shows, especially Networld+Interop, are a great way to stay in touch with the industry without spending a lot of time digging through magazines. In three days, you can refresh your general knowledge of the entire industry and collect enough business cards to build a small house with.

14 Accountability

"Well, see, the motorcycle is an expense because it gives me an experiential frame of reference for high-speed networking."

This chapter is a transcription of a conversation with Steve Klovanish, a certified public accountant and former agent of the Internal Revenue Service. I've broken it up into headings based on the meanderings of our conversation for your convenience. I have specifically avoided the temptation to interpret any of the advice given, but I have edited the conversation to make it more readable. This advice has also permeated the rest of the book (in interpreted form) in the form of recommendations, so some of it will seem familiar to you.

When I first started my business, I used TurboTax to do my taxes. I walked through their wizard interface, plugged in my numbers, and voila! It generated a completely filled-in tax form. I was happy.

Then I started making money. For my '98 return, I filled in the numbers, printed it out, and voila! I had a heart attack. The bottom line was astonishing. I knew I must have done something wrong, so I went through the numbers again and again. There didn't seem to be any way around it.

On the advice of a friend, I gave my taxes to his accountant to look at. That accountant basically rubber-stamped what TurboTax said and lectured me about not paying my taxes quarterly. It was not the sort of advice I was looking for.

My wife is a bookkeeping consultant. She really liked the accountant who is employed by one of her small business clients. This particular accountant was a former IRS agent (now you see the link to this chapter), and if anybody knew how to help with my tax problem, it was he. So I called him in a panic, and he agreed to take a look at my taxes even though there were only two days left to file.

The next day, he called me in and apologized that he'd only been able to reduce my tax liability by fifteen thousand dollars; he wasn't being facetious, he really thought he could have done better. I couldn't believe it. By finding deductions that the software didn't account for, and by recommending some end-of-year deductible investments, he was able to save me the price of a small car.

Needless to say, he'll be my accountant from now on.

Starting a Business

This first segment of our conversation focuses on starting your business. It covers the various types of businesses from a tax perspective.

What are the tax ramifications of the different methods a consultant could use to start a business?

Well, for people who have been an employee and then have moved over to being self-employed, obviously there are a few different financial vehicles that person can ride.

If they want to just be self-employed, they can file what is called a Schedule C on their individual tax return. The bottom line there is that you have income coming in and you get to write off your expenses using Schedule C to deduct normal business expenses, like your automobile, telephone, rent, utilities, and stuff like that. The main kicker that people have to be aware of is the social security tax implications of being self-employed.

When somebody works for somebody else as an employee, they often complain that they grossed this amount but they only netted this amount on their paycheck. This is because their employer took out this thing called social security and Medicare, which is basically 7.65 percent of their paycheck. Once you leave such employment, you become both the employee and the employer so you're looking at paying 15.3 percent of your net income (after you've deducted all your expenses) to social security and Medicare. In essence, you pay both income tax and the full social security tax on the money you make.

Another vehicle you can ride is incorporation. There are two types of incorporation: the traditional C Corp which is a separate entity that pays its own taxes, and the S Corp, which is a hybrid between the C Corp and self-employment that has tax benefits associated with both.

What are the primary differences between an S Corp and a C Corp? I know that S Corps have a limited number of shareholders, but what are the tax ramifications? Do S Corps pay income tax on undistributed income?

All income is taxed at the individual rate whether it's distributed to the shareholders or not. The main difference between an S Corp and a C Corp is that all earnings in a C Corporation are taxed, and if there are profits left over, then the IRS is going to want those profits that have already been taxed at the corporate level to be distributed to the shareholders. When this happens, the profits are taxed again at the individual level as a dividend, or perhaps as a capital gains tax under certain circumstances. So the difference between a C and an S is that with a C Corp you get double taxation.

Most people don't want to go into the C Corp status for that reason. The other reason is the flowthrough; the S Corporation profit or loss (probably loss when you're starting up a business) flows directly to the shareholders personal income tax. This way, as the shareholder, you get credit for your loss against other income in your personal taxes. With a C Corp, that doesn't happen; the loss just sits on the corporate books and affects only the corporation's taxes.

So an S Corp is, in your opinion, the way to go?

Absolutely. Especially in California. Here, the economy's doing pretty well and there's a lot of tax money sitting up in Sacramento, so the Secretary of State said, "You know what? For the next two years, if you incorporate in California, we're not going to charge you any fees." So now is an excellent time to incorporate, especially if you're already working in a Schedule C status. Of course, you're not going to be tax free, and you'll still be subject to the $800 minimum corporate tax unless you show a loss for the year, but you can at least avoid the fees during 2000 and 2001. That'll save you $600 to $1400 up front. Other states vary.

Do you need a lawyer or a CPA to help you incorporate?

No, you don't have to pay anybody to incorporate you. You can go to a bookstore and pick up a book that has all the forms you need and where to send them; it basically shows you how to incorporate yourself. You can save a bunch of money that way. Those books go into detail on the typical deductions businesses use.

What is the personal income tax difference if you operate as an S Corp?

Well, you have a lot more flexibility in managing your taxes with an S Corp. Primarily, when you're self-employed, you pay both income tax and social security/Medicare on your full net income. With an S Corp, you pay both taxes on your salary, but you pay only income tax on distributions of profit (similar to a dividend in a C Corp). So you'll want to minimize your salary as much as is reasonable and maximize your distributions of profit because you aren't taxed as much on that.

For example, when you start out, you don't know what's going to happen financially. You have some ideas and you hope, but you don't have any concrete evidence that you're going to be making money. During that start-up period, you may not be able to pay a salary to yourself. I recommend to clients who are just getting started that they take a distribution of profits rather than a salary until they have reasonable evidence that the company is profitable. You will pay income tax on that distribution, but you won't pay social security.

Of course, once your business is profitable, you must, by law, pay yourself a salary. Reasonable compensation is a huge gray area with the IRS. There are some people who take a million dollars in salary, and the IRS says that's unreasonable because it's too much. Others take twenty thousand and the IRS says it's unreasonable because it's not enough. In some situations, they want the dividend tax, and in others, they want the payroll tax.

Once you start making more than about $40,000, if you haven't been paying yourself a salary you might want to start worrying about it.

So essentially, the IRS wants to tax you and your business at whatever rate provides them with the most income?

Absolutely. The gray area is again, "What is reasonable compensation?" You may, for example, do $100,000 worth of business but only have a salary of $10,000 or $15,000. You can have considerable expenses or costs of goods sold. Accountants tend to think (and the law has upheld this in court) that reasonable compensation is what you would pay somebody else to do the same work as an employee. Now, San Diego has lower wages than most other large cities, so you can reasonably set your salary here at a lower level than you could other places. The bottom line is that I can hire an accountant to do tax returns for $30,000 per year, so I can justify paying myself $30,000 per year in salary and taking the remainder of my income as a distribution of profits. The self-employment tax on that amount is $4500. If my business has $300,000 in income, and I have $30,000 in salary then I'm paying income tax on $300,000 but self-employment on only $30,000, and because of this, I am saving a tremendous amount of money. You can take out as much money as you want, but the idea is to classify as little of that amount as is reasonable as salary so you don't have to pay self-employment on the entire amount.

What about Limited Liability Companies?

LLCs are strictly about liability; most people utilize them for partnerships where even the general partner doesn't have any liability beyond his investment in the company. For tax purposes, they're like a partnership, which is similar to self-employment.

What's the tax difference between a partnership and self-employment?

Not much, really it's just a different form you fill out. You'll fill out a form 1065 for the partnership, whereas you'd fill out a Schedule C for self-employed.

Accounting On Your Own

This segment of the conversation covers accounting practices and recommendations.

Do you have an accounting software package you recommend?

Most people will opt for something like QuickBooks or Quicken; something with limited flexibility that makes it easy to do the accounting. If you choose to do this, then I recommend getting somebody who is familiar with the software and with accounting to help you set up the chart of accounts and teach you how to use the software. That should take an hour or two, and it's cheaper to use that kind of person than it is to use your CPA because your CPA is going to charge you a lot more for that kind of help. But software is obviously helpful to produce the kinds of information your accountant will want, like a P&L (Profit and Loss statement), balance sheets, cash flow analysis, and even payroll.

People should absolutely use something like QuickBooks if for no other reason than to see where their money is going. You write checks of course, but you don't get a feel for where you're spending it until you look at the whole picture.

If you have other people you have to pay, most accountants will tell you that it's cheaper to use a service (like ADP, Paychex, or whatever company operates in your area than it is to run payroll yourself with a product like QuickBooks Pro, because if you make a mistake in payroll, the penalties are tremendous. Penalties that you avoid paying will more than pay for the entire service for a year.

Payroll is by far the biggest problem that new businesses with employees will have. If they do payroll improperly, they will incur excessive penalties, and if they don't turn that money over to the IRS, it creates tax liens that will affect their credit rating. I've seen more businesses get put out of business by messing up their payroll taxes than for any other tax-related purpose. These are trust fund taxes that are not dischargeable in bankruptcy. They stick with you until they are either paid or negotiated.

Dealing with Taxes

This segment of the conversation discusses tax planning, which is creating a strategy with your accountant to minimize your tax liabilities by understanding tax law and its implications.

Most consultants who are starting out will either use temporary labor or subcontract with other consultants. How do you deal with paying that?

By filling out a Form 1099 at the end of the year and indicating your employee identification number and the amount of non-employee compensation your employee received from you. There's also a transmittal Form 1096 that is sent to the IRS service center where you send your taxes.

But you must watch out for the common-law factors that the IRS can use to retroactively declare a person to be an employee. Most of these factors have to do with how much control you exert over that person. If you pass one or two of those factors, then the IRS can deem that person an employee and you will owe social security taxes for the amount you've paid them.

If you have a person who you have some control over, who comes to your place of business to perform work, or who is not technically a subcontractor, then you should be taking taxes out. The worst case is that you pay the person as a subcontractor, and then that person either doesn't report the income or doesn't pay social security on it, then the IRS can come in and reconvert that person to an employee and make you liable for the taxes. As a former agent, I've seen this scenario happen way too often when people have been too aggressive about paying people as subcontractors.

Often, people who are independent contractors will file for unemployment. The unemployment office will deny their claim because their employer hasn't been paying into workman's compensation. This triggers an automatic investigation, and that person will be converted over as an employee. The people at unemployment aren't concerned with who has to pay; they just point it at the employer and bang, you're it. It's a hard thing to fight.

EMPLOYMENT LAW: IRS FORM 15 CIRCULARS A AND E

These circulars explain employment law. They are available at www.irs.gov, from your local tax office, or at the FTP address shown at the end of this sidebar.

EXCERPTS FROM CIRCULAR E: EMPLOYER'S TAX GUIDE

Generally, a worker who performs services for you is your employee if you can control what will be done and how it will be done. This is so even when you give the employee freedom of action. What matters is that you have the right to control the details of how the services are performed. Generally, people in business for themselves are not employees. For example, doctors, lawyers, veterinarians, construction contractors, and others in an independent trade in which they offer their services to the public are usually not employees. However, if the business is incorporated, corporate officers who work for the business are employees. If an employer-employee relationship exists, it does not matter what it is called. The employee may be called an agent or an independent contractor. It also does not matter how payments are measured or paid, what the payments are called, or if the employee works full or part time.

EXCERPTS FROM CIRCULAR A: COMMON-LAW RULES FOR EMPLOYEE CLASSIFICATION

To determine whether an individual is an employee or an independent contractor under the common law, the relationship of the worker and the business must be examined. All evidence of control and independence must be considered. In any employee-independent contractor determination, all information that provides evidence of the degree of control and the degree of independence must be considered. Facts that provide evidence of the

Continued on next page

degree of control and independence fall into three categories: Behavioral control, financial control, and the type of the relationship as shown below.

Behavioral control   Facts that show whether the business has a right to direct and control how the worker does the task for which the worker is hired include the type and degree of:

➤ Instructions the business gives the worker. An employee is generally subject to the business's instructions about when, where, and how to work. All of the following are examples of types of instructions about how to do work. When and where to do the work, what tools or equipment to use, what workers to hire or assist with the work, where to purchase supplies and services, what work must be performed by a specified individual, and what order or sequence to follow. The amount of instruction needed varies among different jobs. Even if no instructions are given, sufficient behavioral control may exist if the employer has the right to control how the work results are achieved. A business may lack the knowledge to instruct some highly specialized professionals; in other cases, the task may require little or no instruction. The key consideration is whether the business has retained the right to control the details of a worker's performance or instead has given up that right.

➤ Training the business gives the worker. An employee may be trained to perform services in a particular manner. Independent contractors ordinarily use their own methods.

Financial Control   Facts that show whether the business has a right to control the business aspects of a worker's job include:

➤ The extent to which the worker has unreimbursed business expenses. Independent contractors are more likely to have unreimbursed expenses than are employees. Fixed ongoing costs that are incurred regardless of whether the work is currently being performed are especially important. However, employees may also incur unreimbursed expenses in connection with the services they perform for their business.

➤ The extent of the worker's investment. An independent contractor often has a significant investment in the facilities he or she uses in performing services for someone else. However, a significant investment is not necessary for independent contractor status.

➤ The extent to which the worker makes services available to the relevant market. An independent contractor is generally free to seek out business opportunities. Independent contractors often advertise, maintain a visible business location, and are available to work in the relevant market.

Continued on next page

➤ How the business pays the worker. An employee is generally guaranteed a regular wage amount for an hourly, weekly, or other time period. This usually indicates that a worker is an employee, even when the wage or salary is supplemented by a commission. An independent contractor is usually paid by a flat fee for the job. However, it is common in some professions, such as the law, to pay independent contractors hourly.

➤ The extent to which the worker can realize a profit or loss. An independent contractor can make a profit or loss.

Type of relationship Facts that show the parties' type of relationship include:

➤ Written contracts describing the relationship the parties intend to create.

➤ Whether the business provides the worker with employee-type benefits such as insurance, a pension plan, vacation pay, or sick pay.

➤ The permanency of the relationship. If you engage a worker with the expectation that the relationship will continue indefinitely, rather than for a specific project or period, this is generally considered evidence that your intent was to create an employer-employee relationship.

➤ The extent to which services performed by the worker are a key aspect of the regular business of the company. If a worker provides services that are a key aspect of your regular business activity, it is more likely that you will have the right to direct and control his or her activities. For example, if a law firm hires an attorney, is it likely that it will present the attorney's work as its own and would have the right to control or direct that work. This would indicate an employer-employee relationship.

The complete text of these IRS Publication 15 circulars is available at `//ftp.fedworld.gov/pub/irs-pdf/` as files `p15.pdf` and `p15a.pdf`.

What can you do to make sure you don't get into that situation with a subcontractor?

The number one way is to make sure that they also work for other businesses, but each case is different. It depends upon those common-law factors. Again, it's all about your level of control over that person.

So, for instance, if I have a person that I call, and they go where I tell them to go, then they're an employee?

Pretty much, although not necessarily. If you're worried about it, take it up with your lawyer or accountant.

Would writing an explicit contract between the parties help?

I've seen contracts written by top law firms for clients that I've represented before the IRS with this issue, and even they have not stood up because they violated some of the common-law factors. A contract does not secure you against this happening. It doesn't hurt, but it's not an automatic guarantee. The IRS looks at substance over form.

What about when you pay a corporation? Do you need to file a 1099?

No, corporations are exempt from 1099 filings. You just pay them and that's that.

So does that mean that if I hire only corporations, I don't have to worry about employee reconversion?

It's not a factor when you're hiring corporations. If there's an "Inc." behind the business name, the IRS isn't going to look at it. So that's another excellent reason to form your business as an S Corp.

Is there a tax difference between selling services and products?

Not really. The formula remains the same: income minus expenses equals profit.

Collecting sales tax is an issue, however. If you go for a seller's permit or a reseller's license, you have the option of purchasing equipment for resale without paying sales tax on it.

Other people opt to pay the sales tax when they purchase it so they can provide it to their clients without having the reseller's license. That way they don't have to deal with the state Board of Equalization (in California; other states have similar agencies).

Is that legal? It's how I've always done it, by purchasing material tax paid for my clients and then billing them the expense, but I always wondered if I was doing something illegal.

It is absolutely not illegal. In fact, it's one of the best ways to handle passing through material so that you don't have to deal with taxation issues. As long as the sales tax has been paid, it's paid. When you get your reseller's permit, they will give you a book of rules. Read it. If you have any questions, ask the people behind the counter; that's what they're there for.

The bottom line here is that the only way you're going to have a problem with sales tax is if you use a reseller's permit. If you don't use one, you will never have an issue with sales tax.

So unless you're putting through a massive volume of material, you don't see any reason why a consultant or an independent contractor would even bother with a reseller's license?

That's correct. You'll be dealing with a number of tax agencies as business owner: the IRS, the state taxing authority, and the state sales tax board. Among those, the one I'm the most worried about as an accountant and as a former IRS agent is the sales tax board. They are the most powerful organization in terms of their ability to levy fines against you, and they are extremely difficult to defend yourself against. They can look at a few scraps of paper and extrapolate your net sales and what you owe them. If you don't have books and records, or if you're trying to hide books and records, you have no defense. The appeals for them are a kangaroo court; they have almost 100 percent win rate.

With the IRS, the higher you go up, the more fairly your case will be looked at. That's not the case with the state sales tax board. If you can help it, don't deal with sales tax. It's a trust fund tax that will follow you if you ever get behind the ball; so if you have to, always pay it, and always be on time.

What deductions do you recommend that the typical S Corp or self-employed person should take?

The simple answer is any and all. Anything that's remotely related to what you're doing for business is a legitimate business expense.

The main thing for people that are going into business is documentation so you can substantiate the claims you make on your tax forms. That means your receipts and your cancelled checks or credit card statements.

It's not a bad thing to be audited by the IRS. If you have the documentation to substantiate what you put down on that form, you'll have no problems. In this line of work, substantiation will save your soul when it comes down to an audit. When you're audited, you're on record from that point on. If they looked at your returns and the IRS decided that you did fine, and there's not problem with your return, then in the future, if they pull your number to be audited again, they'll see that you passed an audit in the past, then they won't waste their time looking at you again.

So they're going for the most money they can get, and if they see that you've successfully defended your filings in the past, they won't bother?

It's not so much the money as the question: your returns were selected for audit because of some questionable practice, and if you've answered that question in the past to the satisfaction of the IRS, then there's no need to answer it again.

IRS people, contrary to what most people think, aren't motivated to screw you. If there are taxes owed, the agent is happy with that. If there's a refund due, the agent is happy with that. If everything balances out, they're happy with that. It's really about answering the appearance of impropriety than anything else. They're acting purely as impartial investigators.

Being a former agent, and being a regular person, it's public perception to extrapolate on an audit. If you're at a cocktail party it's exciting to say "Oh yeah, I was audited, but I beat those guys at their own game." That's not even the reality of it. Chances are there was a two-day audit, and everyone was cordial.

If you're ever audited, though, don't talk to the IRS. Go through your accountant or your lawyer. On the off chance that you get an overzealous agent, they can extrapolate more information from a naïve individual than they can from an accountant or a lawyer. You don't want to say anything that can be twisted, or accidentally admit to anything.

How to Find a Good Accountant

This section discusses the differences between accountants and tax lawyers, and asks questions about how to find a good accountant.

What's the difference between a CPA and a tax lawyer?

A CPA has passed an exam given by the state board of accountancy that is directly related to accounting and tax law. An attorney has passed the state bar. Basically, a tax attorney looks at the abstract of law, what the law is, whereas an accountant looks at the details of the law to get the financial formulas that apply to the situation.

To be honest, a tax lawyer and a CPA that specializes in taxation are just about the same thing. The only difference is that the lawyer can represent you in tax court and the CPA can't; but if the CPA is doing their job correctly, the case will never go to court. If there is some sort of criminal activity going on a tax return, then you definitely need a tax attorney because then you have attorney-client privilege, which you don't have with a CPA.

How does a person find a good accountant? The referral method?

That's truly how it is. Ask somebody you know. Ask somebody you trust who runs a small business (and who has the same ethics you have) whom he or she recommends. If you truly don't know anybody, then do a couple of interviews with CPAs and go with the one you like best.

It's important for your accountant to match your ethical beliefs. There are accountants who see the law as black and white, and there are accountants who see the law as gray. If you're a black and white person, you won't be comfortable with a gray accountant.

Too many accountants are free flowing with the money that's being spent; if there's $20,000 to be paid, they don't care because it's not their money. But accountants who are customer service–oriented are going to work to save you as much as they can. They'll provide you with options for you and dig deeper to knock that bottom line down for you. Recommendations are the best way to go to find an accountant.

What should you expect to pay an accountant?

Different services are different. Returns are usually a set fee; for example, if you have an S Corp, the accountant would say, "We charge $700 for that." In other cases, accountants might work on contingency if they can get you a return or reduce a liability. It's up to the accountant to be up front. You should shy away from people who are afraid to quote you fees over the phone. If you are explicit with your needs, there shouldn't be any need to come in for an interview because you often feel obligated at that point.

You might look for an accountant who is just starting out because you'll get a break on fees. It also gives you the chance to grow old with your accountant. In the same vein, if you're more conservative, you may find that a young accountant is too aggressive or haphazard. You can also find a lot of mature accountants who worked for large firms or the IRS and have broken out into public accounting. They are often the perfect candidates because they can relate to a broad range of clients, young and old, and they have the experience. At the same time, they are starting their business, so they're less expensive. Once an accountant has all the work they want, price is no longer an issue for them and they won't negotiate. Watch out for the gouge factor with these guys.

I often see clients come in who are afraid to look stupid. There are no stupid questions. Accountants really enjoy the consulting aspect, answering the questions and giving people ease of mind. The result of the work we do is a tax return that the client doesn't want to look at and doesn't want to pay, much less pay an accountant to prepare. So our satisfaction comes from answering questions and providing peace of mind.

So when should a small business owner normally see their accountant? At the end of the year? At tax time?

Once you're ongoing, the main time to talk to your accountant is before the year's end, in November or December. Once you know what your tax situation is going to look like, ask your accountant what you can do before the year's end to minimize your tax liability. The only thing that you can do to reduce your liability after the end of the year is invest in certain retirement plans. Tax planning is more important than tax preparation.

Making Investments

This section discusses investments both as a tax avoidance vehicle and for retirement planning.

As an accountant, do you give any investment advice?

That depends on the qualifications of the accountant. CPAs are financial people, but some follow the markets more than others. A law was passed last year that allows accountants to have a securities license so that they can advise on financial investments like IRAs, cafeteria plans, mutual funds, and so forth. If your accountant is qualified, you should absolutely ask for his advice. He can say, "You've got this pool of capital sitting here that you really should invest in this or that vehicle." Your accountant knows more about your financial situation than a broker would, so they can give much more appropriate advice. Most accountants aren't going to give advice on specific stocks or day trading, even though we all wish we'd had Qualcomm stock at the beginning of 1999.

So you'd look to an accountant for more long-term investment advice?

Absolutely. Accountants make their money off of tax work, so they aren't motivated to churn your investment accounts to make a commission. The more money you make, the more your accountant will make, so they're much more interested in your overall financial picture. A broker will tell you to turn several different ways because he makes a commission on each trade. An insurance agent will tell you that you have to get his latest whole life policy because his commission is highest on it. You're not going to get a straight shot with people who are paid based on something other than your overall financial position.

What standard retirement vehicles should a person look at?

Self-employed people should be looking at a SEP IRA. A SEP IRA allows you to invest 15 percent of your income up to $30,000 per year. Most IRAs are for people who are not self-employed, and they're limited to $2000. How much income you make as an employee also limits your IRA deduction.

There's no big cost to having a SEP IRA, but depending upon how you invest it, like in a defined benefit plan, there are administration fees that are costly to the tune of like $2000 per year. So most people who are self-employed do a SEP or a Keogh, which has different percentages up to 25 percent.

If your accountant doesn't know about these specific vehicles, he should refer you out to a bank or a brokerage.

Do you have the ability to manage the IRA yourself?

Yes, you can manage the IRA yourself. You can put it in a mutual fund, into a stock fund, or individual investments. When you fill out your application, be it at Merrill Lynch or Bank of America, they will ask you what you want to do with the money in the IRA. You can say you want 25 percent in a bond fund, 25 percent in a stock fund, or whatever. You control the money; you don't get to see it, but you control it.

The bottom line is that it's a tax deduction that reduces your income tax. The taxes come out when you remove the money at retirement.

What's the difference between different IRAs?

A lot of people get involved with Roth IRAs, which are nice, but they aren't tax-deferred. You pay tax on the money before it goes into the IRA, so you don't get the immediate deduction, but you don't have to pay tax when you pull it out.

In my opinion there really is no financial difference between a Roth and a SEP IRA. People won't have a lot of deductions when they're older because their house will be paid off and the kids will be gone, but their income will be lower as well once they're retired. When you're retired, you'll be able to take out $25,000 in today's dollars and not pay any income tax on it because of the standard deduction and your personal deductions.

It's about the time value of money. Whether you use a Roth or a SEP depends on where you feel you're going to be in the future. Is a dollar worth more today than it will be worth in the future? Essentially, with a SEP you're investing the tax you would have paid and earning interest on it as well.

Most small business owners want to get the deduction and worry about future taxes when they get there.

What about buying assets to reduce your taxes?

Well, the main thing is that a lot of people think that if they buy something they get a deduction for it. That's true, but I say it's better not to spend the money in the first place. If you're in a 28 percent bracket, you're paying a dollar for something and reducing your tax liability by 28 cents. If you don't really need that item, you're wasting your money. You're better off paying the tax.

I'll say this to people who own homes: the devil really isn't the IRS, it's the bank. Yeah, they get a mortgage deduction, but they're still paying the interest. You're getting a 28-cent refund for every dollar spent on interest. It's far cheaper not to spend the money on interest in the first place. The best investment you can make is to pay your home off as fast as possible. The deduction isn't worth nearly as much as not paying the mortgage interest.

There's a new Section 179 deduction that allows $19,000 for home office deductions, so people run out and buy a $5,000 computer, office copier, and other assets because they've got this deduction. If they need them, great, but it's still your money you're spending. A lot of people don't get the concept that purchasing something just because it's a deduction doesn't make it free. You're still spending the money; you just aren't paying tax on it.

Conclusion

Form your business as an S Corporation (or incorporate as soon as possible if you're already operating) both to reduce the amount of taxes you have to pay and to eliminate the possibility that the IRS might reconvert you as an employee of one of your clients. Forming as an S Corp allows you to avoid paying self-employment tax on your entire income, and it allows you to avoid the double-taxation problem of the traditional C Corporation. Limited liability corporations do not provide any significant tax benefit.

Use QuickBooks or Quicken to handle your day-to-day accounting needs, and use the cash flow reporting mechanism in that software to watch your financial outflow. This software can create all the reports your accountant will need to file your taxes.

If you can avoid it, don't use a reseller's permit. Purchase items tax paid so that you won't have to deal with your state's sales tax board. Never play around with trust fund taxes like sales tax and payroll tax. More businesses are shut down by tax agencies for this reason than for any other.

Find an accountant who matches your personality. If you aren't happy with your current accountant, find somebody else. As with any consulting arrangement, the referral method is the best way. Talk to your accountant before the year's end so you can take advantage of last-minute deductions before they're no longer available to you.

Use a SEP IRA to reduce your taxable income and provide for your retirement. You can manage the money yourself, and since it's invested before taxation, it'll grow faster. You'll pay the tax on it when you take it out during your retirement, when you'll be in a lower tax bracket than you are now.

15 The Law

"It's just really unusual to meet someone whose hourly rate is higher than mine."

This chapter is the transcripts of question-and-answer dialogs with Marc S. Bragg, Esq., the general counsel for a client of mine. These transcripts are paraphrased in most cases (to get rid of the "umm," "ahh," and "what were we talking about"), but they are otherwise uninterpreted—you're getting advice straight from the source. This advice has also permeated the rest of the book in interpreted form as recommendations, so some of it will seem familiar to you. In any case, you should also consult with an attorney of your choosing regarding complex issues.

LEGAL TERMINOLOGY

This chapter contains quite a bit of legalese, so I thought (actually, my editors thought) I should start with a terminology sidebar you can refer to in case you need to.

Actual Damages Actual measurable injury sustained by the plaintiff. For example, if a plaintiff's computer was destroyed by a defendant, the replacement cost of the computer and any unique attachments or unique software (if that value can be determined with reasonable certainty) are actual damages. The actual loss is synonymous with *compensatory damages*. Generally, these damages are "direct"; that is, they are examples of the type of injury that arises naturally from a contract breach and can be ordinarily expected to result from the breach.

Arbitration A non-judicial process for resolving civil disputes, wherein the parties agree to resolve their differences without the rigors of full-blown litigation. Often, this process ends up resulting in a resolution that is more like a compromise. The parties can agree to be bound by the arbitrator's decision, which is called a *binding arbitration*. If the arbitration is non-binding and one party doesn't agree, they can appeal the arbitrator's decision to the regular court and participate in the generally lengthy and expensive process of civil litigation.

Breach of Contract Failure to perform a condition or term of the contract.

Consequential Damages   In this context, these damages may result from the consultant's breach of a contract and include any loss that results from the general or particular requirements of the client, which the consultant knew about (or, given the consultant's expertise, should have known about) at the time the contract was entered into. If the consultant provides a product, these damages are those that cause injury as a result of any breach of warranty.

Continued on next page

Contract   In the legal sense, a contract is promises between two or more persons obligating each to do a particular thing. In the practical sense, it is the writing that contains the parties' agreement, the essential terms: competent participants, subject matter, consideration, and mutuality of agreement and obligation. Most contracts applicable to consulting would be *conditional contracts*—executory contracts in which some future act is to be done and in which performance depends on particular conditions.

Damages   An amount of money awarded to a person injured by another. This is the monetary compensation, or indemnity, recoverable in court by a person that has sustained a loss, the amount of which is determined by the nature of the harm, detriment, or injury, whether to the person, property, or rights, resulting from a wrongful act or omission.

Defendant   The party defending a lawsuit.

Discovery   The phase of litigation during which each party gets the opportunity to learn what the other party knows and what evidence they possess. Usually, during this phase, each party learns what the other party believes, or will contend, actually occurred.

Expectation Damages   Synonymous with consequential damages. For example, if the plaintiff expected to go online with an e-commerce Web site and could prove sales, but the developer failed to complete it (and time was of the essence, and the developer was so informed), the developer could be liable for the amount of money the client could prove to have made with the site.

Exposure   The practical limit of monetary liability, or loss of rights, as defined by the total amount a party could actually pay, or the intellectual property rights that could be lost.

Fraud   Deceptive entry into a contract, whether by words, action, or omission to act in the presence of a duty to do so. Fraud occurs when one of the parties to a contract knowingly and intentionally decides to misrepresent themselves or their intent in order to deceive the other party, and the other party relies on the misrepresentation.

Incidental Damages   Damages that are commercially reasonable expenses incurred as a result of a breach. For example, these may be the additional commercially reasonable costs a client might incur in completing a job if the consultant does not do so in a timely manner and the client is not otherwise in breach of the contract.

Lawsuit   A legal action commenced in court and arising from a civil dispute.

Liability   A legal obligation as to all character of debts or obligations.

Continued on next page

Limitation of Damages   A contract term limiting the amount of damages in the case of breach. This may be accomplished by identifying *liquidated damages*—a predetermined amount, reasonable in light of the anticipated harm that could be caused by a breach when that harm would be difficult to prove. A term fixing an unreasonably large liquidated damage is void and construed as a penalty.

Litigation   The process of a lawsuit.

Negligence   In the legal sense, this is an unreasonable action in the circumstances or an omission to act in the presence of a legal duty to do so, and it results in harm to the property, person, or the rights of another.

Oral Contract   A contract that is not in writing, partly in writing partly verbal, or that is incomplete in the writing and then completed by oral expression, or a written contract modified later by words.

Proximate Damage   The natural and consequent, or foreseeable result of an action. If a foreseeable damage can be reasonably certain to occur from a particular action, a legal duty may arise precluding the taking of that action.

Plaintiff   The party suing.

Punitive Damages   An award intended to punish the defendant (for example, fraudulent activity). Punitive damages are generally an amount sufficient to teach the defendant a lesson and must be awarded relative to the defendant's worth, as well as the actual or compensatory damages sustained by the plaintiff.

Reliance Damages   Damages that consider an amount necessary to return the party to the position occupied prior to the harm. When that involves property, or changes in the position of the injured party that cannot be reversed (for example, old computers thrown out, or software that was not saved is deleted), then a monetary equivalent may be assessed. Or, for example, if a plaintiff lost a certain amount of money because of a bug in software written by the defendant, reliance damages in the amount of the loss, if ascertainable, could be awarded in a lawsuit.

Speculative Damages   Damages that are not reasonably certain, but are rather conjecture, contingent, or improbable (not recoverable).

Tort   A private injury or wrong, other than a contract breach, for which the law provides a remedy. Three elements are common to all tort actions: 1) a legal duty owed by the defendant to the plaintiff, 2) breach of the duty, and 3) damage as a proximate result of the breach.

Continued on next page

Trust-Fund Taxes   Generally employee withholding taxes—money which is never property of the business but which the business is required to collect, hold in trust, and then pay over to the applicable authority. Also includes sales tax.

Venue   The county where the court with jurisdiction over a particular case is located.

Written Contract   In legal terms, a legally enforceable written agreement.

Marc S. Bragg is a general practice lawyer whom I know through mutual association with the same client. Mr. Bragg is working on the forefront of technological law on cases and research that help establish the rights of intellectual property owners in cyberspace; he is familiar with both sides of these issues. A body of very interesting (and not always intuitive) case law is developing in that area, and he shares this at the end of this section. If you perform any sort of Web development, that case law will be of particular interest to you.

I've interrupted the flow of the conversation with headings that indicate where the discussion is going, mostly because my editors don't like long tracts of undifferentiated text. You may find it handy to reference certain elements of the discussion.

Contract Components

This portion of the dialog concerns contracts: why they're necessary, what they should consist of, and what makes a good contract.

What is a contract?

A contract is simply an agreement that is enforceable in court between two parties to do or refrain from doing certain things.

Why is a contract important?

Well, in order to receive any benefit from a bargain that you make, there needs to be some understanding between the people bargaining of what is expected from each side. Essentially, when you work and provide services, either as an employee or as a consultant, there is some agreement, some understanding between you and the person paying, regarding the exchange of your services for their money. A contract, a clear contract, is important in order for you to receive your benefit of that bargain with the least amount of hassle, and if there is a hassle, to reduce your costs in that dispute. If the contract is an oral contract, if there's nothing on paper, it can tend to be ambiguous and vague; people's memory of what was said tends to fade, and interpretations of meaning can vary considerably. Also, if you are selling goods, the law recognizes certain restrictions on being paid for those goods when the contract is not in writing.

Written contracts are important because they dispel ambiguity and they specify (hopefully) those things that are subject to misinterpretation. The black and white doesn't tend to change as quickly.

There are basically two types of contracts (whether the agreement is in writing or not) in the sense that some contracts are unilateral one-sided (a promise), and others are reciprocal or bilateral, (a promise in exchange for a promise). Most work contracts are reciprocal in that they provide a promised payment for promised work, yet they are also executory, in that there is some work to be performed, in the future. If the payment was made in full prior to the work, we might call that unilateral, there is now only a promise of performance that is due.

What legal terms are important to include in a contract?

Basic or essential terms must be present for there to be a legal contract. All other terms are to define the intent of the parties. The essential terms, at a minimum, would identify the parties, the object of the contract, legal consideration, and mutuality of agreement and obligation. Additional terms become necessary as the law changes to fit and define the rights of the parties in varying circumstances. For instance, especially for consulting contracts where the needs of the client sometimes cannot be identified until the project is underway, there should be provisions stating that the contract constitutes the entire understanding of the parties (in other words, except what is written in the contract, there is no obligation on the part of either party), and that the contract can only be amended by something in writing. This prevents a plaintiff from claiming that some further oral contract, like a promise you made or something you said you'd do in passing, or one you made out of frustration during the day when a particular part of the project became impossible due to unknown and unforeseeable events, becomes a stipulation of the contract.

It's always good to include payment of attorney's fees (i.e., that the losing party pays all attorney's fees) because that is not assumed by default.

It is wise to include terms that require any dispute in connection with the contract or its object go to arbitration for resolution. Arbitration is a more friendly and less expensive method of resolving a dispute. It means essentially that both parties agree to accept the opinion of the arbitrator as to how to resolve the dispute rather than going to court. In a binding arbitration, the decision of the arbiters is final. In a non-binding arbitration, the decision can still be appealed in court, but since, in most cases, the arbiter's impartial decision is generally believed to be the same result as the judge or the jury would achieve; most businesspeople don't pursue the issue past arbitration if their motives are purely economic and professional. Arbitration generally provides for a three-lawyer panel, though single panels are not unusual, as well as the plaintiff's and defendant's lawyer. Resolution time is generally quicker, and if settlement is a possibility, an arbitration can often crystallize the benefits of settling at an earlier stage. It's also nice, from a consultant's point of view, to cap the damages to the face value of the contract, so that the plaintiff can't recover damages in excess of what they've paid you.

There are many other terms that might also be considered, but again, these need to be tailored to specific needs.

Why do contracts specify where the contract will be adjudicated?

For the party's convenience. If you don't specify the state of jurisdiction, and the venue (county) for arbitration or court, then you could wind up being forced to travel to the other party's venue if you get sued. As long as you specify in the terms of the contract where the contract will be adjudicated, you can avoid this additional time and expense drain. If not, certain rules will apply to determine the venue, including such factors as where the contract was entered into, where the harm occurred, where the evidence is located, the convenience of the witnesses, and where the plaintiff and defendant are located. You don't want to have to travel to your client's home venue to either sue them or in response to a lawsuit because then they get an automatic cost and convenience advantage.

What does the term Implied Warranty mean?

In many states (especially California), there are merchantability warranties, and even where they are not expressly stated in the contract, the law says they might be implied for the benefit of your client. The reason being that there is a belief: you being the expert, are in a better position to know whether what you are designing or building is capable of serving the needs as described by the client, and if not, then, you shouldn't skirt that responsibility just because there is no clause in the contract requiring you to do so; the object of the contract, what you are doing, is the most important part from the client's point of view. Merchantability warranties assure the client that what you are producing or have sold is suitable for the intended use. You can limit implied warranties by providing a specific warranty, or by including a waiver of implied warranty, but in the absence of any language on this warranty, it is generally implied. Waivers of implied warranty are only effective to a point, however. They become ineffective when you simply can't perform the task you said you could perform. At that point, the plaintiff can claim that the waiver simply wasn't executed in good faith. Also, in some consumer situations in certain states, merchantability is not waivable. Generally, consultants work in a commercial environment, both parties are in the contract for business purposes, and so the merchantability can be waived. This is especially important where the functionality of your part of the services is dependent on the proper performance of some other supplier.

What does good faith actually mean in relation to contracts?

It is intangible. No formal or technical meaning. It means that you are operating from a reasonable basis; in other words, that you honestly believe what you are saying or representing, without purpose or intent to take unfair advantage in entering into the contract, and in the performance of the contract, that the effort you've made is what anybody in your industry would have exerted.

Does a contract really have to spell out everything? I use a simple half page statement of terms, but I've seen other contracts that look more like a book. Which is better?

Small contracts are fine in most cases. When both parties are operating in good faith (that is, neither party actually sets out to screw the other party from the get go), a small or simple contract with essential terms and clarity of purpose is more than sufficient. It all comes down to the intent of both parties. If the intent is to get reasonable work performed, than nothing more than the few specific terms we've talked about is really necessary. However, if one of the parties is intent upon being litigious, cheap, or vengeful, that's where a longer contract offers more protection. In those rare cases, however, you're still going to spend a lot of money in litigation no matter how the contract is written.

What kind of problems do people run into with contracts that they've written?

You don't know how good a contract is until it gets tested in court. Every term in a contract is always open to two interpretations: the interpretation of the plaintiff and the interpretation of the defendant.

The most important purpose of a contract is to make sure that the intent of both parties has been expressed.

From the perspective of a consultant, the most important things to spell out are scope of work, satisfaction for completion, and terms of payment: What am I required to do? When is it to be accomplished? How do we agree I've satisfactorily completed it? How much are you going to pay me? How often am I going to be paid? What are the conditions of receiving payment?

From the perspective of the client, the most important terms are terms of completion. One of the best things you can do in a contract is spell out the conditions under which the contract has been completed as a set of definitive test results. In the contract, specify a set of test criteria that can be shown to definitely satisfy the contract. When each testable criterion has been accomplished, an agent of the client should sign off on that test element, indicating that it has been completed and accepted. This way, when the complete set of test criteria have been accomplished, the contract is definitely over and final payment is unambiguously due. The contract should include agreement on what sort of standards should be applied to the testing as applicable. If the sign-off cannot be obtained, an objective mechanism, where possible, should be identified to satisfy the condition.

Can you think of any specific problems you've seen with contracts in court?

Ambiguity and vagueness are the two biggest enemies in interpreting contracts. If contracts are clear, the language is normal English, and it adequately covers the subject, term or condition, no interpretation is necessary and no oral evidence is necessary to ascertain its meaning or the intent of the parties. The next biggest problem is the contract doesn't cover a problem that arises.

You know, things like when somebody takes on too much work and can't complete it, or when somebody else needs to modify the contract because what they agreed upon initially no longer works for them. Finally, the next biggest problem is generally the parties. Emotions run high.

You should consider including terms for how you're going to modify the contract, for example, in the case of change orders or other circumstances that might change during the performance of a contract. This is especially important in the fast moving field of technical network consulting, where technology changes so quickly that what was appropriate at the start of work could be completely obsolete at the finish.

Advice for Starting a Business

This portion of the dialog concerns those legal issues you should take care of when you start your business: what type of business you run, the importance of various insurances, legal issues surrounding employees, and finding a lawyer if you need one.

Selecting a Type of Business

Similar to the discussion in Chapter 14, this section shows a lawyer's perspective on establishing a business.

Before a person begins contracting, what legal issues should they consider?

Presumably, you're in business to make money. Equally important, if not more so, is keeping the money when you get it. The most basic consideration is how you're going to conduct your business so that you can protect either what you earn, or what you create. There are various forms of business entities: sole proprietorships, partnerships, corporations, or limited liability companies.

What difference does the type of business make from a legal perspective?

In a sole proprietorship, the proprietor, you, has all the liability. Everything you own as an individual is subject to attachment to a lawsuit. This means that if you lose a lawsuit, some or all of your assets, depending on the amount of the judgment and the value of your assets, would be transferred to the winning party. A sole proprietor operates as his business—there is no legal difference between the individual and his business.

In a partnership, you have two or more people owning the business as partners; they share equal or distributed rights in management, operations, profits and losses. It's as if each person was a sole proprietor in business with each other person. Each is generally equally responsible for all debts and obligations and acts of the other within the scope of the partnership activity; therefore, all the assets of all partners can be subject to a lawsuit and attached by a judgment.

There's a special variety of partnership called a limited partnership. In this type, general partners act as the managing or operating partners, and the limited partners are partners that share in the profits and losses, like investors, but they do not manage or operate the business. Consequently, while the general partners retain personal liability, the limited partners limit their liability to the amount they've invested in the business. If a limited partner takes a role in management, their characterization changes regardless of what they might call themselves, and they can be construed as general partners and be equally liable with the other general partners. Though rare, if you share in the profits and losses of a business, have some authority, or appear to have that authority with the consent of the known owners, if not clearly spelled out, you may be construed as a general partner to third parties.

Another type of company is the limited liability company, which is similar to a corporation on the issue of liability protection, but rather than shareholders, it has members that are entitled to their respective interest in its assets, and it affords protection for personal assets otherwise endangered by company liability. Starting an LLC typically requires less paperwork than a corporation; and essentially, they're like liability limited partnerships. However, there are taxation issues with LLCs that are not completely resolved—how tax benefits are assigned either to the LLC or to the individual members. The rules may vary from state to state.

Finally, there's the corporation, which is still believed to be the best vehicle for protection of personal assets from company associated liability. In any activity for which the corporation is liable, only the assets of the corporation can be attached.

What's the difference between a C Corp and an S Corp?

In an S Corp, the income and losses (but not liability) pass through to the shareholders. In a C Corp, income and losses stop at the corporation, which receives its own taxation benefits. Profit from the corporation, is paid via dividends to the shareholders. Shareholders can also be employees, in which case they can also be paid salary as an employee. Generally, the decision to switch from an S to a C depends on the structure and tax advantages.

What sort of business should a consultant start as?

Depends on the individual's circumstances. My advice would nearly always be to begin as a corporation because of the liability protection even though it's a little more of a headache. I would start as an S Corp since you get the liability protection and it's easier to manage the finances. Typically, when you start a business, your corporation has no track record, history, or credit. You're probably going to have to sign for credit personally anyway, which means your personal assets could be attached in a recovery attempt associated with any loans you acquire; however, as long as you adhere to the corporate formalities (that is, holding yearly meetings, keeping minutes, filing proper tax returns, and not taking your money out of the corporate checking account, and so forth), you're protected from liability generally as to your clients. If you fail to act as a corporation, or respect the corporate formalities, you could lose the liability protection and be individually responsible; those instances are rare.

General Liability Insurance

This section describes the legal advantages of various types of insurance including general liability insurance. See Chapter 7 for more information on insurance.

Do you have any other legal advice for a consultant?

Buy an umbrella general liability insurance policy for the work you do, with specific riders for those areas where you have exposure. A knowledgeable insurance agent can help you figure out what those areas are and the policy limits of coverage you should carry.

According to some advice I've heard from people who aren't lawyers, if you're incorporated you shouldn't worry about GL because in the worst case, the corporation is lost, not your assets. Is that true?

Not really. First, as your company grows, your corporation acquires assets. Money in the bank, equipment, cars, etc. Also, why ruin a successful corporation with a lawsuit when insurance would pick up the bill? Finally, what if the plaintiff "pierces" the corporate veil and you become personally liable? Insurance premiums are generally very inexpensive compared to judgments when it's time to pay. If the plaintiff can show recklessness in the operation of the business or evidence that you actually operate improperly, your liability protection is gone and you would need insurance to protect you.

What sort of problems could cause a corporation to lose its liability protection?

When you incorporate, you must hold an organizational meeting, first shareholders' meeting, and a directors' meeting to elect officers and directors, and issue shares. If you're not recording things properly, if you aren't keeping the minute book properly, if you aren't holding yearly meetings, if you aren't paying your franchise or payroll taxes, or if you're taking money directly out of the corporation for personal use, you could jeopardize your corporate protection. In those cases, it may become possible to pierce the corporate veil and attach the assets of the owners. So in all these cases, general liability insurance comes into play. It's cheap protection—like they say, "insurance is always cheap when you need to exercise it, but expensive when you don't."—in other words, insurance you don't use seems like a waste of money until the one time that you need it.

How much general liability insurance should a person buy?

The short answer is the total value of your assets. If you're working in an area where the amount of damage you could cause could be substantially more than the value of your assets, you should increase your liability insurance because you don't want those judgments following you around. In essence, it's whatever you think your exposure is.

Employees

This section explains the law as it pertains to employees and employment insurance.

Any other advice for starting a business?

If you have employees, you must carry workers' compensation insurance. A lot of people don't realize that for some reason and don't carry it, only to find a person gets injured on the job, and the employer has not only broken the law, but now has exposure.

Another thing that's critical if you have employees is handling withholding taxes correctly. You've got to make sure your withholding tax forms (Form 941) are filed correctly and that the taxes are paid in. Witholding taxes are the type of taxes that will follow you around forever if there is a judgment against you. Trust-fund taxes are one of the very few things you can't even discharge in a bankruptcy, so it's critical that you take proper care of withholding taxes.

Small business owners tend to try to use whatever money is available now thinking that they'll pay taxes later. When later never comes because the business is failing, they've dug themselves a hole they can't get out of.

If you hire subcontractors, or independent contractors, there is no withholding requirement on your part, and no workers' compensation coverage necessary. But be sure they are independent contractors. You need an agreement that clearly identifies their capacity as such. Even then, however, an individual providing you with their services could be construed as an employee with all the attendant responsibilities. How do you know? Various facts come into play, but primarily the issues considered are: 1) do they determine their own hours of operation? 2) do they determine the order and manner of work flow? 3) are they paid by the hour or by job? 4) are there particular skills required to perform the job, or is it unique? and 5) are they required to be at the employer/contractor's premises to perform the job?

Finding a Lawyer

This section explains how to find a lawyer. As with any professional service, referrals are the recommended method.

How should a person try to find a lawyer if they need one?

Referrals are the best method, the same way you'd find a consultant. If you have a little time, go to a law library and see who's done good work in your area. For basic incorporation and contracts, most lawyers can help, but when you start getting into more complex larger jobs, you'll want somebody with transactional experience.

You can go to a large firm (or even to some boutique law firms) and find specialists in very narrow fields of law, but they're going to be a lot more expensive, and the quality of advice you get isn't necessarily going to be any better than a more general practice lawyer well versed in the specialty. A general practice lawyer is fine to get started.

Would this person be considered a corporate lawyer?

A lot of lawyers could be called corporate lawyers. It used to be that the lawyers who were employees of corporations were corporate lawyers; these days, if a lawyer practices in the area of corporate law, they're a corporate lawyer.

Liability

This section explains the legal issues arising when a client has a problem with the work you've done.

Most starting consultants are worried about the issue of their own competence. Is there a way to gauge when you're ready to start?

Competence is a big issue. When you hold yourself out as a professional, even in an unlicensed field like network integration where there's not a lot of standardization, there's still the contract issue: what you said in the contract that you could do, your client's reliance on that representation, and often, the unspoken belief that you have the expertise to accomplish the task.

What types of damages are there? What can you be sued for?

There are tort damages and there are contract damages. You hit me in your car, that's a tort. You get frustrated with your client's computer and use a hammer to correct the software; that's a tort. If you breach a term of the contract, that could lead to contract damages. Tort damages come into play when there's no agreement or contract between the parties involved and the law recognizes a consequent injury.

Typically, in a contract, your going to be dealing with contract damages, although tort damages can come into play in certain situations, such as interfering with someone else's contract. The contract damages are dependent upon the nature of the agreement. There are different types of damages. There are expectation damages, there are reliance damages, and then there are actual damages.

Actual damages are self-evident: they can be expressed as "how much did I lose?" Reliance damages can be expressed as "I lost this much because I relied upon you to provide something." Expectation damages are lost opportunities, where one could prove with reasonable certainty that an opportunity for profit was lost due to a breach of a contract term. For example, if your client could prove you were aware they were depending on you to complete a specific job that was predicate to their completion of their contract, that you knew of this, and the damage was ascertainable, you could be liable for their lost opportunity.

Tort damages are for things like misrepresentation, negligence, or intentional fraud. In a case of intentional fraud or intentional misrepresentation, punitive damages can come into play. The worst case is when somebody can prove intentional misrepresentation or fraud against you.

Fraud is when you intentionally intend to deceive someone, and they reasonably rely upon you. So, for example, if I told you I could deliver software when you knew I couldn't do it, that's not fraud because it's not reasonable reliance. To prove fraud, a plaintiff has to prove intent to deceive, which is different than negligent misrepresentation ("I thought I could, but I can't."); they have to prove reasonable reliance; and they have to prove that damages have occurred.

What to Do When Faced with Lawsuits

This section details what you should do if a client sues you. Although I've never been sued, nor do I know a consultant who has, consultants are exposed to the possibility of lawsuits based on their performance.

If a consultant gets sued, what should they do?

If they have insurance, tender the claim to the insurance carrier. That's what general liability insurance is for. The insurance company will typically hire a lawyer to defend it, settle it, or do whatever they feel is appropriate. When you buy insurance coverage, because the carrier pays for your conduct, or harm, they generally have the right to settle the claim, even if you believe you were in the right.

There are different types of exclusions from general liability policies, the most common of which are misrepresentation and fraud. In these cases, you're acting outside the scope of your policy, in which case, the insurance company will generally deny coverage or defend with a reservation of rights. This means that if the insurance company (or if tendered by the insurance company to the court for a determination of your and your insurance company's rights under the insurance agreement) determines that fraud or misrepresentation (or any other exclusion) has occurred, then you may owe the insurance company the money they've spent defending you, and they will not be required to continue.

If it's a covered claim, they'll generally hire a lawyer and cover the costs associated with defending the lawsuit. Typically, you convey settlement authority to the insurance company, so if they decide to settle, even if you feel you've done nothing wrong and you don't want to settle, they have the right to do it because it can reduce their costs.

When you take out a general liability policy, try to retain the right to choose your lawyer if you have a preference. Insurance companies will generally allow this unless they have a good reason not to. In that case, you can limit your costs in terms of time and distraction.

What if you don't have general liability insurance?

You need to find a lawyer. If it's a small claims matter—less than $7000 or $8000 depending upon the state—then it's usually settled without lawyers. For example, you can't take a lawyer into small claims court in California, but in Pennsylvania you can. In most small claims matters, you retain an automatic appeal right, everybody gets to air their claim, and the judge typically cuts damages somewhat fairly within the limits of the law.

For beginning consultants, most contractual damages should be small claims matters unless you land a big contract at the outset. Often, large companies have pre-prepared contracts drafted by their attorneys. You will want to have your attorney review and revise. Many people feel that because a contract is typed or pre-printed, it can't be modified. Any contract can be modified before it is signed, either by being re-printed or in handwriting. Don't be bullied into accepting terms that are unfair just because the contract is on a form that you're told can't be changed.

Retaining a lawyer is going to cost anywhere from $150 to $350 per hour. If you sue a client, you may find it costs you $30,000 to recover $20,000, depending upon how aggressive the defendant wants to be. You have to look at the case, look at the defendant, counsel with your attorney, and ask yourself "What's the cost of going through the process, and when it's all over, am I actually going to come out ahead?" Is the lost business time worth the investment?

Litigation vs. Arbitration

This section discusses litigation, the process of a lawsuit, and arbitration, a simpler alternative that can be used in contract disputes to lower costs.

What does the average contract cost to litigate?

It depends entirely upon the complexity of the disagreement. If it's a simple case of not being paid for services that both parties agree were provided, then litigation is a simple matter.

More often, there's disagreement about what was delivered, and that makes litigation more difficult. Often there's a misunderstanding between the parties about what was supposed to be delivered. The consultant delivers what he thinks is within or defined by the scope of work, but the client isn't satisfied because that's not what they had in mind, or it doesn't function as was first thought or expected.

In those cases, the parties may have to retain experts to put a valuation on the delivered product, to determine how closely the product conforms to the scope of work, and so forth. Experts can typically cost between $3500 and $5000 up to the time of the trial, and then during the trial they're paid by the hour. You'll need an expert witness for each area of technology involved in the contract, so it can get quite expensive, and if it's a new area of expertise, it is all the more expensive and difficult to obtain.

This is why it's so crucial for the contract to clearly define what's expected and to define completion criteria that are not subjected to the discretion of the customer, because, in the case of a establishing a Web site, for example, you could go on forever without making the customer happy.

Hopefully, it wouldn't cost more than $10,000 to litigate a $50,000 contract, but it easily could and actually depends entirely on how ornery the defendant is, and how efficient the attorney you hire is. If the defendant is unresponsive, or if they've got an attorney who is a real jerk and they dig their heels in, then you have to keep going to court to compel them to move the process along. Suddenly, you are looking at a year and a half to two years, or more if a complex case, before you're going to get any kind of settlement or your day in court. Everything can become very messy very quickly. Clarity up front is the best solution.

This is also why arbitration clauses are so important; they can reduce the size of this mess. You can get in front of an arbitration panel of three attorneys pretty quickly and everything may be resolved much faster than in the litigation process. If your client is unwilling to arbitrate at the inception of the contract, you should pause and ask yourself, and them, "why?"

Am I right in assuming that just because you've specified an arbitration clause in the contract, that the parties haven't given up their right to litigate in the event that they aren't happy with the arbitrated decision?

That depends on whether you agreed to binding or non-binding arbitration. If you contract to binding arbitration, the decision of the arbiter can't be appealed back to court to start over again. Any judgment, however, can be lodged with and enforced by the court.

Even non-binding arbitration is useful however. Most people, once they suffer through the process and realize how much effort and money they've spent, tend to acquire some business maturity, and aren't going to appeal the arbitration, especially when the odds are that they'll achieve the same result anyway. Individuals, attorneys and companies that are litigious are, unfortunately, a cost of doing business.

Completion and Getting Paid

This section describes the other side of lawsuits: cases where you might need to sue a customer who refuses to pay you. It includes information on specifying completion criteria that will make it difficult for a deadbeat customer to defend themselves.

How could a consultant define completion criteria that aren't subjective?

For example, in the case of a creative effort like creating a Web site, it's typical to contract for three efforts, and out of those three efforts, the client agrees to select one, or the contract is terminated. If you're busy, you can charge for these efforts, if not, they might be gratis. This gives the customer choice, but at the same time limits the amount of work you're on the hook for.

Other ways to define completion are to stipulate that the client will provide a design, and in the absence of that design, they get whatever you provide whether they like it or not. It's hard to put test criteria on design since there's not really any qualitative metric that could be applied to it, unless it is somehow technological, mechanical, or capable of measurement and there are benchmarks that can be applied.

Other methods include having mileposts along the way, or having the customer review your progress along the way; this way you get the customer's signoff during the creative process as much as is reasonably possible. This signoff confirms to you that they're approving your continuance down this line of development, and limits the amount of "rework" you might have to do. You're best off getting paid as you reach and satisfy these milestones, if you can work it into the contract, because this limits the amount that you can be ripped off—if the customer has problems paying, you'll know at the first milestone rather than at the end. This method should also limit the amount of the contract that's in dispute to the most recent milestone.

Essentially, with milestones you're breaking up a contract into small interior contracts that are dependent upon the proper execution of their predecessors. Writing a contract with milestones is easy to do if you think of it as a continuum of small contracts.

Your contract should also specify the cost of additional work or changes to the completed product (adds and changes) so that the client can get exactly what they want and understand up front what it will cost them to make changes. As well, changes that you couldn't anticipate but that are require to complete the task, should be compensated. Adds and changes happen all the time, and it's very common for beginners to forget to charge for them. Frequently, when you get started, you will be performing a lot more work to satisfy customers until you get the hang of contracting.

The only thing most consultants are going to sue a client over is non-payment. Is there any way to fast-track that process?

Not really. An agreement to arbitrate is the quickest way. There are some procedural mechanisms outside of arbitration, in court, but they rarely achieve the desired result. For example, if the only disputed issue is non-payment, and even the amount is not in dispute, and there are no other issues as to your performance in dispute, you may receive a *summary judgment.* Summary judgments are issued by the court when there are essentially no issues of fact in dispute and you are entitled to judgment as a matter of law. This is rare. Essentially, the defendant has to admit that they're liable, owe you the money, and simply haven't paid. The best way is to arbitrate. The litigation process tends to exhaust resources, fiscal and human. Consequently, even if you win, you are not always able to collect.

So if you can walk in to court or arbitration with a page full of signed off test results from agents of, or the customer themselves, they're going to have a hard time disputing what you're owed and you've made the job for the arbiter, judge, or jury, easy to find in your favor. That narrows down the whole discovery process, which is generally the most expensive part of litigation. Discovery is the process of conducting all the inquiries, depositions, interviews, and investigations necessary to determine the facts in a case. If you can get the customer to sign off on the various portions of a contract, you may be able to get in front of a jury to determine what the damages are much more efficiently and quickly. As for the legal issues of liability, then there's very little question, especially if your client participates with you in designing the sign off criteria, and then has employed it.

The best thing to do is set the contract up well; make sure it is clear, make sure it covers your conditions of future performance, and make sure it has test objectives and sign-offs for the customer as you proceed.

Intellectual Property

This portion of the discussion concerns intellectual property, like copyrights, trademarks, and patents.

I wrote code for a client. Who owns it?

That depends on what you negotiated. If it's work for hire, you wrote it, but the client holds the copyright.

How do you determine if you're working for hire?

You specify it in the contract. Issues of copyright ownership, license exclusivity or non-exclusivity, etc. should all be nailed down in the contract. As the author, you can license the code to the client to use but reserve the right to license elsewhere, license it exclusively to the client, license it exclusively for a period of time or in a specific market, or you can sell them the copyright outright. You can pretty much do with it as you please, or as you and your client agree. You should adjust your price accordingly.

If there's no contract, are there any litmus tests for what constitutes work for hire?

Yes. It's going to depend on the nature of the job, the nature of the work, and your legal relationship with the entity you are providing the services for; that is, are you an employee or an independent contractor? Essentially, it's going to get down to each person testifying as to what their intent was, and how closely the product matches that intent. It's going to be "what was the deal?" Is this the type of code that can't be used anywhere else? Or can it be used in other areas? Is this the way the author normally works? Does he or she have other copyrights to code? Is he or she writing similar software or code for another client? Or does he or she already have pieces of the code that are proprietary or copyrighted? A lot of factual issues are going to come into play, and as they are in dispute, it's up to the judge, arbiter, or jury to determine what was intended.

The best way to determine issues of copyright is simply to contract for those interests in the written agreement. You'll also want to file a copyright registration with the U.S. Copyright Office if you retain the copyright. Registering a copyright costs $30 dollars, and it's extremely easy to do. You obtain a common law copyright on anything in which you have an authorship interest that is not work for hire, and it's a defendable copyright. But you can't go into federal court without a federal registration, and there are different statutory damages that you can't get without that registration. It's easier to protect your rights with a federal copyright.

TIP Register your own copyrights with the U.S. Copyright Office. Check out www.loc.gov/copyright for (much) more information about copyrights.

WORK FOR HIRE

Work-for-hire copyright ownership laws affect consultants relationships between both their clients and their own helpers or contractors. Unfortunately, there are no simple instructions on how to clearly determine the ownership status of a work made for hire. The laws on the subject are a complex mixture of statutory definitions and interpretations of cases decided by courts.

WHAT IS COPYRIGHT WORK FOR HIRE?

Under the Copyright Act of 1976 (Title 17 of the United States Code), a work is protected by copyright as soon as it is created in a fixed form. Only the creator or author of the work can rightfully claim copyright and receive all the attendant legal protections. Although the general rule is that a person who creates a work is the author and initial owner of that work, there is an exception when another party hires the author to create the work. Depending on the relationship between the parties, copyright ownership may belong to the hiring party.

WHEN IS A WORK CONSIDERED A WORK FOR HIRE?

If a work is created by an employee within their scope of employment, the creator's employer owns the copyright in the work. Lawyers call any work produced during this employment period a "work made for hire." Since the employer-employee relationship determines ownership in the work, it is important to clarify each party's status when exchanging labor for compensation. Detailed analyses exist on how to determine if a creator is an employee or independent contractor, but it is beyond the scope of this discussion. For more information, read Circular 9, "Works Made for Hire" under the Copyright Act of 1976, published by the United States Copyright Office.

Continued on next page

Copyright law also assigns copyright ownership to a hiring party when a work is specially ordered or commissioned. However, special limitations apply. Works created by independent contractors are treated as works made for hire if the parties sign a written agreement before work commences and the independent contractor creates a work in one of the following categories listed under the Copyright Act: contributions to collective works (e.g. anthology), audiovisual works, translation, supplementary works (e.g. forewords, etc.), compilation, instructional text, tests or test materials, or an atlas.

If a work is created by an independent contractor that does not fall under one of the above categories, the copyright in the work automatically stays with the creator.

PRACTICAL CONSIDERATIONS

Computer software programs are not listed as one of the work for hire categories. Legal commentators say that computer software programs do not constitute a collective work or compilation. Most attorneys recommend that computer consultants, or companies who hire independent contractors to create or contribute to computer programs, should obtain a written agreement that assigns all copyrights in the work to the hiring party.

WORKING WITH THE CLIENT

Savvy consultants working with clients should clarify whether the copyright in the commissioned work is being transferred to the client along with the program. If the consultant intends to give the copyright in the work to the client, the consultant may sign a work-for-hire agreement with the client before commencing work.

Such an agreement clarifies both parties' expectations that the independent contractor is not an employee and that the hiring party now owns the copyright in the commissioned work in exchange for paying compensation. For examples of independent contractor agreements, see *Software Development: A Legal Guide, 2nd Ed.* by Stephen Fishman, (Nolo Press, 1998).

Depending on the situation, a consultant may want to retain ownership of a proprietary software program unless the client pays extra for the rights. Or the consultant may work out an arrangement in which the consultant grants the client an exclusive or non-exclusive license. A license is similar to renting out property. In this case, you rent out the copyright use in the work for a specific use or duration.

Continued on next page

WORKING WITH YOUR OWN INDEPENDENT CONTRACTOR

Many consultants forget to work out ownership issues with their own helpers or independent contractors. This is important because if a consultant assigns rights to a client, the consultant must guarantee that he or she legally possesses all of those rights. The best way to protect yourself is to have all independent contractors, no matter how casual the relationship, sign a work-for-hire agreement. If you are concerned that the work-for-hire agreement will not be considered valid, you can hedge your bets by inserting language into any work-for-hire agreement that states, "if for some reason such created work is determined not to be a work made for hire, the independent contractor assigns in advance all his copyright in such works."

How about trademarks?

Trademarks also can be obtained from common law and/or federal registration. Common law rights accrue when you begin to use the mark in connection with your product or service and in commerce. If you're just using it locally, you might just have a statewide right to the mark. If you apply to register the mark, you would identify the mark trademark (^{TM}), or servicemark(^{SM}) for a service mark. Only when the federal registration occurs are you entitled to use the registered trademark (®). When you register a trademark with the U.S. Patent and Trademark Office, you get presumption of your rights in the ownership and exclusivity of that mark within the applicable industry. Those rights are refutable if somebody else can prove prior and continuous use of the mark, which is rare.

What if I want to register a trademark but I find out somebody is already using it?

Trademarks are generally specific to a certain industry unless they are famous; if you're not in the same industry, you may be able to use it as well. If you have a trademark you think is especially valuable, you should go to Thompson & Thompson and request a trademark search. This service costs about $350, and provides a very thorough search of everything that's been published, registered, pending, and cancelled, about a mark, including Internet related use.

DO YOUR OWN TRADEMARK SEARCH

You can easily perform your own trademark search using these methods:

➤ Search the United States Patent and Trademark Office (USPTO) trademark directory directly at `www.uspto.gov`.

➤ Search the Thomas Register at `www.thomasregister.com`.

➤ Search the entire Internet for applicable uses using AltaVista at `av.com`.

➤ Search the domain name directory at `www.register.com`.

What about patents?

You need a patent attorney. You can patent certain code but there are restrictions, including the amount of time after public dissemination in which you must apply for or obtain it.

Is there any value in a software patent?

Yes, if it has application value.

Any other intellectual property rights issues that you think would be appropriate to discuss with budding consultants.

Well, cyberlaw implications, domain names, Web site copyright issues, such as linking, deep linking, and framing, have recently and understandably gained a lot of interest. For example, if you take someone's trademark or copyrighted material, and sandwich it between other characters in a domain name, then that maybe a violation. But if you take the trademark and put it in the relative file path after the domain name, that's generally acceptable; it's not disseminated out to the public in the same way and unlikely to cause any confusion in the marketplace.

Deep linking, which is the act of linking to images or text embedded within another's Web site without their permission is a copyright violation. The violation is the copying of the protected work, enabled now by the link. In other words, if you include the Quake logo on your home page, but rather than copying their logo to your local hard disk, you've simply included a reference to the publisher's Web site where you know the logo is stored, you're still violating copyright law, and possibly trademark law, because you've copied it into your home page via the link, and you have represented the logo as yours, or some affiliation, sponsorship, or ownership.

Copyright violations occur from the act of copying. If you don't actually make a copy of a work into your own Web material, such as in opening a new window or clicking a link and going to that site to view the material, you most likely have not committed a copyright violation.

Opening a window inside a frame, or framing of another's copyrighted or trademarked material, very well could cause a copyright or trademark violation, irrespective of whether that's the default operation of the Web browser. You should be certain you've got permission from the Web sites you frame in your Web site to avoid this problem. Many, in fact, don't mind, they want the traffic.

This body of case law is being developed right now. It's very fascinating, and there are a lot of issues developing that don't fit very well into traditional copyright and trademark law.

Conclusion

Always work with a written contract. A good contract specifies that it is the entire agreement between the parties, defines how disputes will be resolved (arbitration or litigation, venue, and assignment of attorney's fees), and caps the damages at the value of the contract. If you include testable criteria in the contract as proof of completion, you'll make it much easier to win your case if you have to sue a client for payment.

As soon as you know your business is going to succeed, incorporate as an S Corp to protect yourself from lawsuits. Once your business has significant assets to protect, get a general liability (GL) policy with riders for errors and omissions to protect you from lawsuits.

If you get sued, turn the suit over to your GL insurer. Otherwise, you'll need to find a good lawyer to defend yourself.

Before you establish your business, ensure that you are not infringing another company's trademarks by doing a trademark search on the name you choose. Once your business is well established, consider registering your trademark. If you write code for a client, your contract should clearly spell out who owns the code. If there is no specification, you will normally retain the copyright as the original author. Watch out for accidental copyright violations in Web sites you design—it is not legal to frame or include copyrighted information from another server in your Web page no matter where the content originated.

Appendix A
Job Contracts

This appendix shows three types of proposals/contracts. The first is a proposal for a new network, the second shows a contract for a retainer, and the third is a simple quote appropriate for existing customers.

New Build

This proposal is in the form of a quote. Unlike a normal contract, this contract allows a customer to select how much of what type of work they need because work elements are broken down by type. In this case, if the user wanted to contract for another server or additional clients, they could simply fill in the new number and calculate the new price. To initiate the job, the customer simply signs the contract and faxes it back to me.

I use the date I wrote the job proposal as the job's unique identifier because I frequently perform multiple contracts for the same customer. Using the date avoids looking amateurish with a Job number like "Job 0003."

Proposal 960930

To

Digital Widgets
7408 Any Street
San Diego, CA 92121

For

Design and Integration of Windows NT Network

At

Primary and Remote Facilities

3643 Another Street San Diego, CA 92111. Tel: 619.555.7141

Proposal for service support contracting by and between Netropolis and Digital Widgets to include labor to be furnished according to the following terms:

Job Site

Digital Widgets
7408 Any Street
San Diego, CA 92121

Scope of Work

Build Server

Furnish all labor required to build Windows NT Server to Netropolis specifications. Netropolis shall respect the manufacturer's warranty on components and will provide diagnostic and replacement labor free of charge for any defective component still covered by its manufacturer's warranty.

This cost occurs once for each server installed.

Total Cost:
$200 per server

Estimated Additional Costs:
$3100 for each adequate server

$5100 for each premier server (twice the hard disk throughput)

Integrate Network Digital Data Link

Furnish all labor required to

- Install two network hubs

- Install bridge (if necessary) between locations

- Attach Windows NT Servers to hubs

- Install fiber-optic transceivers

Netropolis Proposal 960930

This cost occurs once.

Total Cost:
$750

Estimated Additional Costs:

$1500 for two 16-port Ethernet Hubs w/100Mbps link

$500 for bridge

$300 for two fiber-optic transceivers

$3000 for contracting to install building-to-building fiber link

Install and Configure Windows NT, Per Server

Furnish all labor required to

- Bring Windows NT Server 4 online

- Configure Microsoft Exchange Mail client for use internally

- Configure Remote Access Server to connect to Internet

- Set up automated tape backup

This cost occurs once per server.

Total Cost:
$525 per server

Estimated Additional Costs:
$650 for Windows NT Server 4

Install and Configure Client Workstation

Furnish all labor required to

- Install and configure network interface adapter

- Install client network access software

3643 Another Street San Diego, CA 92111. Tel: 619.555.7141

- Configure Exchange client (Windows only)
- Attach client to premises wiring
- Set up user account

This cost occurs once per client.

Total Cost:
$120 per client

Estimated Additional Costs
$120 for 10/100Mbps Fast Ethernet Adapter

$35 for Windows NT Server 4 Client License

$100 per drop for Category 5 UTP installation

Job Prices

Task	Quantity	Cost	Extended
Server Build	1	200	200
Server Configure	1	500	500
Network Infrastructure	1	700	700
Client Configuration	30	120	3600
	Total	5000	

Terms:
Net 10 days upon completion of each phase.

Discount of $1500.00 given for purchase of One Server + 30 Client package.

Complete Package Total Cost: $4875.

3643 Another Street San Diego, CA 92111. Tel: 619.555.7141

<u>**Netropolis Proposal 960930**</u>

Completion Tests:

Log on using a typical user account from a client computer.

      Completion witnessed: _____ Date _____

Store a file on the server in a secured group folder.

      Completion witnessed: _____ Date _____

Log on using another user account and verify that the file is not accessible.

      Completion witnessed: _____ Date _____

Transmit e-mail message between two user accounts and two client computers.

      Completion witnessed: _____ Date _____

Back up the contents of the server hard disk to tape.

      Completion witnessed: _____ Date _____

View a public Web page.

      Completion witnessed: _____ Date _____

Provisions:

1. This contract shall be subject to and construed under the laws of the State of California as if all parties entered into this contract within its jurisdiction.

2. Should any provision of this agreement be found invalid, illegal or unenforceable under present or future law, the remaining provisions of this contract shall remain in force and the invalid provision shall be automatically replaced with a legal provision of similar intent.

3. This document comprises the sole and complete statement of obligations on the part of all parties.

4. All wording in this contract shall be interpreted according to its simple and fair meaning.

5. Any disagreement that arises concerning the interpretation of this contract shall be resolved according to the methods of the American Arbitration Association.

6. Netropolis respects the manufacturer's warranty on any material provided and shall provide such labors necessary to diagnose and replace defective equipment. However, the customer may be liable for diagnostic charges if the manufacturer's warranty on affected equipment is expired or if no hardware fault has occurred.

7. Netropolis shall not be liable for any delay or inability to perform under this contract due to any factor not under the control of Netropolis.

8. Liability on the part of Netropolis shall be limited to the reimbursement of costs for the contract under which liable activity occurs. Under no circumstance shall liability on the part of Netropolis be greater than that specified in this clause.

3643 Another Street San Diego, CA 92111. Tel: 619.555.7141

<u>**Netropolis Proposal 960930**</u>

Acceptance

The following duly authorized agents of Netropolis and Digital Widgets
hereby enter into this contract:

Netropolis

21 November 1996

_____

Matthew Strebe   Date

DIGITAL WIDGETS:

_____

Henry J. Tillman   Date

Retainer

This proposal uses the same basic template to establish a retainer contract. Retainers allow customers to fix their budget costs and provide guaranteed income for consultants.

Proposal 970929

To

Digital Widgets

7408 Any Street

San Diego, CA 92121

619.555.5300

Fax 619.555.7714

For

Computer and Network Emergency Service

And

Maintenance Retainer

At

Digital Widgets Miramar Facility

Netropolis Proposal 970929

Proposal for service support contracting by and between Netropolis and Digital Widgets to include labor furnished according to the following terms:

Job Site

Digital Widgets
7408 Any Street and adjacent facilities
San Diego CA 92121

Response Period

Weekdays, 6:00 a.m. through 6:00 p.m. All other times by appointment.

Specific Equipment and Proper Operational Status

Windows NT Domain DIGITAL WIDGETSNET and attached clients, servers, and network devices.

Scope of Work

This contract covers existing equipment and the addition of client computers. Additions of servers and network devices (e.g., routers, bridges, hubs, gateways, and special function servers) constitute changes to the architecture of the network and are therefore outside this scope of work.

The covered scope of work includes the following:

- Furnish all labor required to restore to proper operation the specific equipment located at the above premises during the applicable time period.

- Install client networking and operating system software as directed by Digital Widgets employees to support their work.

- Recommend changes to the network architecture to support growth and other necessary changes.

- Provide remote (telephone, e-mail) technical support to employees of Digital Widgets upon request.

- Act as an agent for Digital Widgets to network vendors when directed by Digital Widgets.

- Assess and report to Digital Widgets the operational status of the specific equipment periodically, at least once per service month or when specifically directed by Digital Widgets.

Special Terms

Netropolis shall

- Respond within 30 minutes to requests for service by the Digital Widgets employee(s) designated as the point of contact for Digital Widgets.

- Initiate repairs within two hours of requests for service.

- Notify Digital Widgets of all repairs, changes, and reconfigurations made to the specified equipment.

- Make such arrangements necessary to ensure continuous response coverage during the period specified above.

- Maintain a communications infrastructure capable of complying with this scope of work.

Digital Widgets shall

- Provide all materials necessary to complete the scope of work as identified by Netropolis in a timely manner. Hardware purchases and software licensing are the sole responsibility of Digital Widgets, although Netropolis may on occasion elect to provide hardware or acquisition in order to expedite service.

- Recognize the risk shouldered by Netropolis in specifying an unlimited labor scope at the prices specified in this contract by minimizing requests for service and on-site delays to the extent possible.

- Assign a specific point of contact to gather and promulgate information to Netropolis about specific equipment failures at the initial response time. Although Netropolis will respond to any employee's request for service, special provisions of this contract may

3643 Another Street San Diego, CA 92111 Tel 619.555.7141

be evoked based solely upon contact initiated by the employees designated by Digital Widgets and affirmed by Netropolis as the point of contact.

Total Cost

The sum of $50 per client computer, $200 per server or special purpose computer, and $200 per wide area or Internet link.

Terms

Net 15 days after the beginning of a service month. Invoicing will occur at the beginning of the service month.

Provisions

1. Either party can nullify this contract through simple notification during the last week of a service month.

2. This contract shall be subject to and construed under the laws of the State of California as if all parties entered into this contract within its jurisdiction.

3. Should any provision of this agreement be found invalid, illegal or unenforceable under present or future law, the remaining provisions of this contract shall remain in force and the invalid provision shall be automatically replaced with a legal provision of similar intent.

4. This document comprises the sole and complete statement of obligations on the part of all parties.

5. All wording in this contract shall be interpreted according to its simple and fair meaning.

6. Any disagreement arising concerning the interpretation of this contract shall be resolved according to the methods of the American Arbitration Association.

7. Netropolis respects manufacturers warranty on any material provided and shall provide such labors necessary to replace defective equipment.

<u>**Netropolis Proposal 970929**</u>

8. Netropolis shall not be liable for any delay or inability to perform under this contract due to any factor not under the control of Netropolis.

9. Netropolis shall in good faith execute the terms of this contract. However, no warranties are provided. This proposal does not imply insurance of any nature. Should Netropolis, after a good faith attempt, fail to restore to operation the equipment specified herein, Netropolis shall recommend further action but shall not be liable for the cost of any further actions necessary.

10. Liability on the part of Netropolis shall be limited to the reimbursement of the monthly service retainer for the month in which liable activity occurs. Under no circumstance shall liability on the part of Netropolis be greater than that specified in this clause.

Acceptance

The following duly authorized agents of Netropolis and Digital Widgets hereby enter into this contract:

Netropolis

_____   29 September, 1997
Matthew Strebe   Date

Digital Widgets:

_____   _____
Henry J. Tillman   Date

Simple Quote

I use this simple quote form (based on a default MS-Word template if I remember correctly) to provide simple quotes to existing customers when I'm covered by an existing contract.

Quote
18MAR97

To:

Digital Widgets
7408 Any Street
San Diego CA 92121
619.555.5300 Fax 619.555.7714

Ship To:

SALESPERSON	CONTACT				
Matt	John O'Dea				

QUANTITY	DESCRIPTION	UNIT PRICE	AMOUNT
1	Install & connect 10MB & 100MB hubs in new building	$300.00	$300.00
15	Install & connect 15 networked PCs	$100.00	$1500.00
1	Install 10MB & 100MB Network Interface adapters in Server	$400	$400
1	Test systems as installed for proper operation	$0	$0
1	Personnel training for network systems	$0	$0
1	Documentation of system as installed	$0	$0

SUBTOTAL	$2200.00
SALES TAX	0
SHIPPING & HANDLING	0
QUOTE TOTAL	$2200.00

If you have any questions concerning this quote, contact: Matthew Strebe, 619.555.7141.

THANK YOU FOR YOUR BUSINESS!

3643 ANOTHER STREET • SAN DIEGO, CA 92111• 619.555.7141

Appendix B
Job Documentation

T his appendix shows what I do for job documentation. This specific document simply shows the configuration of a server and an as-built network diagram.

FIGURE B.1 Sample as-built diagram

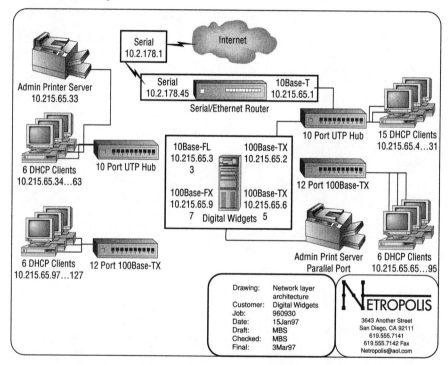

NT PDC Installation Options

Name: Network Administrator
Organization: Digital Widgets
Product ID: 11111-OEM-1111111-11111
License Mode: Per Seat

Server Name: DWPDC
Server Type: Primary Domain Controller
Password: d^w#I*d$g(e)ts
No emergency repair disk created
No accessibility options
All Accessories
All Communications
No Games
No Multimedia
No Windows Messaging
Network Participation: Wired
Internet Information Server installed
Network Adapters:
Allied Telesyn AT1700
Allied Telesyn AT1700
Intel 82557 based 10/100
DEC PCI DECchip 21140
Protocols:
TCP/IP
NetBEUI
Additional Services:
DHCP Server
TCP/IP Printing
Network Monitor Tools and Agent
RIP for Internet Protocol
Simple TCP/IP Services
Network Components
  DECchip 21140: Autosense
  AT1700 (1) I/O PORT: 300h
  AT1700 (2) I/O PORT: 320h
  Do you wish to use DHCP? No
TCP/IP Settings:
  DECchip: 38.215.65.2
  Intel: 38.215.65.3
  AT1700: 38.215.65.5
  AT1700: 38.215.65.6

User Accounts Created

Clingren (Administration, Executive)
Jbutler (Administration, Executive)
Jwilliams (Administration, Bookkeeping)
Jodea (Administration, Bookkeeping)
Kklause (Administration, Executive)
Rconwell (Mechengineering, Electronics, Science)
Bpi (Electronics)
Ewatson (Electronics)
Jbrunsch (Electronics)
Sfriesenhahn (Electronics)
Tcollins (Electronics)
Arabinovich (Manufacturing)
Aoganesyan (Manufacturing)
Brhafezi (Manufacturing)
Bdhafezi (Manufacturing)
Bapotovsky (Manufacturing)
Blane (Manufacturing)
Cfuimaono (Manufacturing)
Cstewart (Manufacturing)
Dmedvedenko (Manufacturing)
Goganov (Manufacturing)
Iyutsis (Manufacturing)
Mhafezi (Manufacturing)
Phasty (Manufacturing)
Szhao (Manufacturing)
Shahn (Manufacturing)
Ysha (Manufacturing)
Chickcox (Mechengineering)
Cisaacson (Mechengineering)
Jlueschen (Mechengineering)
Rsmith (Mechengineering)
Washburn (Sales)
Dknuteson (Science)
Fpdoty (Science)
Jcozzatti (Science)

Disk Structures Created

```
4GB partition "C:"
20GB partition "D:"
```

File System Structures Created

```
D:\COMPANY shared as "COMPANY"
  DOMAIN USERS:FULL CONTROL
D:\COMPANY\SOFTWARE
  DOMAIN USERS:READ
D:\COMPANY\DOCUMENTS
  DOMAIN USERS:FULL CONTROL
D:\USERS shared as "USERS"
  DOMAIN USERS:READ
D:\USERS\<USERNAME>
  <USERNAME>:FULL CONTROL
```

INDEX

Note to the Reader: Throughout this index **boldfaced** page numbers indicate primary discussions of a topic.

Do You Have What It Takes to Become a Consultant?

Take this quiz. As long as you answer "A" for each question, you are on your way.

1. If you went a month without making any money, you would...
   A. Learn to love mac & cheese
   B. Get divorced
   C. Starve to death

2. Have you ever brought a weapon to work?
   A. No.
   B. Yes.
   C. Does it count if I bought it at work?

3. Do you believe that you've been contacted by non-human intelligent beings of any sort?
   A. No.
   B. Yes.
   C. I have strange scars I can't account for.

4. How many pets do you own?
   A. 0–4
   B. 4–8
   C. 9+

5. How many times have you been convicted of a felony?
   A. 0–1
   B. 2–3
   C. 4+

6. With whom do you live?
   A. Self, domestic partner, roommate, kids
   B. Parents
   C. Other members of my commune/church

7. Complete this sentence: I believe the world is...
   A. Round/spherical
   B. Flat
   C. Hollow, with an interior sun and a sub-technological society living in peace on the inside

8. How often do you shower?
   A. Daily
   B. Weekly
   C. Monthly

9. Why do you want to be a consultant?
   A. For the independence
   B. Sounds cool to say you're a consultant
   C. Because I keep getting fired